REVOLUTIONS AT HOME

A VOLUME IN THE SERIES
Childhoods: Interdisciplinary
Perspectives on Children and Youth

Edited by
Rachel Conrad, Alice Hearst,
Laura Lovett, and Karen Sánchez-Eppler

REVOLUTIONS AT HOME

The Origin of Modern Childhood
and the German Middle Class

EMILY C. BRUCE

UNIVERSITY OF MASSACHUSETTS PRESS
AMHERST & BOSTON

ISBN 978-1-62534-562-2 (paper); 563-9 (hardcover)

Designed by Deste Roosa
Set in Garamond Premier Pro and Attleboro Gothic
Printed and bound by Books International, Inc.

Cover design by Derek Thornton / Notch Design
Cover art by Joahchim Campe, *Neues Abeze- und Lesebuch,* 1807. Euro 18 18733,
Cotsen Children's Library, Department of Special Collections, Princeton University Library.

Library of Congress Cataloging-in-Publication Data
Names: Bruce, Emily C., author.
Title: Revolutions at home : the origin of modern childhood and the German
    middle class / Emily C. Bruce.
Description: Amherst : University of Massachusetts Press, [2021] | Series:
    Childhoods : interdisciplinary perspectives on children and youth |
    Includes bibliographical references and index.
Identifiers: LCCN 2020053169 (print) | LCCN 2020053170 (ebook) | ISBN
    9781625345639 (hardcover) | ISBN 9781625345622 (paperback) | ISBN
    9781613768143 (ebook) | ISBN 9781613768150 (ebook)
Subjects: LCSH: Children—Germany—Social conditions—18th century. |
    Children—Germany—Social conditions—19th century. | Middle
    class—Education—Germany—History—18th century. | Middle
    class—Education—Germany—History—19th century. | Children—Books and
    reading—Germany—History—18th century. | Children—Books and
    reading—Germany—History—19th century. | Child development—Germany.
Classification: LCC HQ792.G3 B78 2021 (print) | LCC HQ792.G3 (ebook) |
    DDC 305.2350943—dc23
LC record available at https://lccn.loc.gov/2020053169
LC ebook record available at https://lccn.loc.gov/2020053170

British Library Cataloguing-in-Publication Data
A catalog record for this book is available from the British Library.

A portion of chapter 4 was previously published as "'Each Word Shows How You Love Me':
The Social Literacy Practice of Children's Letter Writing (1780–1860)" in *Paedagogica
Historica* 50, no. 3 (2014): 247–64. Reprinted by permission of the publisher, Taylor &
Francis Ltd., http://www.tandfonline.com.

To Bertram Camp Bruce
and Susan Porter Bruce,
with all my love.

CONTENTS

CONTENTS

ACKNOWLEDGMENTS

This book tells the history of how children learned in the Age of Revolutions, and these acknowledgments tell the story of how I learned to research and write the book. Still, they are far from comprehensive and certainly do not come close to capturing the depth of gratitude and affection I feel for the people named in these pages.

Thank you first to the extraordinarily able Matt Becker, as well as to Sally Nichols, Rachael DeShano, Julie Shilling, the University of Massachusetts Press editorial board, and all the UMass production staff. Thanks as well to Beatrice Burton for indexing the book (How many authors luck out with a high school classmate who happens to be a brilliant historian and indexer?).

This project owes debts to archivists and librarians across Europe and the United States (see the full list of institutions in the bibliography). I would especially like to single out the welcoming, well-informed assistance I received at the Georg-Eckert-Institut für Schulbuchforschung, the Deutsches Tagebucharchiv, and the Landesarchiv Baden-Württemberg, as well as from Elke Strang (Landesarchiv Schleswig) and Andrea Immel (Cotsen). The work of librarians across the University of Minnesota (UMN), especially Peter Bremer, LeAnn Dean, Sandra Kill, Naomi Skulan, and Angela Vetsch, has been vital. My sincere appreciation extends as well to the support and friendship of Laura Burks, Terri Hawkinson, and Sharon Severance in the UMN Morris Division of Social Sciences Office. Thank you to Alisande Allaben, John Hamerlinck, Roger Wareham and the rest of the UMN Morris Grants Development Office.

The archival research essential to this book was generously supported by the National Academy of Education and the Spencer Foundation; the UMN Twin Cities Department of History and the Graduate School; Hella Mears and the UMN Center for German and European Studies; the Deutscher Akademischer Austauschdienst; the Central European History Society; the Friends of the Princeton University Library; the Imagine Fund within the Office of the

Executive Vice President and Provost at UMN; and the UMN Morris Dean's Office. In an *American Historical Review* essay titled "On Acknowledgments" (February 2020), Emily Callaci rightly describes the listing of fellowships a "rare privilege" that is often limited to white middle-class US citizens; I only wish the indispensable support this research received were more broadly available.

In previous work, I described the chance to study with my doctoral advisor Mary Jo Maynes as a "winning lottery ticket." I still feel that way. Her enthusiasm, curiosity, knowledge, and friendship are unmatched. My approach to history was also developed by the phenomenal teachers at University Laboratory High School, Williams College (especially Alexandra Garbarini, Libby Kieffer, and Chris Waters), and UMN Twin Cities (especially Anna Clark, Regina Kunzel, Patricia Lorcin, and Jack Zipes). In addition to learning always from the students it is my honor to teach at UMN Morris, I have specifically benefited in writing this book from the hard work of several undergraduate research assistants: Grace Atkinson, Ford Benjamin, Elise Klarenbeek, Sarah Messer, Christina Muñoz-Piñon, and Destiny Schultz.

Giving thanks for all the support offered to this book project by family and friends seems an insurmountable task, and although I have named individuals here only once, many belong in multiple categories. Together, my family and writing center work have taught me to cherish feedback on in-progress work. In addition to acknowledging the two anonymous reviewers for the University of Massachusetts Press, I am grateful for the time and insights of Joseph Beaver, Jennifer Deane, Charise DeBerry, Maureen Gallagher, Kathryn Goetz, Joseph Haker, Heather Hawkins, Nate Holdren, Marissa Holst, Karen Hughes, Jennifer Kang, Kathleen Kearns, Ursula Lang, Katie Levin, Karen MacQueen, Brooke McAdam, Kristen Nichols-Besel, Cristina Ortiz, Michelle Page, Emma Reynolds, Mateusz Świetlicki, Ann Waltner, Barbara Welke, and Kate Williams.

Writing in parallel is one of the great joys of my career. Thank you for the advice and accountability, comrades: Lisa Bevevino, Merc Chasman, Adrienne Conley, Adam Coon, Rebecca Dean, Steve Deslauriers, Elizabeth Dillenburg, Teresa Gowan, Melanie Huska, Elliot James, Sara Lam, KK Lamberty, Tim Lindberg, Ellen Manovich, Nic McPhee, Heather O'Leary, Sharon Park, Alyssa Pirinelli, Nade Sotirova, liz Thomson, Elizabeth Venditto, and Kevin Whalen, as well as other members of the UMN TC Modern History Workshop, the UMN C4W Dissertation Writing Retreat, the UMN Faculty Writing Hunker, the YaSOA Research Circle, and the UMN Morris Junior Faculty Writing Support Group.

Other friends and colleagues shared their book proposals with me, suggested sources, commented on conference presentations, advised me on the publishing process, provided feedback at workshops, fed and hosted me, and offered inestimable encouragement and good cheer: Kristine Alexander, Tracey Anderson, Chris Atkinson, Anne Barber, Priyanka Basu, Tammy Berberi, Victor Berberi, Adam Blackler, Ann Borman, Ed Brands, Sheri Breen, Dave Brown, Sarah Buchanan, Steve Burks, Alice Burton, Rob Denton, Satis Devkota, Sarah Chambers, Kelly Condit-Shrestha, Tracey Deutsch, Colleen Dogotch, Ann DuHamel, Julie Eckerle, Dan Emery, Janet Ericksen, Liz Everton, Qin Fang, Katharine Gerbner, Becca Gercken, Susan Gilbert, Jenn Goodnough, Troy Goodnough, Harvey Graff, Steve Gross, Roland Guyotte, Kiel Harrell, Betsy Hearne, Rollie Henrichs, Sarah Howes, Angela Hume, Josh Johnson, Rachel Johnson, Arne Kildegaard, Athena Kildegaard, Michael Lackey, Dave Letzler, Leslie Lindberg, Argie Manolis, Jane McBride and members of the First Church Chancel Choir, Joe McDonough, Eli Meyerhoff, Ana Miller, Brad Miller, Pavla Miller, Angelica Mortensen, Jecca Namakkal, Ben Narvaez, Heather Peters, Sarah Riskind, Windy Roberts, Jennifer Rothchild, Eric Roubinek, Jimmy Schryver, Nick Skulan, Birgitte Søland, Alaya Swann, Lucy Thiboutot, Tisha Turk, Gary Wahl, Aaron Wenzel, and Liz Zanoni.

Working on this project for the past decade has made me lean significantly on family. Thank you for the inspiration and affection: Bert Bruce, Susan Elizabeth Bruce, Dave MacQueen, Bernie Porter, Cyndi Smith Porter, Kent Porter, Mike Porter, Rhoda Porter, Bill Todd, Catherine Bruce Todd, Karen Williams, and everyone I could not name here. My amazing brother Stephen Bruce read many sections of this book—some many times—and had to hear about it even more.

In the early twentieth century, my great-grandmother Isabel Hoover Bensberg ("Issy") left after two years of high school for a position as Second Assistant Librarian in Fresno, California. An oft-repeated family account of her service to children in the early 1910s included the memory that among the young Armenian immigrants she told stories to in the library basement was William Saroyan, the future novelist. However, this seems unlikely, as Saroyan lived in an orphanage in Oakland from 1911 to 1916. But the moral of the tale is not that you should keep the professional historians in your family away from cherished myths. The intergenerational transmission of storytelling and prizing children is what ties Issy's history to the one I narrate in this book. Her relations have long peppered their memories of youth with Issy stories, remembering her dramatic flair. My own early reading and writing was shaped by the kindest version of the educational ideals charted in this book. My family valued curiosity and adventure, emotional closeness, storytelling, and question-asking. While for many people, the experience of modern childhood is not so positive, I remain grateful beyond measure to my earliest teachers—my parents. This research simply would not have been possible without the encouragement, advice, financial support, defining conversations, and keen editing supplied by Susan and Chip Bruce. The book is therefore dedicated to them.

REVOLUTIONS AT HOME

SENTIMENT AND SELF-CONTROL

Approaching Childhood in the Age of Revolutions

As a material object, the diary that Marie Seybold kept from 1830 to 1831 weighs very little. Written in a compact hand, the text extends across two slim, unadorned notebooks, with uneven lines separating each of five or six dated entries per page. Both volumes of the diary are small enough to rest on an archivist's palm.

As a personal record of Marie's education, opinions, and daily experiences from age ten to eleven, the diary is freighted with meaning. It documents the practices that shaped how a middle-class German girl grew up during an era of radical transformations in the ideology and experiences of childhood. In their professional careers and social network, the Seybold family exemplified the emerging class of the *Bildungsbürgertum*, for whom children's education was essential to securing bourgeois success. *Bildungsbürgertum*, although sometimes used narrowly to describe individuals in the civil service, medicine, and law, more fully captures a German social class preoccupied with education and self-formation (*Bildung*).[1]

Marie's diary is thus useful as an archival record of the social habits and pedagogic practices of this increasingly influential group. But her diary furthermore reveals contests over children's agency as part of that education.

March 9 [1830]

> Today it was such beautiful weather that we went walking
> until it was almost 3 o'clock. In the afternoon we were with
> Frau Doktarin.

10.

> I know nothing to write about today other than that it
> always rained.

11.

> Today—it rained again the whole day.
>
> <u>This should not be a weather almanac!</u>

12.

> In the afternoon we brought Father the first primrose
> from the garden and a little bunch of violets with many
> blooming buds.

13.

> This morning I learned how to bind off and cast on stock-
> ings. After dinner there was lightning and thunder.[2]

Although an adult reader criticized her repetitive account ("This should not be a weather almanac!"), Marie continued to write very similar, short entries, often still preoccupied with the weather. Marie's diary thus adds evidence to the story told through the prescriptive ideology of adults. It confirms what anyone who interacts with or has been a child knows: children do not always behave the way adults expect them to. At the same time, Marie kept track of her days in this form because adults required it of her; she made choices and expressed herself within clear constraints, which even included a contradictory requirement to be more independently creative. Marie's diary illustrates the tension between governance and agency that colored children's education as she was growing up.

Judged from one vantage point, Marie's life was ordinary and unremarkable. She spent her childhood in a provincial town; she eventually married a man who worked in the prosaic sectors of beet sugar production and dairy farm studs. But it requires only a slight shift of perspective to recognize a life lived in momentous times. A hundred miles from her hometown of Brackenheim, Marie's cousins were separated from their parents for two years after they fled the Jacobins' 1793 occupation of Alsace.[3] Later, a different Seybold cousin served as the represen- tative of Heilbronn at the short-lived reformers' parliament in Württemberg during 1848 and 1849.[4] Marie's story is thus bracketed by intimate family ties to the upheaval of the French Revolution and the failed revolutions of 1848.

Beginning in the late eighteenth century, a series of dramatic transformations occurred in German ideologies and practices of childhood. As these changes disseminated from educated middle-class German families across European society in the nineteenth century, they spread the notion of childhood as a life stage that was critical to self-formation. The new childrearing regime was in part a process that adults enacted on youth, one that hinged on motivating children's behavior through affection and on cultivating internal discipline. But there is more to the story than adult strategies—children themselves negotiated these approaches in practice. *Revolutions at Home: The Origin of Modern Childhood and the German Middle Class* brings together a rich collection of documents created for and by young Germans to show that children engaged with new educational practices in transformative ways between 1770 and 1850. Through their reading and writing, they not only embodied but helped construct the modern child subject. In this book, I argue that the active child reader who emerged at this time was not simply a consequence of expanding literacy but was, in fact, a key participant in defining modern life.

By tracing both the history of changing mentalities and the history of children's lived experience in Germany in the late eighteenth and early nineteenth centuries, the book aims to illuminate the roles children played in transforming modernity. It unpacks how affection and didacticism worked together in children's socialization and how young people's own choices mediated the reimagining of childhood. Relying largely on the writing of adults, historians have identified the formation of modern subjectivities across a range of settings from theological disputes to commerce to political associations. Meanwhile, the emerging field of childhood studies has contributed rich but sometimes ahistorical analysis of the child's development and social roles. *Revolutions at Home* brings together these methods and perspectives on children's lived experiences to open new paths through debates about Western modernity.

The position of children as a central preoccupation of modern institutions and processes—the family, the state, mass schooling, class stratification, industrialization, imperialism, and so on—has been well documented.[5] What is less understood is the part children played, not only in their own experiences, but in the development of modernity itself. There is now a need for research that combines the cultural history of changing sentiments with the social history of children's lived experience. The development of modern childhood and the history of education have traditionally been understood as processes that adult elites enact on youth, but in practice children's own choices and experiences mediated their socialization in families and schools. Examining what eighteenth- and nineteenth-century German children read and wrote brings to light both the nature of their experiences and children's role in constructing modernity.

IMAGINING THE MODERN CHILD

In the middle of the eighteenth century, even though more children were learning the rudiments of literacy, few books were designed with young readers in mind. How, then, did an active education become the defining feature of middle-class childhood a century later? This transformation is something of a *Bildungsroman*: a coming-of-age story not for one individual, but toward the formation of a new child subject. From the end of the Enlightenment, middle-class educators, parents, and children themselves cultivated that subjectivity through new practices until it became a hegemonic ideal by the end of the nineteenth century. This book will explore that development in detail. To begin, the emergence of the modern child subject may be briefly characterized by the following features.

Childhood was increasingly positioned as critical to the formation of the self. Pedagogues and parents particularly emphasized the cultivation of self-control—although this notion of self-mastery was primarily intended for elite, white, male children. While educators were concerned about protecting children's innocence and guiding their purportedly malleable moral development, at the same time they idealized the power and creativity of individual intellect. More than ever before, adults at least claimed to care about entertaining children in active ways through their education. Therefore, they were preoccupied with capturing children's attention and shaping their learning response.

The domestic setting of education (especially for early childhood) grew in importance, and sentimental attitudes and aesthetics increasingly colored children's learning. Young people's social networks also changed in character and significance across this era. Finally, new genres, texts, and practices opened opportunities for children to exert agency in their education and leave traces of that agency as they resisted, negotiated, ignored, heeded, imitated, and reframed these pedagogic efforts.

THE AGE OF REVOLUTIONS

Although it was an age of new horizons and thrilling possibilities, the instability of virtually every aspect of life in the mad century of unprecedented transformation bridging the year 1800 cannot be doubted.

—*Christopher Johnson and David Sabean,* Sibling Relations and the Transformations of European Kinship, 1300–1900, *2011*

The twin political and economic revolutions of late eighteenth-century Europe could not have come about without a revolution at home. Family labor practices changed, the ideology of separate spheres took shape, and women played key roles in the intellectual life of the Enlightenment. While these developments have been well documented, children's contributions to this site of revolution have gone overlooked.

Contemporaries saw themselves as living in a time of great change during what historians call the "Age of Revolutions" today. Invoking Eric Hobsbawm's plural term has now come to signify a host of overlapping historical developments including violent political change around the globe, the dissemination of ideas about popular sovereignty and natural rights, the development of secessionist independence and written constitutions, the rise of nationalisms and early decolonization, the first efforts to abolish the slave trade, and the productivity and (uneven) prosperity of the Industrial Revolution.[6]

The era was certainly one of tumult and contradictions. On the cusp of time periods conventionally defined as early modern and modern, traditional and innovative ideas about how children should be educated coexisted sometimes in conflict and sometimes in surprising harmony. The history of reading also illustrates this dialectic, as oral communication and traditions were not displaced everywhere by the rise of print but persisted in new and old forms alongside increased literacy.[7]

Politically, the effects of the French Revolution and subsequent uprisings varied across Europe, but nevertheless were widely felt. The German states of Central Europe were reshaped in their borders, administration, linguistics, military, politics, and more. And the events of 1789 and following decades changed family life across the continent and led to new understandings of the relationship between society and the state.[8]

In response to the threats of political unrest, states took up several defensive strategies, including the project of mass schooling for children from the popular classes. The purpose and effects of eighteenth-century literacy campaigns were also conditioned by absolutism and the German Enlightenment, Richard Gawthrop has argued. First, he writes, "Absolutist governments realized that they needed to do more than merely impose an external discipline on their subjects."[9] A modernization program required the cultivation of self-discipline to serve the state's needs. Second, the ideals that German Enlightenment thinkers promoted depended on willing diligence. As Gawthrop observes, the Enlightenment was committed "to educating subjects who would conform to the demands placed on them by 'modernization,' not in a spirit of mechanical obedience, but 'from a rational understanding of rights and duties.'"[10] The same political situation motivated middle-class liberals to develop different educational strategies for their own children, but both mass schooling for lower-class children and changing bourgeois childrearing practices indicate that children's reading and writing practices were an essential means of becoming modern in Europe.

Meanwhile, industrialization reshaped European family life in a number of ways, starting with the rapidly growing markets of the late eighteenth century that created new kinds of child consumers, and changing occupational structures that demanded new forms of child socialization.[11] Additionally, urbanization altered many families' daily life and relations; indeed, increasing numbers of the children in this study lived in cities. Innovations in technology, including for print, affected various aspects of daily life. Household forms adapted in some social classes in response to industrialization, although the various arrangements of families remained diverse and complex in this period.[12] Class cultures of family life also evolved in response to industrialization and prompted bourgeois families to cultivate privacy.[13] Children and youth as producers and consumers helped drive the Industrial Revolution.

CENTRAL EUROPE ON THE MARGINS OF REVOLUTION

Beginning a century before unification, this era still saw Germany as a social and cultural imaginary. However, we should not attribute too much to those famously numerous political borders. For example, contemporary maps of the Holy Roman Empire often marked large areas as "Germany," despite the quasi-sovereignty of small interior states.[14] I follow the lead of recent scholarship that considers the region as a whole even before 1871, seeking, as Jason Coy puts it, "less to provide assessments of the empire's Staatlichkeit, than to examine the empire and its institutions as a framework for political and intellectual interaction."[15] This book draws from a broad set of regions, including Schleswig in the north (which then belonged to Denmark); various places in Prussia, especially in and around Berlin; Saxony in central Germany; Westphalia and Lippe in the west; Bavaria and especially Baden-Württemberg in the south; as well as publishing houses in Vienna. For families of the Bildungsbürgertum, class and language were in many ways more salient unifying categories than the regional differences that separated them.

While Germany has been seen as marginal to the political and economic revolutions of the eighteenth century (which are conventionally understood as centering in France and Britain, respectively), Central Europe held outsized importance in the transformation of the family and educational practices that supported a revolution in selfhood. German literacy rates were high compared to the rest of Europe: for example, by 1850, 85 percent of Prussia's population could read and write, compared with 52 percent in England and 61 percent for only reading in France.[16] German readers also lived at the crossroads of the early modern European book trade, with centers in Leipzig, Hamburg, and Vienna, and already enjoyed more than two hundred newspapers in publication before 1700, far more than anywhere else in Europe at the time.[17] Central Europe is the origin of the modern bourgeois Christmas celebration as a family event, an iconic element in the imagined "good childhood" of our modern era.[18] It was two German brothers, Jacob and Wilhelm Grimm, who made the European tradition of fairy tales an essential component of children's reading around the world.[19] German companies dominated the global toy market in the later nineteenth century.[20] Germans played a key role in the development of schooling throughout the eighteenth and nineteenth centuries in Europe, as well as in promoting Friedrich Froebel's *Kindergarten* movement around the globe.[21] School reformers like Horace Mann came from North America and across Europe to examine Prussian schools in particular as a model.[22] It is true that the transformation of childhood was in some respects a class-specific but cross-European phenomenon.[23] Nevertheless, I suggest that German educators and families led the way during a revolutionary moment for the ideology and practices of childrearing.

REVOLUTIONS AT HOME

Childrearing and children's education served as a crucial mechanism through which the European public sphere was produced in the nineteenth century. By centering children and childhood, I offer an important new perspective on longstanding questions about the history of the family, gender, and generations. Decades of scholarship have demonstrated that the family does indeed have a history as an object, site, and agent of change.[24] As an institution, the family is not separate from social and political life, and the contention that the family is a site of history is closely linked with research that has dismantled a false dichotomy between public and private spheres. Some of the most essential work in this area has emerged from debates around the writing of Jürgen Habermas. Even though Habermas has been criticized for reifying a divide between public and private, he is himself preoccupied in *The Structural Transformation of the Public Sphere* with the connections from the family to the market and civic discourse, because he sees the bourgeois public sphere as constituted through the bourgeois family. He writes, for example, of "the ambivalence of the family as an agent of society yet simultaneously as the anticipated emancipation from society."[25] Belinda

Davis and other feminist critics of Habermas and subsequent scholarship have usefully highlighted his silence on how the public sphere is gendered.[26]

Revolutions at Home uncovers how modern bourgeois subjectivity was cultivated across the life course, starting with the education and active participation of young children. In this way, the work harmonizes with Daniel Cook's *The Moral Project of Childhood*, which looks at mothering discourses and middle-class Anglo-American children's consumption to argue that childhood was constructed through bourgeois taste and a Protestant moral architecture in this same era across the Atlantic Ocean.[27] Other scholars have looked to the home as a site for producing modern selfhood.[28] David Hamlin, for example, has shown how, even if the middle-class European family did become more private over the course of the nineteenth century, the public world of economics, politics, and society nevertheless depended on families. He argues that "the modern, autonomous individual was simply not conceivable without the family."[29] Indeed, he suggests, seeing family life as the origin of the self is what made it a domain of concern for contemporary observers.

The formation of self that I trace in this book was a reflexive, social process for children, whose dependency makes those relationships even more transparent in the historical record. As Jerrold Seigel writes, "To regard people as partial agents of their self-existence is not at all the same as to assert that they need only themselves in order to effect it."[30] Germans during the Age of Revolutions themselves saw children simultaneously as agents of their own self-cultivation and as fundamentally embedded in social relations. Therefore, in my consideration of children's agency, I follow the lead of David Sabean, who cautions against assumptions about the psychodynamics of personhood, which promise "the possibility of studying the emotional experiences and subjective lives of those to whom we give our attention."[31] He suggests that the historian should conceive of selfhood more usefully in terms of a person's constitution within a matrix of social relations. This book locates the child within a household, as part of extended family and social networks, and through the influences of educational texts.

EDUCATING THE MODERN CHILD

The nature of learning and self-development were conspicuous issues in the decades surrounding 1800. Writers of this era understood themselves to be living in a "pedagogic century," particularly in continental Europe. There, enthusiasm for reforming instructional methods in service of a superior, freer humanity absorbed scholars across intellectual and political divides.[32] Indeed, that passion was so extreme it invited satire. In Rococo artist Jean-Honoré Fragonard's 1780 painting *Education Does Everything* (figure 1), for example, a young girl dresses up two dogs in human clothing and poses them in a parody of Enlightened instruction.[33] The child's gender also suggests a caricature of progressives who called for the intellectual uplift of girls and women.

FIGURE 1. *Education Does Everything*, engraving by Nicolas de Launay, c. 1790, based on a painting by Jean-Honoré Fragonard. Purchase, Roland L. Redmond Gift, Louis V. Bell and Rogers Funds, 1972. Courtesy of the Metropolitan Museum of Art.

How Enlightenment pedagogues educated their own (elite) children diverged sharply from the aims of mass schooling, which reified social class distinctions and shored up elite power.[34] Targeting young children of the peasantry and working classes, school reformers sought to grow a malleable workforce in service of the state and economic development.[35] While my focus in this study is on the emerging pedagogy for bourgeois children that embodied ideals widespread today about responsive teaching and active inquiry, it is key to remember that these new expectations formed during the Age of Revolutions in contrast to the repressive modes of instruction delivered to the popular classes in the German *Volksschule*.

More bourgeois children and youth did start attending schools in the late eighteenth and early nineteenth centuries, but the aims and practices of these institutions varied widely. Confessional differences between states led to some religiously administered and some secular institutions, often both in the same town. The terms and curricula for different levels were far from consistent across regions in the late Enlightenment, as Juliane Jacobi has tracked.[36] Schooling also differed by gender, of course. Many of the boys and young men mentioned in this book left home to board at secondary schools, including military academies such as the influential Hohe Karlsschule in Stuttgart (founded 1770).[37] Fewer young women received formal secondary education in Central Europe until later in the nineteenth century, but the percentage of girls attending school was definitely on the rise during this period. In Prussia, for example, a total of between 250 and 350 public girls' schools from 1827 to 1864 ensured at least one secondary school for girls in every Prussian city or large town and even in some smaller towns.[38]

It was through the pedagogic philosophy aimed at middle- and upper-class children, intended to be practiced across educational settings, that the Enlightenment aims of cultivating sentiment and self-control in young people fully emerged.[39] Enlightenment philosophers placed the child as symbol at the center of political discourses about reason, governance, and the self; at the same time, some directed their attention to child development itself, reimagining childhood as a vital stage of life cordoned off from adulthood.[40] Two of these writers demand special attention here because of their international reach.

Building from John Locke's assertion of the innate morality of humans, Swiss reformer Johann Heinrich Pestalozzi radically argued that educators should attend to the individual needs of each child, and he emphasized observation and experience over received knowledge.[41] In the German context, Pestalozzi's philosophy was popularized through experimental schools and a proliferation of teaching and parenting manuals. Readings of Pestalozzi by John Dewey, Rudolf Steiner, and Maria Montessori have ensured that his ideas have continued to shape Western pedagogy through institutions such as Montessori and Waldorf schools, as well as the progressive education movement of the twentieth and twenty-first centuries.

During the Age of Revolutions, Jean-Jacques Rousseau's influence on pedagogy was profound, including in the German case, where his often contentious and sometimes self-contradicting ideas about nature and self-control shaped pedagogic thought. In particular, German followers took up Rousseau's elevation of the human struggle with nature, his intense focus on child development as the linchpin of social reform, and his reimagination of mothering as always separate from and yet essential to the public world.[42] The philosopher Paul Hensel asserted that Rousseau's influence in France "seems almost negligible" compared to his presence in German philosophy.[43] In the German context, Rousseau's work was translated by Joachim Heinrich Campe, who adapted Rousseauian moralizing about the wild world in his widely read adaptation of Daniel Defoe's *Robinson Crusoe* for German child readers, *Robinson der Jüngere* (*Robinson the Younger,* 1779–80).[44]

A cornerstone paradox of eighteenth-century pedagogy was that the parents and teachers who pursued the educational ideals of Rousseau wanted to *instruct* children in the ways of self-knowing Enlightenment, to educate the innately "natural" child.[45] They hoped to develop readers who were sociable, yet independent; writers who were cultivated, yet natural; children who were curious, yet obedient. Above all, they sought to cultivate self-knowledge and self-control in the child.[46]

To convey these messages, many pedagogues were concerned with crafting new mechanisms to capture children's attention.[47] As I show throughout this book, adults were therefore increasingly interested in how to provide an entertaining education. Because reading took effort, German pedagogue Christoph Wilhelm Hufeland argued, "we thus must place such books in their hands that connect pleasure with instruction."[48] Making learning fun would help children devote themselves to their work. Following again in Rousseau's footsteps, others suggested that encouraging "natural" inclinations would engage children's attention. Ludwig Georg Friedrich von Seybold, cousin of Marie above, urged his own daughter to resist the cultivated education of her teacher and mother so that she would not become an "ailing hot-house flower, but rather a free, sturdy child of nature."[49] Ironically, this presumed she would achieve an authentic, unencumbered state by following her father's guidance, in her education as a natural child.

The call for amusement in instruction did not mean that Enlightenment schoolrooms were a paradise of unsupervised children freely following their own various desires. Many Enlightenment pedagogues were concerned with the dangers of unrestrained curiosity and imagination, especially in girls. Philosopher Étienne Bonnot de Condillac warned against young women and girls reading novels because he feared their "tender brains" would not be able to distinguish the real from the fictive and they would spend too much time in asocial isolation; Nicolas Malebranche believed that mothers' overactive imaginations were responsible for the births of monstrous children; and J. H. S. Formey worried that children allowed to play at make-believe would never learn the self-discipline to concentrate and focus their "wandering" imaginations.[50]

Yet Enlightenment pedagogy was authoritarian and dictatorial only to a certain extent.[51] Later Romantic conceptions of the child have overshadowed important changes in attitudes toward children's education that were already developing in the eighteenth century, as William McCarthy has observed. He writes, "Conventional accounts of Enlightenment pedagogy . . . seem wedded to the story that Enlightenment education was a regime dedicated in one way or another to the oppression of the child." McCarthy points out that this conventional story falsely flattens the diversity of approaches in the Enlightenment into a "single-minded enterprise." More importantly, it presumes "that the *effects* of Enlightenment teaching on pupils are in fact known."[52] Until recently, sources for this kind of inquiry have seemed elusive. Understanding the effects and mechanisms of Enlightenment pedagogy in practice, as this book seeks to do, requires analysis of education across settings, including informal home-based learning and formal instruction in schools.

A VERY SHORT HISTORY OF READING

In this book, I build on scholarship in the history of reading, a diverse area that encompasses the history of the book, philosophy, literary criticism, cognitive psychology, and literacy studies.[53] Notably, I adopt the premise that reading is always an interpretive process with multiple agents who make choices about both the writing and reading of texts. To that claim, I am adding a charge to consider young readers seriously as interpreters of texts. As Janice Radway has argued, "reading is not eating."[54] I do not assume that children consumed their reading passively or that children's literacy was a simple matter of learning to decode. Even though no reader is autonomous, children may have been especially free, according to William St. Clair, "to skip, to argue, to resist, to read against the grain . . . to misunderstand, to be distracted, to slip into dreams, to disagree but to continue reading, to stop reading at any time, and to conclude that the reading had been a waste of time."[55] It is this exercise of reading agency that has made the historical study of reception notoriously challenging.

I work from the assumption that while we cannot fully diagnose the interior experience of reading, we should consider the meaningful effects of age, gender, and class in producing different, sometimes unexpected relationships between reader and text. As I trace these impacts on young readers, I situate myself within a critical sociological approach in which reading is understood as "an historic and culture-specific competence which has been regulated institutionally in accordance with particular economic and political interests."[56] Literacy studies also informs my work.[57] In this case, I am concerned primarily not with assessing the literacy attainment of individuals, but rather with *literacy practices*: that is, children's ongoing reading, writing, and learning experiences.[58]

During the years around 1800, just as the modern child subject was coming of age, new modes of reading also emerged that resemble reading practices common today. This was the period of Rolf Engelsing's "reading revolution," in which educated Europeans moved from intensively reading only a few religious books to extensively reading a wide range of secular books.[59] At the same time, literacy as the basic ability to decode and even write text was spreading rapidly across social barriers. Literacy is challenging to measure, not least because those hoping to count it use varying definitions, and it has been subject to discontinuities and reversals over time.[60] Furthermore, the ability to follow the catechism or sign a name was not necessarily a mark of progress for those targeted by literacy campaigns in the eighteenth and nineteenth centuries, as Harvey Graff, David Vincent, and others have justly asserted.[61] But in general, crude measures of literacy across studies bear out a similar trend that mass literacy accelerated in Western and Northern Europe from the middle of the eighteenth to the middle of the nineteenth century. The most reliable numbers may be found in regional studies of literacy rates; national averages conflate key population differences emerging from differing legal regimes, local customs, confessions, and of course the effects of class and gender. For example, in East Prussia, one of the poorest areas in the German lands, the proportion of peasants able to sign their names at the time of marriage grew from 10 percent in 1750 to 25 percent in 1765, and to 40 percent in 1800.[62] During the nineteenth century, Prussians across social categories were consistently more likely to be recorded as literate than people in Austria, Belgium, England, France, Italy, Ireland, the Netherlands, Spain, Russia, or Scotland. By the 1840s, fewer than 10 percent of all Prussian men were recorded as illiterate.[63] To take another German region as an example, nearly 100 percent of children in Baden (in the southwest) attended primary school by the same decade.[64]

But the developments in reading were not just quantitative. What reading meant and how it worked also changed dramatically between the eighteenth and nineteenth centuries. European reading practices were increasingly private and introspective and granted access to wide-ranging information and genres.[65] It took long centuries after the development of the written word for the innovation of silent reading to emerge, although this practice was established by the turn of the nineteenth century. The early modern transition from reading aloud to silent reading built partly on the invention of word separation, as Paul Saenger has shown, and transformed ideas about authorship and privacy.[66] To read independently was a novelty in the modern world. The new, personal way in which texts came to be written and read also affected the classroom, including through facilitating rapid reference reading.[67]

New modes of reading entailed a new moral weight on what reading might mean. Histories of women readers have often focused on cultural anxieties around the "dangers" of women's unsupervised literacy. In Europe around 1800, this anxiety was not only about gender, but often also about age (think of Jane Austen's well-known parody *Northanger Abbey,* in which both the youth and gender of Austen's youngest heroine contribute to her mishaps). Thus in 1841, seventeen-year-old Anna Hasenfratz (one of the diarists discussed in chapter five) decided she ought to write to her older brother, away at university, for permission to read the novels she craved.[68] But many Enlightenment pedagogues also believed that reading books could protect children from vice, and they began to promote book consumption, especially for children, as an explicitly bourgeois rejection of aristocratic dissipation. When fundraising to furnish his utopian school with an appropriate library, Johann Basedow asked his potential patrons to pay a little money for children's books, money that they might otherwise spend on "the tobacco tins, the cases, the furniture, the various collars, the barber, the masquerades and the solos [forms of dress] in color (ladies and gentlemen!), to say nothing of the foreign wines."[69] He positioned the written word not only in company with other commodities, but superior to them.

To feed the demand of these changing reading practices, the German book market grew exponentially during the late eighteenth and early nineteenth centuries. Friedrich Nicolai, a notable eighteenth-century publisher, said the profession required "tireless industry" in knowing the books available, handling them, selling and visiting book fairs, printing, and so on.[70] Indeed, it was a substantial charge, since eighteenth-century German book fairs featured more than 250,000 titles, two-thirds of which were written after 1750.[71] The number of titles for sale at the most famous book market, Leipzig, increased by more than half between 1740 and 1770 and subsequently more than doubled between 1770 and 1800.[72] As the formerly bread-and-butter publication of religious texts declined from 1740 to 1800, pedagogy and geography were among the five genres that each doubled their previous market share in the replacement of theological writing, according to German trade statistics from Helmuth Kiesel and Paul Münch.[73] Education was becoming one of the most reliably profitable sections of a German bookseller's catalog. While for Nicolai a novel typically sold 750 copies in the 1790s, and his more obscure texts were published in runs as low as 225, he gave the 1805 edition of Johann Matthias Schröckh's world history reader (a key text in chapter three) an issue of 5,000.[74]

With the rise of children's book markets, such texts entered more and more children's lives as sought-after commodities.[75] As in nineteenth-century America, domesticity was produced through books as "things to buy, own, and display."[76] Pedagogues encouraged an acquisitive desire for a personal youth library, as in the frontispiece from an alphabet book published by Campe in 1807 that shows children clamoring around their father to grasp his book (figure 2). As publishers began to recognize the purchasing or proxy purchasing power of bourgeois children, they developed various business strategies to capture it. For one, they reissued popular schoolbooks in abridged editions as shorter, cheaper introductions for home use. The final pages of many schoolbooks and periodicals for children advertised other titles the printers hoped would interest young readers and their teachers. Even if adults were purchasing the books, children could read the topics and see the prices directly themselves, making them ubiquitous temptations. And sometimes publishers attached "tie-ins," discounts to other books, to attract the child reader to a new author or genre. For example, Johann Günther Friedrich Cannabich's *Kleine Schulgeographie* (*Short School Geography*), published in at least seventeen editions from 1818 to 1851, prominently advertised a discount on a school atlas from the same printer.

Young people both bought books for themselves to read and read books they had not purchased. Booksellers' records reveal that schoolboys in Rugby during the second half of the eighteenth century were an important market for children's and adult fiction, as Jan Fergus has excavated.[77] But there were certainly other means of acquiring books. For example, sixteen-year-old Anna Krahmer (see chapter five) wrote in her diary on March 1, 1831, that after playing with paper dolls, she and her friend Franziska together finished reading James Fenimore Cooper's *The Red Rover*. Krahmer reported, "It is really a wonderful book. I confess it drew 2 tears from me."[78] It is not clear here whether the book belonged to Anna or Franziska, reminding us to look beyond purchasing lists or inventories for the circulation of texts in an expanding market.

AGENCY AND DISCIPLINE

During the Enlightenment, parents lavished attention on keeping children's books orderly, a telling illustration of the partnership and tension between agency and discipline in the history of children's socialization. One of the central goals of didactic propaganda in this era was to cultivate self-disciplined children.[79] An increasingly important means of demonstrating self-discipline was through the management of material objects and knowledge. For example, in an 1813 birth-day note for his father, ten-year-old Heinrich Wilhelm Weise made an earnest promise: "I will be more diligent this year and I will keep my books in order; if you look at my drawer, dear father, you will find all my books in the greatest order, but no crumbs."[80] At first glance, it appears that Weise thoroughly absorbed

FIGURE 2. Frontispiece, Joachim Campe, *Neues Abeze- und Lesebuch,* 1807. Euro 18 18733, Cotsen Children's Library, Department of Special Collections, Princeton University Library.

the message from Enlightenment pedagogy that obedience and orderliness, in addition to writing beautiful letters as a demonstration of his literacy, were the best way to show his love for his father. But the suggestion of his past behavior not having lived up to this vow reinforces what we already know: that prescriptive messages for how well-disciplined children should act did not necessarily translate to compliant practice. Similarly, while her philosopher husband was traveling in Italy in 1789, Maria Caroline Herder was driven to make a new set of rules for her children, enforcing fines for bad behavior. The list of sins was almost entirely concerned with mess and disorganization, and it specifically named the infraction of not keeping books in order (punishment: one Saxon thaler).[81] This prescriptive evidence tells us that the Herder children, like Heinrich, failed to tidy their books often enough to please their parent, and their mother chose to motivate their supposed self-governance with money. The example also underscores a developing notion that each child in this milieu ought to possess his or her own treasured books—enough to get them out of order. The volume of words spent on this need for orderly books demonstrates both the Enlightenment value of self-discipline *and* children acting outside of adult intentions.

Historians have neglected children's experiences partly because of the persistent challenges of discerning their presence in the historical record. But young people have also been relegated to objects of history because scholars have mistakenly understood children's agency as simple and unimportant, when in fact the ways in which children form opinions, exercise power, and make history are complex and profoundly embedded in social context.[82]

Because agency, voice, and subjectivity have been of special concern to recent studies in the history of childhood, this field reveals common traps for historians. First, there is a desire to discover or even celebrate agency in the historical record, including resistance to or negotiation of disciplinary power. Thus we see the inclination of many historians of childhood and youth to seek out examples of children struggling against the dictates of their education with defiance, parody, or silent refusal. Second, there is a desire to reveal and critique the propagandistic mechanisms of authorities, institutions, and power. Thus we see emphasis on the governance of children through schooling and other disciplinary practices. Even though these two impulses stem from shared historical and political perspectives, they are often in conflict. That is, either we understand children as agents with the capacity to reinterpret and dismiss their socialization, or we accept that teachers, parents, authors, and other adults successfully impose a tyrannical pedagogy on young people.

My approach to reading agency does not look for middle ground between these poles, but instead investigates how agency and discipline worked inseparably to shape the experiences of children and, in turn, their imprint on modern European history. Education does have transformative potential for some individuals, but it has also—and in the same context—served as an instrument of governance and conformity. Children are forces of socialization at the same time and indeed because they are objects of socialization. Moreover, "they are children: individuals inhabiting and negotiating these often conflicting roles as best they can," as Karen Sánchez-Eppler has observed of the early American context.[83]

During the Age of Revolutions, as they do today, children exerted agency when they made choices, exercised power, and resisted authority. Individual children also influenced the perspectives and actions of individual adults (teachers, pedagogues, policy-makers, parents), shaping their ideas about childhood and how children learn. At the same time that education worked as a governing process intended to cultivate a particular kind of middle-class citizen, children were still able to form their responses to this instruction: they might reinforce and participate in the changing ideology of childhood; they might also reinterpret the education produced for them through their own lived experience; and they might subvert adults' pedagogical intentions through misreading, refusing to study, or altering the physical texts of their education. Recognizing the mutual constitution of agency and discipline undermines the story of an orderly trajectory in the history of children's education from an age of absolute didacticism to an age of emancipated inquiry. This book both uncovers earlier practices that promoted children's creativity and imagination and reveals how emerging educational strategies purporting to be liberatory also served as forms of discipline.

As scholars of the subaltern have argued, voicelessness in written records should not be mistaken for historical irrelevance or passivity. Taking children's agency seriously requires new methods and attention to practice. I suggest that children's education is a particularly bright avenue for exploring agency and discipline, since education involves both children's own practices and the construction of childhood by adults. Texts written for youth present an intriguing intersection of adult desires to shape childhood and the agency of the child readers themselves. Education is always an interactive process between teachers and learners. But what was special about the decades around 1800 was the scale and pace of change in these interactions as childhood was redesigned.

My consideration of children's agency does not come without skepticism toward the liberal conception of individuality, which coalesced during the Enlightenment and undergirded much of the pedagogic philosophy of this era.[84] Understanding subjectivities as being historically constituted is still compatible with an investigation of the choices and self-articulations that young people made within social constraints. German children participated in the discursive construction of modern selfhood, not only as future adults influenced by youth identities but also through their own development and negotiation of relational autonomy in childhood.

Historical conceptions of autonomy in general (that is, for adults) are enriched by this approach to considering children as partial agents, partial subjects. Recognizing the constraints on children's agency helps us question ideas taken for granted about adults as historical actors.[85] Indeed, this entanglement between adult and child expressions of choice and power further indicates the continued value of investigating agency. The attempts to govern, discipline, and control children that were fundamental to the historical dynamics of industrialization, class stratification, and colonialism were pursued within the context of children exerting their own will. The perception of agency and subjectivity, however incomplete—this core idea that "I" can be my own person—is essential to understanding the choices and actions people take in history, even, as Tessie Liu writes, "if their bravery rests on uncertain foundations."[86]

CHAPTER OVERVIEW

This morning I wrote to Otto. Herr Bertsch and Herr Lerscher didn't come. This evening I was in the garden. I gave Luise Göhring her book back.

—*Marie Seybold, diary, age ten, July 6, 1830*

When I frequently would like to have a good book for myself, I always first estimate whether so much remains leftover that I can buy the necessary books for [my children] before that. I often wish to possess one thing or another that would serve my comfort: but as soon as I consider that this could go into sufficient payment for a few months to one of the tutors who teaches them in one or another of the arts and sciences; then I happily deny myself these comforts.

—*Christian Felix Weiße*, Der Kinderfreund, *1775*

Because "childhood" is not a conventional category around which archives are typically organized, writing this book has required developing my own archive across nearly twenty institutions in Germany, France, and the United States. The two commonplace moments quoted above from a child's diary and youth periodical, respectively, illustrate some contradictions of bringing together texts for and by children as historical evidence. Ten-year-old Marie Seybold's words seemingly offer the historian "real evidence" of her participation in literacy practices of the nineteenth-century Bildungsbürgertum: writing letters to her brother, taking lessons with tutors, borrowing books from friends, and dutifully recording these activities in her diary. But because this is a limited historical document and not a novel, there are many unanswerable questions: What *was* the book she borrowed from Luise? What was their relationship like? Why did she borrow this particular volume? What books did Marie herself own, and did she ever lend them out? Did these friends discuss their reading together? What opinion did Marie have of the book in question?

By contrast, Christian Felix Weiße describes fictional family exploits across many issues of his periodical in fine detail. The prominence of this passage (in the very first issue of *The Children's Friend*) makes it clear that the new bourgeois family was fundamentally defined by education: Weiße celebrates books as a highly desirable commodity, and as something that the new child subject deserves. This message circulated in a range of prescriptive texts, likely producing varied effects in both adult and child readers of this periodical. But because we only have the text itself, it is difficult to say anything definitive about those reader responses.

What this means is that we need to assemble sources of both types for a multi-dimensional picture of children's lives—and in this example, the central role that reading and writing played in those lives. *Revolutions at Home* places archival evidence from family papers, especially children's own writing, alongside texts written for children. In this way, it intervenes in research on the family and education that has relied on prescriptive, top-down evidence from adult pedagogues. This exploration of practices on the ground is also amplified by rich information in the material produced by adults for child readers.

This book is organized as a series of studies in practices or genres of literacy that constituted children's education through overlapping but varied audiences, chronologies, purposes, and rhetorics. Each chapter attends to changes in both the cultural meaning of childhood and children's social experiences. Each unfolds a different dimension of childhood in the Age of Revolutions, including didacticism, orality, schooling, and domesticity. Bringing together these multiple genres illuminates the full prism of educational experiences that produced the modern child.

Chapter one, "Reading Serially: The New Enlightenment Youth Periodical for the New Youth Subject," examines serial publications for young readers and their families, paying special attention to the fashioning of gendered subjectivities. In the 1770s and 1780s, German publishers rapidly began issuing magazines, weeklies, yearbooks, almanacs, and other serialized readers designed especially for children and youth. I have analyzed approximately sixty of these titles published between 1756 and 1855 and distributed long distances across

Central Europe. Serialized to varying degrees, some of these publications were very short-lived and a few became remarkably successful. Youth periodicals presented a patchwork of essays, fiction, "true" stories from current events, games, poetry, riddles, illustrations, sheet music, and more.

I explain how the commercial expansion of this new genre in the late eighteenth century provided a literary laboratory for developing pedagogic ideas about children's innocence and the cultivation of self-control; at the same time, the growing success of these publications indicated the widespread construction of child readers as a distinct audience. Not only did adults' aim "to amuse and instruct" signal greater attention to child readers' desires and agency, but the spread of such texts offered more opportunities for children themselves to negotiate their reading education.

Chapter two, "Telling Tales: Folklore Transformed for Middle-Class Child Readers," investigates how radical changes in the revision and publication of fairy tales during the early nineteenth century shaped bourgeois child readers' understanding of class and family relations. Viewing fairy tales as neither simple nor static, this chapter traces the transformation of a popular, adult oral form of folklore into reading matter designed for middle-class children. I focus on Jacob and Wilhelm Grimms' *Kinder- und Hausmärchen* (*Children's and Household Tales*), which constitutes a particularly rich corpus of data as one of the most influential collections of fairy tales in the Western world. The Grimms were especially self-conscious about the pedagogic aspects of their project, and their text's seventeen editions published between 1812 and 1857 furnish the means to examine precise changes in the didactic and aesthetic priorities of the tales over time.

I am primarily concerned with the family sociology that children encountered in fairy tales: how parent-child relationships, marriage and sexuality, proper age and gender roles, and the emotional life of families depicted in German folklore were shaped by class. What did child readers learn about family life and class distinctions from fairy tales? In addition to using this genre to explore how the new child subject was constituted in terms of class cultures, I also address the literary-oral hybrid nature of fairy tales as a dimension of nineteenth-century children's culture.

Chapter three, "Reading the World: German Children's Place in Geographic Education," surveys geography texts, world history narratives, atlases, and natural science schoolbooks to examine the formal component of middle-class children's education. Geographic textbook authors in this period often drew on their experience as schoolteachers or on established scholarly reputations in history or classics. These books were used in a variety of settings: Gymnasien and Realschulen (secondary schools); Volksschulen (primary schools); military schools; and at home, with or without private tutors.

I use this corpus to trace how a descriptive, memorization-driven approach to geography instruction gave way to the fashioning of a modern approach around 1800. Now understood as a social science concerned with the dynamic relationship between humans and nature, the discipline demanded an active, problem-based pedagogy. Through examining textbooks themselves, as well as readers' marginalia, teaching curricula, and students' notebooks that reveal evidence of educational practices on the ground, I use the story of geography to exemplify a new, active model of learning for German children.

Chapters four and five turn to writing *by* children in order to paint a more complete picture of literacy practices than an analysis of children's literature alone provides. Enlightenment pedagogues taught and understood reading and writing as distinct disciplines despite their obvious connection, and researchers have continued to study them as separate phenomena. Especially in this era, it is certainly true that not all readers were writers. But for this particular class of the Bildungsbürgertum, writing was an essential tool in the cultivation of the active child learner.[87] Children's writing and writing practice took a variety of forms: formal essays and quotidian notes at school; poetry (both copied and original), often to accompany a holiday letter or drawing; autograph books (*Stammbücher*), in which school friends and family would inscribe short messages or lines of verse in honor of the recipient; and other informal or ephemeral writing that did not leave archival traces.[88] This book focuses on writing forms in a domestic setting, genres associated with home and family.

Chapter four, "Writing Home: Letters as a Social Practice," explains the escalation of children's letter writing from the mid-eighteenth to the mid-nineteenth century by drawing on hundreds of letters children wrote to parents, other relatives, teachers, and friends. The letters come from eight archives and some published sources, representing Berlin, Brandenburg, Schleswig, Lower Saxony, Lippe, Württemberg, and Bavaria. I have collected as many children's letters as I could find, with a central focus on letters written by bourgeois children before late adolescence. Most were short (one to two pages) and carefully composed, though some examples were more informal. Although many were sent through the post, some written for a special occasion were delivered by hand to a relative living in the same household.

Letters show children practicing adult conventions and asserting their important place in the family by reporting on household news, money management, and other practical concerns; demonstrating their bourgeois accomplishments and sentimental education; cultivating associations that would be important in adulthood; and engaging in relational autonomy through a number of different vertical and horizontal relationships. I reveal how children's letters document a lifelong process in the making of class cultures and forging of social ties. I furthermore situate children's education in letter writing as part of the broader project in cultivating able bourgeois subjects.

Chapter five, "Writing the Self: Growing Up with Diaries," explores how young people wrote about their own lives. As has been well documented, diary-writing soared as a technology of the self at the end of the eighteenth century. Yet though it might seem common sense that childhood and adolescence are a pivotal life stage for self-development, few diaries written by youth before the twentieth century have received extensive attention. For this book, I have closely read the little-known diaries kept by six girls and boys between the ages of ten and seventeen in regions across the German lands.

I argue that young diarists wrote regularly as a means of both self-surveillance and self-formation. Diaries could be another canvas for practicing penmanship and linguistic development, or perhaps for mechanically echoing didactic ideas about virtue and discipline. But I show that young writers also used their diaries to forge identities, assert personal taste and opinions, and grow up. Youth diaries thus reveal how modern European discourses of self-expression and self-discipline were practiced and shaped by very young writers.

In the conclusion, I return to Enlightenment educational philosophy and linger on some of the contradictions that animated middle-class children's learning throughout the transformations wrought by the Age of Revolutions. It is these contradictions, I argue, that make it essential we consider children's perspectives and participation. By bringing together documents created both for and by children of the Bildungsbürgertum, this book charts a fundamental shift in the experience of growing up that still guides our world today.

CHAPTER ONE

READING SERIALLY

The New Enlightenment Youth
Periodical for the New Youth Subject

Opening the first issue in April 1776 of a popular weekly magazine by Christian
Felix Weiße, young readers found a dialogue in seven scenes. The story went like
this: While playing with his father's gun, Karl accidentally shot his little sister,
Julie. Seeing her covered in blood, their brother Wilhelm cried out that he would
give his own life for her, and Karl fell in a swoon. Their father demanded to know
who was responsible. His rage was so terrifying, the brothers covered for one
another to prevent a second murder! Then—Julie miraculously revived, claiming
responsibility for shooting herself and refusing to let Karl be punished. Moved
by the children's loving defense of one another, their father relented, grateful to
his mendacious children for preventing him from shooting the culprit.

One could be distracted by this story's shocking content, or read it as an
Age of Revolutions anti-authoritarian allegory. But the uses of this little soap
opera as a pedagogic tool are particularly intriguing. Imagine the German children who subscribed to *Der Kinderfreund: Ein Wochenblatt für Kinder* (*The
Children's Friend: A Weekly for Children*) in the 1770s and 1780s. What can
we surmise about how they responded to "Sibling Love"? Did they recognize
characters from previous serials? Who laughed through the silly opening scene
of Wilhelm's arithmetic mistakes? Who skipped ahead for the fun of rehearsing
the dramatic gunshot itself? What pleasure did child readers find in the vivid,
over-the-top stage directions? If a set of siblings performed this dialogue, did
someone want to play the terrifying father? What happened when girls read
parts written for boys, and vice versa? Who claimed the position of director?

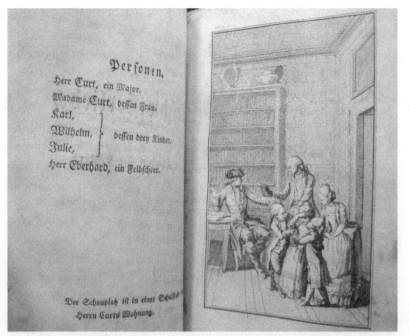

FIGURE 3. Cast list and facing illustration of "Sibling Love" from Christian Felix Weiße, *Der Kinderfreund,* 1776. Kinder- und Jugendbuchabteilung, Staatsbibliothek Berlin.

Various sources furnish evidence of reading practices around dialogues such as this one. Family archives document that elite German children often copied, wrote, and performed plays with siblings, parents, and tutors. Folklorists, child development researchers, and our own experiences as children tell us that performance and storytelling of some kind are ubiquitous in growing up. The genre of sentimental drama would have been familiar to eighteenth-century child readers, given its frequent appearance in youth periodicals. We can suppose that siblings receiving *Der Kinderfreund* read this play together even if they did not act it out, since the magazine's subscription list included girls and boys in a wide range of ages. But perhaps most suggestive for considering child readers' practices is what follows after the play: a moral lesson placed in a more realistic setting. The coda suggests that children should apply similar principles to the scenario of a brother lying for his sister after she breaks two porcelain cups.

The play and its framing story point toward the same moral guidance: prioritizing compassion for the feelings of others, even if that suffering is caused by a parent's discipline. Beyond that, the lesson also models a way to read, with fictional children from the frame narrative discussing the story they have just heard with their father, identifying personally with its characters, and investing it with meaning for their quotidian life. This new genre of youth periodicals invited children to play an active, imaginative role in their reading, for an education that was more sentimental and concerned with children's amusement than ever before.

In this chapter, I explore how Enlightenment youth periodicals supported the development of the modern child subject. The commercial expansion of a new genre during the years around 1800 provided a literary laboratory for pedagogic ideas about children's innocence and the cultivation of self-control; at the same time, the growing success of these publications indicated the reimagination of child readers as a distinct audience. Forms such as dialogues for children's performance and serialized tales both scripted and responded to changing reading practices. While the texts provide direct evidence of adult values about childhood, children's tastes and changing uses of periodicals influenced the development of a modern children's literature. The stories themselves depicted ideal readers and sentimental family life in line with the new ideology of childhood, but were also subject to a range of possible readings and misreadings. Enlightenment periodicals especially contributed to the emergence of a new kind of reader through the fashioning of gendered subjectivities in texts directed both at girls and at a cross-gender audience. Not only did adults' desire "to amuse and instruct" signal greater attention to child readers' desires and agency, but the spread of such texts offered more opportunities for children themselves to negotiate their reading education.

More than sixty titles published between 1756 and 1855 are surveyed in this chapter, as the publication of youth periodicals exploded at the end of the eighteenth century. After taking a look at the forms and stories found in these texts—that is, *how* they were written and *what* they were written about—I examine the construction of gendered subjectivities in periodicals as a crucial dimension of young people's changing reading practices. Throughout, I indicate ways of thinking about child readers' reception and practices around the developing genre of youth periodicals.

GENRE DEVELOPMENT

In their style and format, youth periodicals of the European Enlightenment owed a debt to the moral weeklies that, building on an English tradition, had been published for adults since the early eighteenth century.[1] The 1770s and 1780s witnessed an explosion of magazines, weeklies, yearbooks, almanacs, and other serialized readers especially redesigned for children and youth.[2] I suggest that the swift adoption of periodicals by pedagogues demonstrates a growing preoccupation with children's literacy practices as a cornerstone of constructing the modern child subject.[3] Pedagogic use of serial publications also underscored this era's reimagination of childhood as a separate stage of life that required its own books. Periodicals quickly generated new texts that could guide child readers to moral action and emotional expression. These publications also carried the pedagogic aims of the Enlightenment into the home.

TYPICAL CHARACTERISTICS

The definition of a youth periodical during the years around 1800 was not narrowly fixed. Some periodicals were very short-lived and some single books were so frequently updated in subsequent editions that they functioned in ways similar to magazines and yearbooks. For example, Nadine Bérenguier describes Madame Jeanne-Marie Leprince de Beaumont's influential *Magasin des enfans* (*Children's Storehouse,* first published in 1756) as a conduct book, which it certainly was in its moralizing content. The French word *magasin* meant then more a warehouse or treasury than did its later cognate, *magazine.* But this sense of collecting and anthologizing material over time was reflected in Leprince de Beaumont's search for future subscribers and promise to issue future annual volumes. In this way, it was a foundational model for many later periodicals and children's books from German, French, British, and American publishers. I suggest that we should attend both to the form of such a text and to its function in children's education.

Beyond these variations, what did a typical Enlightenment youth periodical look like? (See Appendix A for the tables of contents from two exemplary publications.) Some form of serialization was key, though I have included titles that were published as frequently as twice weekly and as infrequently as annual yearbooks. Some only survived about a year, but longevity increased moving into the nineteenth century.[4] A few titles introduced at the end of the period under examination here lasted in some form into the early twentieth century. Most Enlightenment-era magazines and weeklies had short runs, but surprisingly wide distribution. Some were short-lived because their creators moved on to other projects but did become more popular from year to year.[5] The volumes were usually small—often pocket-sized—and ranged in the quality of their paper, printing, and presentation. As with fairy tales and schoolbooks, technological innovations throughout this period increased the number and interest level of accompanying illustrations. Some included fold-out copies of sheet music for folk and art songs, supporting their cultivation of bourgeois arts. Many of the earlier periodicals still followed the old practice of an opening letter of dedication to a royal patron.

AUTHORS AND READERS

Authors of youth periodicals, both men and women, often asserted their natural authority as teachers or parents in order to connect with the child reader audience.[6] For example, Leprince de Beaumont's time as a governess in England prompted her to write the *Magasin des enfans*. She explicitly offered this experience as evidence of her knowledge of children and as a moral authority on their education. Meanwhile, Weiße painted a picture of his narrator surrogate in the first issue of *Der Kinderfreund* as a self-sacrificing father whose only pleasure in life was his children.[7] Writing on the use of this same device by French conduct-book authors, Bérenguier calls it "the Crucial Role of Experience."[8] Bérenguier perhaps takes these claimed biographies too much at face value, since authors were often performing fictional parental roles; nevertheless, some previous connection to children's education was a common background for the women and men of letters who turned to producing amusing periodicals in their pursuit of a youth audience.

While some of the periodicals I have examined were explicitly aimed at young children below the age of ten, in many cases the imagined audience of these periodicals was older. However, age is one of several boundaries of publishers' intended audience that was permeable in practice. This can be seen in the subscribers' list published in the *Niedersächsisches Wochenblatt für Kinder* (*Lower Saxony Weekly for Children*, orig. 1774) in its 1781 and 1783 volumes. Families of four or five children each were listed by name, spanning enough years to suggest that youth were reading before or beyond the intended age.

SUBSCRIPTIONS

Young readers acquired periodicals in a number of ways, including at shops and book fairs. One early magazine explained in each issue the ideal methods of finding the *Leipziger Wochenblatt für Kinder* (*Leipzig Weekly for Children*, 1772–74):

> In the coming new year, this weekly paper will still be issued on the usual days, namely Mondays and Thursdays, both at the local newspaper stall as well as in the Crusius bookshop in Paulino. Elsewhere it is to be had both at any post office and in the principal bookstores.

The frequent publication of this title is worth noting, as is the range of distribution sites beyond the publisher's main shop. A later volume noted that supplementary materials (a collection of letters by the fictional child protagonists of the weekly stories) were being sold to benefit educational institutions in the Ore Mountains of Saxony.[9]

Eighteenth-century European publishing was often financed by reader subscriptions. In a quintessentially modern turn to middle-class consumers versus a single aristocratic patron, subscriptions were collected by publishers from across wide regions. Serial publications were especially suited to the subscription process, since readers could invest in a title and continue to receive new volumes over time.[10] The first edition of Leprince de Beaumont's *Magasin des enfans* warned readers "who wish the continuation of this *Magasin* that it cannot be printed, unless we are sure of one hundred subscriptions; they are therefore urged to subscribe early."[11] In that case, they exceeded their initial modest hopes, and continued to issue new volumes. To encourage subscriptions, publishers offered special deals, as when the first volume of *Für deutsche Mädchen* (*For German Girls,* 1781–82) noted that subscribers would receive the next volume at their known address for the special rate of four issues at three guilders.[12] The editor Paul Nitsch wrote "with prophetic spirit" that he would like to begin with at least a couple hundred "admirable girls" as readers.[13] Aimed at younger girls, this publication was very regularly printed, missing only one week during Christmas. Even though it was short-lived in its original run, it was popular enough to be collected and reprinted some years later. In fact, many of these periodicals, especially in the eighteenth century, were gathered and reissued in bound volumes.

Even where a list of subscribers seems small to us today, it could be of great value in the eighteenth- and nineteenth-century book trade. When publisher Johann Friedrich Cotta and author Marianne Ehrmann had a famous falling out over the popular girls' periodical *Flora,* Ehrmann created a new journal but Cotta had possession of the original subscription list and was able to continue sending out magazines under the cover of the old title.[14] Subscription proved a useful tool for the cultivation of a community of youth readers. The explosion of the genre was not possible without the financial and cultural investment of German families.

FOUNDATIONAL TITLES

Several titles from the late Enlightenment stood out as especially successful or influential for the development of youth periodicals and children's literature extending into the nineteenth century. They also furthered the construction of a modern child subject through their establishment of normative practices for children's reading and propagation of ideas about children's interiority. These landmarks include some publications already mentioned: Madame Leprince de

Beaumont's *Magasin des enfans* (first published 1756) and its German translation (first published 1761), Johann Christian Adelung's *Leipziger Wochenblatt* (first published 1772), and its successor, Weiße's *Der Kinderfreund* (first published 1775).

Leprince de Beaumont's series for children and young women was not only translated swiftly into German, but also circulated in its original French among educated families in Central Europe.[15] In fact, a French-language edition of the first volume was published in Berlin at least as early as 1782 (by Arnold Wever). Hubert Göbels included the French version of the *Magasin des enfans* in his definitive catalog of German youth periodicals and notes that Leprince de Beaumont's "bestseller" was "surely intended for private reading as well as for school use."[16] In the early years of European children's literature, pedagogues justified the amusement of reading merely as a vehicle for learning, but books like the *Magasin des enfans* opened the door to a new idea that children deserved pleasure, humor, and narrative, not only moral development. In her foreword, Leprince de Beaumont described her primary purpose as "the acquisition of virtue, the correction of vice . . . Everything we say to children, everything we write for them, all that is brought before their eyes must aim at this end, or be skillfully led there by an able master."[17] But she also blamed children's distaste for reading on the choices of books that "we place in their hands."[18] This model of desire and choice did not entail allowing children the freedom to find books to their own taste or, for that matter, to choose not to read at all. Rather, Leprince de Beaumont and subsequent pedagogues called for new moral stories that would also be entertaining (according to adult prescription).

For the most part, the German translation of Leprince de Beaumont's *Magasin des enfans* (directly translated as the *Magazin für Kinder*) preserved the original characters and stories. The translator, Johann Joachim Schwaben, produced the first German edition shortly after the initial publication. Some changes, however, highlight the bildungsbürgerlich vision of childhood. Choosing Dresden as a similar social world to the original text's London setting, Schwaben noted that the characters would not be referred to as "Lady" or "Mademoiselle" but rather by terms befitting the daughters of a German middle-class house, "Fräulein" and "Jungfer."[19] Schwaben's interpretation of Leprince de Beaumont's educational mission was framed in classic terms of the German Enlightenment, invoking both rationality and sentiment: "She seeks in these children . . . to improve their hearts and enlighten their minds, two important things which we should see in every interaction with children especially."[20] He thus contributed to the redefinition of children as morally innocent, pedagogically malleable, and sensitive to emotional influence. Any changes that Schwaben made to the actual stories, he wrote, were motivated by a desire to prevent potential misreading: "It is true that such small errors naturally shape the character of a childish tale ... I simply wished to avoid [errors] in those stories which are presented to children during lessons."[21] This itself reveals an awareness by the author of the imagined child reader's potential agency to take different meanings from the text than those intended. But even more interesting is the following passage, in which Schwaben writes that he was careful to keep the children's speech authentically "childish" even in his translation. His assertion of a "natural" mode of children's speech and literacy was then offered as a script to teach real children appropriate behavior and language.

One of the earliest German youth periodicals was the *Leipziger Wochenblatt.* Though it only ran for two years, the editor Adelung's use of a direct sentimental address to the child reader, epistolary and dialogue forms, and moral-didactic stories serialized across regular, short issues established a popular model for youth periodicals. This framework was notably taken up by Weiße in his weekly *Der Kinderfreund,* an even more widely disseminated publication.[22] By opening the first issue with a reference to what he called the "sadly discontinued" *Leipziger Wochenblatt,* Weiße tried to capitalize on the previous magazine's reputation.[23] His own publication, though similar in format, actually turned out to be more successful, and deepened connections between changing ideologies of childhood and reading practices. He followed it with a book written entirely as letters among the characters he introduced in *Der Kinderfreund,* called the *Briefwechsel der Familie des Kinderfreundes* (*Correspondence from the Family of the Child's Friend,* 1783–92). Weiße, who was already a successful author and well-known in Enlightenment *philosophe* circles, gained his greatest popularity with *Der Kinderfreund.*[24] Pedagogue Samuel Baur wrote in 1790 that "this excellent book founded an epoch in the world of children, and will still remain one of our best children's books long from now."[25]

Subsequent magazines in the late eighteenth and early nineteenth centuries built on Weiße's model in terms of format and expectations for child readers. This was signaled in titles such as Karl Engelhardt's *Neuer Kinderfreund* (*New Children's Friend,* first published 1796). Still other types also emerged. Authors who had been successful in other genres for adults and youth entered the periodicals business, including the well-known Amalia Schoppe and Sophie von La Roche. German youth periodicals specifically written for girls, such as Paul Nitsch's *Für deutsche Mädchen* (*For German Girls,* 1781–82), first began to appear in the 1780s and 1790s. As years passed, more magazines targeted even younger readers. By the late nineteenth century, the formats for children's newspapers and magazines became more standardized, cheaper, and more widely disseminated. *Das Pfennig-Magazin für Kinder* (*The Penny Magazine for Children,* 1834–38), a weekly published by Brockhaus, was a prototype for later magazines that were printed inexpensively in a large page format and then rebound annually to reach an even larger audience. By contrast, the years around 1800 appear as a time of experimentation for pedagogues and literary authors interested in cultivating child readers.

Thus, the rapid expansion of the genre of Enlightenment youth periodicals itself reveals a newly intense focus on the education of the modern child. A review from Friedrich Nicolai's authoritative *Allgemeine Deutsche Bibliothek* (*General German Library*, 1775) gives some sense of contemporary awareness of the changing landscape of children's reading: "We are beginning to receive a great wealth of writings for young people . . . thus the young soul finds here such matters through which it must be awakened to the fear of God and love of humanity, once it is able to accept good thoughts and sentiments."[26] Even the reviewers were keenly aware of the potential for molding the child self through reading. More praise followed in this review of the *Niedersächsisches Wochenblatt für Kinder,* but there was also some criticism of its flaws. Ultimately, the reviewer recommended that the publishers of the weekly defer continuing the next volume until success was assured and its usefulness to the target audience proven. The adults involved in the production of periodicals for youth asserted their power to form individual morals and enlighten minds, but because of that weighty responsibility there were debates and differing priorities in how periodicals would be used to educate children.

FORM

Pedagogical debates are not the only means of assessing the transformation of children's education. In this section, I examine different formal elements of youth periodicals—*how* the material was conveyed to young people—and suggest some implications of these strategies for the child's reading experience. The particular and diverse forms of these periodicals highlight different ways child readers might have used and misused them. Some magazines featured serialized stories—were these followed eagerly from the beginning or picked up mid-narrative? How did periodicals attempt to build loyalty to a serial publication among their readership? In the mixed form "variety show" of most texts, it is easy to see how readers might independently pick and choose a poem to reread here, an essay to skim there, or a play to perform. Nevertheless, authors tried to direct their audience through the prefaces included at the beginning of many magazines, which also attempted to exert control over the relationship between author and reader. Frame narratives were also commonly deployed to model ideal reading practices and moral behavior, usually in a family setting, and dramatic dialogues took on special importance for children's reading. Taken together, these elements of form and style created a new kind of reading environment for youth.

PERIODICAL STRATEGIES SHAPE CHILD READER RESPONSE

As is evident through this book, reception is not easy to assess, neither in the past nor the present. But authors of Enlightenment youth periodicals continually worried about how their texts affected child readers. Weiße encouraged children to write to him with their responses to *Der Kinderfreund,* "even to say what you dislike about my weekly magazine."[27] He promised to respond to their complaints and edit the magazine in response. Madame Leprince de Beaumont even claimed to have tested her manuscript for the first volume of the *Magasin des enfans* with some real girls of her acquaintance. "I needed other judges, and I searched for them among my pupils of all ages. They all read my manuscript. The child of six years was entertained by it, as well as the ten-year-old and fifteen-year-old."[28] Leprince de Beaumont had worried (with some degree of false modesty) that the book's success with adults meant she had missed her target audience, but this response from young readers encouraged her to publish.

When making decisions about how to organize periodicals, authors and pedagogues considered the possible uses children might make of them. When he translated the *Magasin des enfans* into German, Johann Joachim Schwaben explicitly praised Leprince's mode of morally guided literacy. In his added introduction, he described the exchanges between the fictional girls and their teacher that structured Leprince de Beaumont's text: "The children think, speak, and act according to their inclinations, their disposition, and their reason. She praises and encourages them for what they have done and said correctly, or helps them to be right and punishes them when they err and make mistakes. Therefore, one discovers in [this text] not only the chief weaknesses and deficiencies of their stage of life, but also the ways and means of how one could lift them up and improve them."[29] Schwaben imagined readers of his *Magazin für Kinder* taking a similar approach so that they would learn from these supposedly realistic models of both good and bad behavior. But forms such as dialogues that included erring or disobedient children could also lead to a kind of counter-reading that authors did not intend; similarly, the diverse genres that made up individual issues of a periodical could easily allow bored child readers to skip any pieces that did not captivate them.

In a nostalgic reflection, Hubert Göbels deftly evokes the potential meaning of a short, serialized publication for the child recipient of one of these regularly published little volumes. He writes of children's periodicals, "Who did not encounter these in his youth, these items for collecting & trading that were so easy to transport in the jacket pocket or schoolbag? Which one could consume secretly, even by the shine of a flashlight and possibly entirely under the bedcovers?"[30] The intimate reading that Göbels describes may reflect a more modern practice from his own childhood in the early twentieth century, but by the early nineteenth century this emotional resonance between children and their magazines was beginning to spread as an ideal for how children should read and desire books. A serialized, inexpensive periodical could be marked as a child's own, the next issue of which she might await with excitement, share with friends, or keep for herself.

Scholars have suggested that publishers chose to serialize stories or novels from already popular authors as a commercial strategy.[31] Weiße emphasized the serial format of his new publication in a not-so-subtle exhortation of his child readers to buy into the magazine if they wanted to receive more of it: "I want to share my children's amusements with you weekly . . . The appetite with which you will collect it from the publisher and read it will soon persuade me whether I should continue these little family amusements or should break it off."[32] The frequent schedule of *Der Kinderfreund* was intended to propel interest in the title. The growing popularity of serial stories for children was also reflected in the format changes of Paul Nitsch's *Für deutsche Mädchen* over the course of its short run. Opening with several discrete stories and poems contained within one sixteen-page issue, by the second year more and more of the weekly was taken up with long stories "to be continued" in the next issue. Not only does this imply that Nitsch could assume a consistent readership over time, but it also allowed for an enduring relationship of the youth reader with continued characters and themes. Similar effects on children's reading practices of serialized periodicals could be observed in titles that were regularly reissued in new editions, or by the promotion of well-known authors by publishers. Books and periodicals were becoming understood and marketed as essential commodities for middle-class children themselves to desire.[33]

YOUTH PERIODICALS AS VARIETY SHOW

As the typical tables of contents listed in Appendix A demonstrate, periodicals presented children with a wide range of genres and styles—a literary variety show. Despite the ephemeral nature of some magazines and weeklies, this meant that some volumes could be kept almost as reference books, to be dipped back into later for pieces of music, poetry to memorize, or the earlier issues of a serialized story. This indicates a fundamentally different relationship with printed texts than that of an early modern young student studying linearly and orally from a select number of volumes fully directed by a teacher. Adalbert Merget suggests that the variety of forms served to enliven and tie together the family stories that Weiße used as a framing device: "The instructional pieces from the various fields of study mentioned above were woven into the family life events which are the basis of the book."[34] To Merget, this diversity of forms made periodicals naturally appealing for a family audience. Göbels points to an alternative explanation of the grab-bag style of youth magazines and weeklies—their market appeal. He writes that authors "sought to win over the reader not only with enticing titles; they also took no small trouble to bring their magazine to men (and women!) through the means of variety in the individual articles."[35] And indeed, Weiße made the mélange of material in *Der Kinderfreund* one of its selling points, promising in the first issue to include interesting engravings and sheet music in future installments.[36]

Some youth periodicals contained illustrations inside each issue, but these were rare before the 1830s. Most visual information came in the form of frontispieces at the beginning of each issue. By far the most common theme of frontispieces in Enlightenment youth periodicals was reading, specifically in a domestic setting. Whether in a book-lined study or a bucolic landscape, these opening illustrations made it clear that a child's world should be built from books and family. The 1776 frontispiece of the third volume of Weiße's *Der Kinderfreund,* for example, showed an energetic group of six boys and girls of various ages, most holding small pamphlets in their hands, apparently preparing to perform a dialogue together with their teacher or father. Though many of the pictures emphasized literacy as tool of middle-class sociability, some also stressed the child's individual, personal relationship with books.

Though all-male groups were unsurprisingly more common than all-female groups, many periodical frontispieces for a mixed audience showed boys and girls together. An illustration of women and girls alone often depicted a sentimental scene, as in the fourth volume of Weiße's *Der Kinderfreund* (the 1776 edition). In it, a mother kisses one child with another literally hanging on to her apron strings. Perhaps the most interesting illustrations came from the combination of these messages, as in the 1781 illustration from the seventh volume of *Der Kinderfreund* (figure 4), which depicts a physically affectionate sister and her brothers clearly receiving the same instruction in astronomy from their tutor.

FIGURE 4. Frontispiece of Christian Felix Weiße, *Der Kinderfreund,* 1781. Kinder- und Jugendbuchabteilung, Staatsbibliothek Berlin.

Alongside illustrations, music was also common in youth periodicals, with the lyrics of songs on various subjects included amid the essays and stories. Several publications also included actual sheet music as a fold-out addition. These songs were usually fairly simple, offering a melody line with keyboard accompaniment and a few verses. For example, Christian Carl André's *Der Mädchenfreund* (*The Girl's Friend,* 1789–91) provided the lyrics and notation for such songs as "To Youth," "The Worth of Religion," and "Diligence."[37] Music was one of the "extras" that made certain periodicals more attractive, and likely contributed to determining the price of different editions and republications. The inclusion of sheet music and songs as poetry supported the cultivation of bourgeois accomplishments in child readers, and the musical styles also reveal a nascent folk nationalism. Music was thus another way in which youth periodicals were a useful tool for training the ideal bildungsbürgerlich German child.

Beyond illustrations and music, the list of common forms that made up typical youth periodicals was long. Poetry included both digests of highbrow work by authors like Johann Wolfgang von Goethe and Friedrich Schiller as well as newly composed didactic odes to various virtues. Riddles were not uncommon, alongside their specialized form, charades. Games were also sometimes on offer, including instructions for parlor games and the rules of popular card games. "True tales" were popular in some periodicals, as in the account of a courageous pregnant woman who saved a runaway coach from disaster in "The Great Presence of Mind of a German Woman: A True Story," from one of the 1799 issues of *Flora*.[38] Essays were quite common; these were directly addressed to children, sometimes serialized across issues, and concerned largely with qualities of character and family relationships. Academic subjects were offered in a few titles, with content on religion, history, botany, and geography, as in Christian Gottfried Böckh's weekly *Kinderzeitung* (*Children's Magazine*, 1780–83), whose content ranged from comments on the products of Russia to questions for his readers about an anecdote from Saxon history.[39] Finally, book reviews could be found in some publications, encouraging children to acquire similar texts from the publisher—and cultivating them as buying readers.[40]

What effect might such a wide-ranging mix of material have had on children's reading experiences? The reviewer of the *Niedersächsisches Wochenblatt* in Friedrich Nicolai's journal expressed mixed opinions about the value of the diverse genres and material included in that magazine, writing, "Sometimes the authors have the children write to one another, sometimes they engage in discussions, at times they present a fable or a song, at times something from natural history, at times from history, and finally at times something from mythology. Of course, we must also admit that not everything has equal value. The poetic pieces in particular were not all written or chosen with sufficient taste."[41] It is true that the pressure of producing or collecting so much content for each of these titles on a weekly or monthly basis not only led to short publication runs but also produced quite a lot of third-rate, place-holding items. But more importantly, this patchwork nature of most youth periodicals generated a different kind of reading experience than the limited and highly directed literacy in which children engaged before this period. The variety of forms constituting the typical issue demonstrates the emergence of an active child reader, both because it reveals authors' attempts to shape a sophisticated but "childlike" reading subject, and because it indicates a kind of practice for children that allowed for more imagination, problem-solving, mistaken reading, fantasy, performance, personal connection to stories, and non-linear reading.

PERIODICAL PREFACES CONSTRUCT AUTHOR-READER RELATIONSHIPS

While in textbooks the prefatory remarks were usually addressed to adults (teachers or parents), the forewords and opening lines of most periodicals were notably addressed to children. Though adults certainly would have been understood as a secondary audience, this supported children claiming these periodicals as their own. Authors and publishers used prefaces to imply an intimate, sentimental relationship with their child reader that usually continued through subsequent issues, especially through the use of apostrophe (direct speech to the imagined reader). Authors also used prefaces to instruct children how to read (and how not to), and those prescriptions can be revealing.

The phrase "my dear readers," ubiquitous in periodicals, was usually addressed to both genders ("meine liebe Leseren und Leserinnen") rather than defaulting to the usual masculine plural. This kind of language both imitated and modeled the new ideal of domestic intimacy for children, especially since it often occurred in a fictional family setting. In the piece "The Young Woman among Youths" from Nitsch's *Für deutsche Mädchen,* the author, who signs as "R," adds a caveat before beginning a dialogue with a girl named Doris.[42] She writes to her readers, "You will pardon me, though, for speaking with her somewhat informally. We understand each other."[43] And in fact, the dialogue is somewhat flippant, with banter and kind-hearted teasing between Doris and the voice of authority. Both this style and the request for her readers' pardon invite children into a sentimental relationship with the author. André expressed a similar wish in the first issue of his *Der Mädchenfreund,* writing that he wanted to get to know his readers.[44]

Some prefaces recommended that the text be shared with siblings or read alongside a parent, implying both that group reading experiences were possible and also that some authors feared children were indulging too much in the dangers of solitary imaginative reading. Editors also invoked an extended community of child readers. As a common formal element of most youth periodicals, authorial prefaces contributed to crafting the ideal child reader subject, one who both delighted in and eagerly anticipated future periodical reading, but who also read in socially acceptable ways that would lead to personal moral development.

Frame narratives were a popular device for youth periodical authors; by far the most common was a frame of siblings reading or performing the inner story with a parent or tutor as guide. The outer story modeled the proper setting for children's reading—at home—and how to apply it to a moral life. Just like frames in adult literature, from the *Odyssey* to *Frankenstein,* frames in youth periodicals sought to manage the reader's perspective and attention. Unlike in other literature, however, narrators in the frame stories of Enlightenment periodicals were always presented as reliable guides for child readers. In *Der Kinderfreund,* Weiße suggested in his foreword to the first issue that children might not understand everything in the weekly magazine on their own. To that end, he created a surrogate fictional family to explain the content while engaging in their own minor dramas, characters with whom he expected the real child readers to identify. For example, after the story of near sororicide with which I opened this chapter, Weiße's fictional family reflected on what they had heard in the play. The teachers in the frame narrative explained to those surrogates for real child readers what lesson they should take from the drama to their real lives.

Frame narrative settings were also used in youth periodicals to instruct child readers in bourgeois sociability.[45] Girls and boys were trained in rituals of discourse as a civic virtue, but, crucially, one located at home. These little discussions of young people in a schoolroom or a group of siblings that framed the primary content of periodical literature modeled for child readers how they should participate in these forms of sociability as part of growing up. Weiße brought various tutors and family friends into the scenes of his fictional frame family as foils for the frame narrator father's discussions.

Though frame narratives are a common device in literature, one crucial new aspect of their use in periodicals for children at the end of the eighteenth century is that the frame child was also presented as a flawed being. Just like the real child reader, the characters who were engaged in the reading, performing, conversing, and reciting that made up the action in periodicals were prone to error and yet redeemable. Weiße wrote in his introduction of the frame family that his purpose was "to help you to get to know my children and our friends: because their conversations quite often reflect their character, and to have as ever the virtues or faults of my children and their improvement as my aim."[46] As surrogates for and reflections of the imagined reader, this was a different interpretation of the old "model child" story. To be sure, the purpose was still to govern children's behavior and expression through their education, but the possibility of a generally good but realistically flawed self was now allowed as part of the modern child subject.

As frames were tangential to the main content, unsupervised children did not have to read the frame story at all. They could skip the moral lessons and go straight to the more dramatic parts. Alternatively, some children might grow quite attached to the characters of the outside frame, following them from issue to issue like an Enlightenment soap opera. In frame stories with the moral instruction of children at the center, the real reader might identify with or admire the "bad" behavior of the frame children, whatever the author's intent. Or in establishing the model of a perfectly loving, sentimental middle-class family, frame narratives might make real readers conscious of absences or problems in their own lives. But these discussions could also guide how a child would learn to read (especially insofar as the frames were also a model for the parents or teachers reading alongside the children), suggesting the safe utility of group reading and adult supervision.

DIALOGUES SCRIPT CHILDREN'S READING

Dramatic dialogue was perhaps the most transparent way in which new youth periodicals facilitated active reading by children. Pedagogues transformed the adult genre of drama to realize their ideal of engaged, educated children taking an active role in learning. But the common use of plays in periodicals also reflects a broader practice of performance and imaginative play by children themselves, beyond the strict dictation of adults.

Just as letter stories in children's magazines owed a debt to epistolary novels of the eighteenth century, their dialogues developed out of a common literary form: sentimental drama. Rather than excerpting current plays or classics for a general audience, however, periodical authors wrote new dialogues with young characters and translated the style to what they believed to be "childlike" expressions. They also highlighted a special pedagogic concern—that fictional dialogues should motivate child readers to moral action. Dramatic dialogue provided a key instrument for authors interested in eliciting and managing the youth reader's affective response. Pamela Gay-White and Adrianne Wadewitz call this "socializing theater in the domestic sphere" and observe that dialogues in texts for children draw explicitly on the social conversation mode of Locke and Rousseau.[47] This was borne out repeatedly in youth periodicals, whether dialogue was used as one of a variety of forms as in Weiße's *Der Kinderfreund* or served the entire piece as in Antonia Wutka's *Encyklopädie für die weibliche Jugend* (*Encyclopedia for Female Youth*, 1802–16). As a form, drama allowed for the paradoxical teaching of spontaneity, encouraging children to rehearse out loud the emotions and responses they ought to express as children of the Bildungsbürgertum. In the cases of Wutka and Leprince de Beaumont, the dialogue format made it possible to place their didactic messages in girls' voices. For Weiße, the plays included in his magazine especially contributed to the pedagogy that Birgit Prilisauer names his "playful learning process."[48]

The inclusion of dialogues in periodicals also allowed for children's expression of reading agency as they literally "acted out" these stories. Stage directions in the periodicals indicate that these dialogues were clearly intended to be performed, or at least read aloud with siblings and friends. In "The New Year's Wish" from the *Neujahrsgeschenk für Kinder von einem Kinderfreunde* (*New Year's Gift for Children from a Child's Friend*, first published 1778), the character of Lottchen was meant to give part of her performance "in a sing-song tone."[49] Dialogues offered readers the possibility to assume different characters, take on the authority of direction, and enjoy the pleasure and humor of the physical action.

Just as children's play today is influenced by various media, the importance of theatricals to family life around 1800 can be seen in archival evidence. For example, the Breitenburg children in Schleswig regularly wrote dialogues to be performed at the holidays, such as the "Christmas Dialogue between the Two Young Counts Detlef and Hans" (1769) and the "Dialogues between August and Conrad" (1784).[50] In considering a youth-authored play from the Bakunin family archive during the same era, John Randolph writes that fourteen-year-old "Praskovia's *Prologue for the New Year 1790* is easy to dismiss as domestic ephemera.... Whatever Praskovia's literary inspirations or personal motivations, however, we should not forget the political dimensions of her choice."[51] For Randolph, the content of children's dramas can tell us about political life on an enlightened Russian estate. Such texts also demonstrate the interplay of children's agency and adult expectations in the use of dialogue as a literacy practice.

CONSEQUENCES OF PERIODICAL FORMS FOR CHILD READERS
From the use of apostrophe to forge intimate, direct links with child readers to dialogues that elevated children's voices, the stylistic techniques and formal elements of the new youth periodicals document the changing reading practices of middle-class German children at the end of the eighteenth century. Over this period, some aspects of form adapted in response to new visions of how children should read, such as the transition from parent-addressed prefaces to texts entirely directed at children. Others, like serialized stories that sought to connect reading subjects with the subject of reading, became more widespread as periodicals for young people themselves grew in popularity. Though much of the content may seem predictably didactic on the surface, the variety of forms employed in youth periodicals underscores their goal to engage the reader's attention and to cultivate a new kind of child subject.

STORIES

What content did these youth periodicals deliver? This section turns to the material itself for answers about the interpretative process between text and reader. Some of the most common themes in these periodicals included: filial obedience, sibling love, and other social relations such as friendship;[52] the beauties of nature, holidays, historical topics, and orientalist tales of faraway lands; and character virtues like courage, gratitude, and compassion, often told through fables. What do the stories, essays, and dialogues reveal about children's reading practices? How did they facilitate or constrain the active child reader? Here I explore the messages about character formation, sentiment, amusement, and the dangers of reading offered by youth periodicals as they and their young readers worked together to construct the modern child subject.

THE READING CHILD SUBJECT

By transforming reading into an active, engaged practice for children, pedagogues hoped to use texts like these periodicals to foster character development and subject formation, thus cultivating a new child self. This ideal subject was defined in a number of ways evident in children's reading material.

First, the child should grow up into a self-controlled middle-class adult able to contribute to society. The dangerous alternative was tied to illiteracy in a report from J. G. Reinhardt's *Der Mädchenspiegel* (*The Girl's Mirror*, 1794), "On the Use of Reading and Writing." In this sad tale, a dishonest man discovered that Anastasia, who had inherited some money, could neither read nor write. Drawing up a fraudulent loan agreement, he disappeared with her money and she was unable to get justice in court. The story ended with Anastasia's lament: "'Oh, if only I had learned to read and write!' And from that time she told all children to go to school diligently, where they could learn to read and write."[53] Yes, Reinhardt redundantly extolled the virtues of literacy via the written word, but this dramatic story may have caught the attention of bourgeois girl readers contemplating their own financial futures.

Second, the child reader's individual intellect was prized through the encouragement of diligence, especially in education. Chapter four documents this preoccupation with diligence in the reports of real child writers recounting assiduous study in their letters to family. Industriousness was also one of the most discussed personality traits in youth periodicals, but it held different meaning across social categories. The trick was to cultivate appropriate engagement but not undirected curiosity, and the work that children could expect to undertake was gendered and classed. Readers of *Der Mädchenspiegel* received a clear picture of the virtues of women's work in "Die kluge Wahl": "A clever man wanted to marry, and came into a house in which there were two sisters. The first was pretty, enjoyed preening herself, and did not enjoy doing useful work. The other was hardworking, did all of the housework, and made sure everything was kept in the strictest order. Which of these two is he likely to have married?"[54] A virtuous woman (and girl) mastered household responsibilities and avoided vanity. Her industriousness was measured in domestic terms.

Third, children's innocence and their moral-ethical development was a preoccupation of these texts. Christianity held uneven significance in early children's literature, much as it did in the youth diaries I analyze in chapter five. Leprince de Beaumont for example, was deeply concerned with restoring religious faith to the core of girls' education, but had to finesse a confessional challenge that may have contributed to making her work popular with a diverse German audience. Though she herself was Catholic, the girls she taught in her capacity as a governess in England were Anglican. As Bérenguier has observed, religious education was always tied to enlightened academic instruction in Leprince de Beaumont's periodicals.[55] She hoped to find in her readers "a child who is religious through reason."[56] The cultivation of appropriately devout child subjects was explicitly tied to literacy. In the story "The Little Praying Boy" from an issue of the *Neujahrsgeschenk,* young Gottlieb was shown learning the purpose of prayer not only through conversations with his exemplary loving father, but also explicitly from reading a little religious book designed for children.[57]

Fourth, the ideal child subject was defined not only by virtues necessary for future success, but also through relationships. Obedience and affection were newly intertwined in the modern ideology of parenting and ubiquitous themes in the essays and fiction of youth periodicals (as well as the letters examined in chapter four). Frequently, this dual ideal was as explicit as in the title of a poem from the *Neujahrsgeschenk:* "Love and Obedience to Parents."[58] In support of appropriate bourgeois sociability, the child subject was expected to cultivate compassion and generosity. This kind of selfhood was social and philanthropic, deeply implicating children in the making of class cultures. One example modeling middle-class generosity for children can be seen in the piece "The Charity of Some Young Girls," from an 1806 issue of Johann Christian Dolz's *Bildungsblätter* (*Educational Pages,* 1806–11). It reported on two young girls who saved their pocket money to purchase material for winter clothes that they sewed themselves to give to poor children in the Ore Mountains region of Saxony. What is especially interesting here is the link the author makes between moral development and *reading* about bourgeois philanthropy. The piece opened with the question, "What good child would not gladly hear or read something about such young people, who are invigorated by this beautiful spirit of good deeds?"[59] It closed by underscoring the same sentiment, suggesting that reading about these girls might encourage other children to make small sacrifices for the pleasure of charity.

SENTIMENT

Children's books have long provided a domain for the popularization and contestation of sentimentalism. At the end of the eighteenth century, the significance that writers of the sentimental placed on the reader's affective response mirrored the attention that authors, pedagogues, and parents gave to managing children's emotions. For some, this sentimentalism came as a kind of "conditional love," as when Weiße wrote in *Der Kinderfreund,* "I love all children most affectionately, as long as they are good, devout, industrious, and obedient children."[60] Some Enlightenment pedagogues resisted sentimentalism and sensibility in children's periodicals out of concern for reason.[61] Self-control and obedience continued as important moral threads in the ideology of childhood into the nineteenth century, but sympathy and sensibility became increasingly important for a bildungsbürgerlich child in the age of sentimentalism. Hina Nazar has challenged the false dichotomy between rationalism and sentimentalism. She writes that sentimentalism "importantly shaped one of the Enlightenment's principal legacies to the modern world: the ideal of autonomy or moral self-direction, which began to compete with an older morality of obedience in the eighteenth century."[62] I argue that writing for children particularly exposes the tension between sentimentalism as a moral force and as a seductive threat. Pedagogues appreciated stories and dialogues as instruments for eliciting the child reader's compassionate response to the suffering of others, but they also worried about the dangerous power of independent or indulgent, overly emotional reading.

In Weiße's *Der Kinderfreund,* the fictional children "naturally" loved and respected their narrator-father, who wrote in the first issue, "For I hold the principle that one should make childhood as joyful and prosperous as possible, and should make each type of instruction a game. . . . For this reason they love me, my friends, and their teachers with their whole souls, as I [love] them; and as long as they do no act rashly from childish lapses, they are seldom ungrateful enough to injure me through disobedience or recalcitrance."[63] As in the play from *Der Kinderfreund* with which this chapter opened, the form of the family drama modeled ideal affectionate family relationships for middle-class child readers, a setting that invited itself to the sentimental.

The attention to balancing pleasure and instruction that emerged at this moment in new genres such as youth periodicals especially lent itself to sentimentalism because of the possibilities offered by learning through reading fiction. Writing on eighteenth-century children's books, Wadewitz observes that pedagogues hoped reading touching or shocking stories would help children craft a "sensible self."[64] In German periodicals, reading was presented as a diversion that would encourage children to make judgments and consider their own behavior in the context of the characters' choices. Weiße used his pulpit of *Der Kinderfreund* to teach by reaching children's emotions and sympathies as well as by cultivating their rational self-discipline. Sentimentalism, as refracted in children's books, was also deeply connected to sociability, and inflected by gender, religion, and class. Wutka's *Encyklopädie für die weibliche Jugend* trained child readers in highly affectionate language both among the girls, as part of an early nineteenth-century approach to romantic friendships, and with their teacher, as part of the new model of pedagogic relationships. These two periodicals present two different settings: the middle-class family arranged around a patriarch in *Der Kinderfreund,* and a Catholic community of girls learning from their peers in the *Encyklopädie für die weibliche Jugend.* But both intended to use a sentimental reading education to cultivate compassion for others' suffering and a benevolent social self.

Like sentimental literature and drama for adults, sentimental children's books especially focused on stories that the authors believed would cultivate readers' sympathy for the suffering of others. So in Enlightenment youth magazines, the "model child" character was most often identified through sympathetic social relationships, as with the fictional children of Weiße's *Der Kinderfreund.* The narrator's oldest fictional daughter, Charlotte (age eleven), was described at the opening of the first issue as naturally good-hearted. However, Charlotte had to be reminded occasionally of her own good nature and compassion, modeling the construction of an ideal child. When she teased her younger siblings, it was out of playfulness rather than cruelty, her fictional father fondly remarked.[65] Thus Weiße's readers were reminded to show their own good hearts by proxy, in preparation for reading a series of stories that would solicit that compassion. The narrator of *Der Kinderfreund* also claimed that his familial responsibilities made him a good teacher and observer of human nature because fatherhood "naturally" inclined him toward sympathy for others' needs.

AMUSEMENT

Enlightenment youth periodicals aimed to entertain a new class of readers. But did they really succeed in amusing their audience? In a communications study of girls' magazines at the end of the twentieth century, Petra Nickel dismisses texts like Nitsch's *Für deutsche Mädchen* as prototypes of modern publications that are not really concerned with pleasure: "The goal here was not to entertain youth, but rather to mold them in the pedagogic or religious understanding of that time."[66] But a closer examination of these periodicals in their own context shows a different picture. In fact, even though the moral didacticism of such texts stands out to twenty-first-century eyes, their blend of stories, plays, games, songs, and more brought a new degree of imagination, humor, and drama into children's reading lives at the end of the eighteenth century.

Pedagogues did hope that children would imbibe knowledge and moral values along with pleasure. In his introduction to the German translation of Leprince de Beaumont's *Magasin des enfans,* Schwaben explained his perspective on how the fun of fairy tales and other stories could motivate learning: "One knows how much children love tales such as these, and how attentive they are while listening to something wondrous."[67] He also stressed to his adult readers the importance of making clear to children what was real and what was not, a prescription that indicates anxiety about children's imaginations.

The inclusion of game rules in various periodicals tied reading education to new means of entertaining children. For example, J. D. Mauchart's collection, *Neue Hesperiden* (*New Hesperides,* 1804–7), was almost entirely dedicated to social games. It presented the rules and materials necessary for various educational games suitable to a "game evening," followed by dialogues or stories to be shared on a "reading evening." The "Spielabende" in the first volume included natural history guessing games with an elaborate table of options, as well as instructions for constructing a "large, easy, and cheap" game table (figure 5); the "Leseabende" of plays and fables was followed by a section of riddles, also intended for group reading entertainment.

Other than games and riddles, possible sources of amusement for children in periodical reading included illustrations and music; humorous dialogues; attachment to recurring, familiar characters; the pleasure of story, conflict, and resolution; the endless realms of imagination to which these stories might open the door; escape from quotidian surroundings; the interpretative process of reading itself; and the acquisitive satisfaction of a child possessing his or her "own" book.

Of course, some authors' claims about the fun their texts would surely give to children are not so plausible. Leprince de Beaumont suggested in a convoluted fashion in the first issue of the *Magasin des enfans* that her students applied themselves to their education because they found true happiness in obedience to their parents and their teachers.[68] But even if it seems unlikely that all children chose to please their parents from a pure motivation of personal happiness, there is other evidence that some children found pleasure in this kind of reading. Particularly persuasive is widespread anxiety on the part of pedagogues that child readers might sometimes be having *too* much fun with books. The danger of pleasurable reading was the flip side of entertaining moral lessons.

DANGERS OF READING

The exponential growth in publishing for children at the end of the eighteenth century, of which youth periodicals were a part, spread anxieties about children's reading among the very authors and pedagogues who were producing these texts. They recognized a threat in reading that was solitary and unsupervised, or reading that led children toward immoral content. Independent reading might allow children to escape into fictional worlds outside the mediating influence of social authority. This fear reflects the centrality of reading in the vision of a modern, free-thinking child subject.

One kind of danger was that children could take the wrong lessons from otherwise well-intentioned material, which was especially problematic with

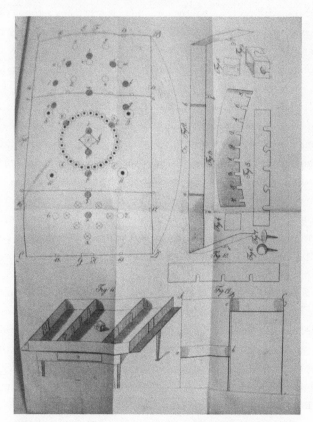

FIGURE 5. Fold-out diagram for constructing a game table, *Neue Hesperiden*, 1804. Kinder- und Jugendbuchabteilung, Staatsbibliothek Berlin.

fiction. Ute Dettmar observes that Weiße was criticized for including stories of "anti-heroes" in *Der Kinderfreund* with whom his child readers might identify, "undermining the moral-didactic intention" of the author.[69] Opening up children's reading to the possibilities of engaged, imaginative reading also meant accepting the possibility that they could make their own meanings out of the text.

Books could also be dangerous because of the information they contained, as with the young men and women so obsessed with dancing that they walked around with collections of dance figures in their pockets described in one issue of Engelhardt's *Neuer Kinderfreund*. Young people learning how to handle the pleasures of literacy and dancing alike aided appropriate bourgeois socialization. Engelhardt writes, "For you, dancing should be recreation after work, cheering up in the long evenings, but not at all a business." He allowed for the scandalous behavior of carrying around dance music and books in dancing-masters, who devoted themselves to that purpose, but argued that it was dishonorable for young people with professional futures: "In this way many a young man who would have, had he trained his capacity and talents, become a useful member of human society, neglected the hours of more serious instruction and self-education, pursued dance, and then regretted too late this confusion of the pleasant with the useful. In this way many a young girl has trilled dance melodies all day, lived and moved in English dances and waltzes, found pleasure nowhere except at the ball, and became a passionate dancer."[70] This caution could easily have been applied to novel-reading and other pleasures in which children and youth might over-indulge. Engelhardt's own advice was contradictory, as he uses a periodical that was also accompanied by sheet music, stories of balls, and essays on social life encouraging appropriate relationships between young men and women—to warn against the dangers of social dancing and dance books.

To prevent the wrong kind of reading "which might deprave children's hearts," parents had to be involved, according to the 1797 prospectus for a French periodical, the *Courrier des enfans* (*Children's Post*): "Many fathers today do not dare to place a book into the hands of their children without knowing beforehand what it contains, and under what principles it was edited. Can we blame this measure of prudence?"[71] It was certainly a common practice for parents to select books and periodicals for their children after consulting pedagogic advice. Of course this also reveals a clever marketing strategy on the part of publishers, who co-opted social anxiety about children's unsupervised reading in order to justify advertisements for periodicals as a better moral guide.

In her first volume of the *Magasin des enfans*, Leprince de Beaumont drew heavily on biblical accounts for her material. In the preface, however, she justified her choice to use the Bible selectively or even censor it by invoking a relatively new understanding of children's innocence, and tying that to the emerging principle of reading as pleasure. Children, she wrote, "should not suspect that I want to educate them; this principle allowed me to keep back everything which might bore them. Do I not have the same privilege with those things which I regard as morally dangerous?" This attitude also reveals the pedagogue's awareness that children had a license to misread or to read the wrong way. Leprince de Beaumont provided examples of Bible stories that could be "misunderstood" by child readers—stories that children might interpret in ways not sanctioned by enlightened Christian morality. What if the tale of Jacob and Esau taught children that lying and fooling their parents was acceptable? Leprince de Beaumont then remarked cryptically that there were even more examples of potentially harmful Bible stories that she chose to exclude, but would not mention these by name. Even though the preface was addressed to adults, she was clearly concerned that children might also read this explanation, since "it is dangerous to excite their curiosity too much."[72] Indeed, it seems likely that this tempting ellipsis would send some children straight to the source to uncover these scandalous stories. Anxiety about the dangers of reading prevented neither the expansion of children's literacy education nor the possibilities of transgression.

THE NEW READING GIRL

Gender was a crucial aspect of defining the modern bourgeois child subject, both in the ideals promoted by authors and in the reality of girls and boys' reading experiences. Germans understood reading as a powerful device in the dissemination of evolving gender ideologies. Pedagogues wanted bourgeois girls to participate in new literacy practices alongside their brothers, but in different ways and to different ends. Still, in gendered reading of periodicals, what adults had to say was not the only determinant of girls' experiences, and the contradictions of these texts could be read against the gender grain. Though full of dicta intended to govern young women's desires and behavior, the earliest books for girls foreshadowed the introduction of more creativity and entertainment. Furthermore, they also asserted a kind of equality in education that was later foreclosed in girls' reading material.[73]

The importance of gender to the set of historical dynamics under examination in this book is especially apparent in periodicals because so many serial texts targeted specifically at girls and young women swiftly appeared in the eighteenth century. Dagmar Grenz makes the important point that girls' periodicals were not always counted in general book catalogs or review journals, so it is difficult to be sure precisely how many titles were circulated.[74] Though early texts such as *Für deutsche Mädchen* targeted older girls and young women, periodicals and other books for young girls became more common by the 1790s. Not only did more serial publications emerge for girls, but this era also saw an unprecedented flurry of writing for and about women, including on their education and vocations.[75] In this final section of the chapter, I address some paradoxes of girls' reading, examine the use of "exemplary lives" as a pedagogic instrument, and offer four specific illustrations of gender dynamics in girls' periodicals.

THE PARADOXES OF GIRLS' READING

Reading girls were surrounded by a set of ambiguities and contradictions in Europe at the end of the eighteenth century. The stories and essays of Enlightenment youth periodicals served as a vehicle for gendered ideologies about the separation of spheres and women's essential nature as mothers and wives, governing girls' choices and teaching them how they should feel and behave. This was at times as particular and even petty as the question posed in *Der Mädchenfreund*: "Should one walk with the toes or the heel first?"[76]

Despite these directive prescriptions, the second half of the eighteenth century was also the moment in Europe when reading was becoming understood as something internal and subjective. The places and modes of reading grew more and more private, intimate, and even sometimes illicit. In this sense, literacy was both an instrument of gendered socialization and also a constrained path toward emancipation.[77] Thus the odd marker of eighteenth-century children's books: one of the common characteristics of a bad, disobedient child in fiction was *curiosity*;[78] at the same time, one of the key ways children were supposed to demonstrate filial obedience was through *learning*.

Girls' reading in the years around 1800 was also shaped by the central paradox of liberal feminism. Scholars have pointed to the utility of writing in women's lives for asserting an autonomous self, contradicting everything Enlightenment philosophers such as Rousseau had to say about the poverty of women's individuality and agency.[79] As Joan Scott has elucidated, while efforts for women's equality sought to efface differences between the sexes in politics, they were forced to articulate goals in terms of that very same sexual difference.[80] The limits of expanding girls' education are exemplified by pedagogue Joachim Campe's unease on the subject. Campe did not intend to extend radical Enlightenment notions of choice and the individual fully to girls, and his work was thus "characterized by different contradictory tendencies," per Grenz.[81] Works like his *Väterlicher Rath für meine Tochter* (*Fatherly Advice for my Daughter,* 1789) contributed to a revolutionary educational context in which unprecedented attention was being paid to girls' learning, even if it was intended for the narrowly constrained purpose of training wives and mothers.

I argue that it is not simply that girls had no access to the masculine, liberal individual selfhood of Enlightened education. Rather, the individual most pedagogues wanted to cultivate in a girl was a compassionate, devoted, *selfless* person directed toward serving others. Both boys and girls were taught to be sensitive and devoted to their families, but ideal womanhood required disregarding individual personalities and desires—the selfless self.

Furthermore, bourgeois girls and boys alike were subject to "the pedagogic double ideal."[82] The reimagination of childhood as a separate stage of life and concern for the child's individual spirit produced contradictions: that youth should be cultivated to be natural and instructed to be self-controlled. Girls, especially as young children, were supposed to be authentic and unaffected, to enjoy the freedom and pleasures of a protected childhood. At the same time, it was the purpose of education (and reading) to raise cultivated bourgeois subjects who would be socially useful. Pedagogues tried to resolve this dual mission by investing in the entertainment value of their moral tales. Authors like Leprince de Beaumont wanted their child readers to be inspired by entertaining paragons and *choose* to behave. In the foreword to the *Magasin des enfans,* she writes, "We tell children over and over: nothing is more naughty than lying, than getting angry, than being gluttonous, disobedient. Who would not believe that these vices are very rare in the world, given the care that we give to defending against them in children? They should have a horror of these faults, and they actually would have, if instead of inserting the maxims that we have prattled on about on this subject in their memory, we had penetrated their reason."[83] It was crucial for the authors of this new genre that moral choices not be enforced didactically from above but instead freely arrived at by independent, educated children.

The act of reading itself was a site of moral contradictions. Reading was a powerful pedagogic tool, to be sure. But it was therefore potentially equally powerful as a seduction to undesirable behavior.[84] In the intersecting relationships among author, text, and reader, what would be the consequences of lost authority? Though this is something philosophers, theologians, and political leaders have worried about across historical contexts, girls' reading seemed especially dangerous to some eighteenth- and nineteenth-century commentators. Girl readers of *Für Deutschlands edle Töchter* (*For Germany's Noble Daughters,* 1801) were cautioned against the growing dangers of "indiscriminate and superficial" reading: "These days reading belongs to the fashionable pleasures of the fair sex; but, just as fashion changes clothes from year to year, so does the fashion of books change for these [readers]." The editor even urged that "females should only read a little, and only a little at one time."[85] At the same time, the editor suggested that reading his periodical would guard against the over-cultivation or corruption of other books. Danger arose not only from the unsuitable or radical content girls might encounter through reading, but from something deeper in the practice of reading. As girls began reading independently and silently, the adults around them worried that their individual relationship with the written word was itself damaging.

Enlightenment youth periodicals provoked but did not answer perennial questions: What should be the most important affective relationship in a young woman's life—female friendship, sibling love, or motherhood and marriage? Were amusement, novelty, humor, and romance mere vehicles for moralizing didacticism, or should these constitute a truly new form of entertainment? If girls must be cultivated as readers, could they also be figured as rational, thinking individuals of the Enlightenment, and if not, what were the limitations on that autonomy?

EXEMPLARY LIVES AS PEDAGOGIC INSTRUMENT

Portraits of exemplary lives filled books written for girls, especially before the mid-nineteenth century. Stories of heroic women were told as models to edify and entertain youth. However, "true histories" of remarkable women from the past, such as political leaders and religious figures, were largely confined to textbooks and biographical galleries intended for use in the schoolroom. Texts designed to amuse, like these periodicals, usually portrayed fictional paragons of virtue or vice.

In periodicals, the individual women whose biographies were held up as models generally came from one of three groups: Greek and Roman myths, tales of princesses and other young nobility, and reports of fictional and real individuals not unlike the readers whose merits or flaws were presented as ideal or cautionary. This last type was the most common, and is well illustrated by the story "A Little Girl Shows Great Courage" from a 1779 volume of the *Neujahrsgeschenk für Kinder.* It told of a girl who swam to rescue twenty people from a capsized ship near Regensburg.[86] At the same time that her heroic action was signaled as extraordinary, the newspaper-style reporting on this anonymous girl also described her as an ordinary person with whom the active reader should identify. With amusement-oriented publishing for children steadily on the rise, the model of fictional biographies found in these periodicals came to represent the primary way children read about exemplary women by the middle of the nineteenth century. Furthermore, in textbook publishing over the course of this period, though ancient and medieval heroines such as Dido or Joan of Arc were still included, contemporary female figures, for example, from the French Revolution, were not. While fictional or anonymous girl models continued to appear, heroic women were gradually relegated to the distant past.

THE CONSTRUCTION OF GENDERED SUBJECTIVITY: FOUR ILLUSTRATIONS

The following examples document some developments in the ways in which childhood in the Bildungsbürgertum was gendered. First, a heavy-handed example may be seen in Leprince de Beaumont's *Magasin des enfans* as two characters discussed their dolls and trinkets:

LADY SPIRITUAL:	It has been more than six months since I threw all these things in the fire: I begged Papa to give me all the money that he spent on these bagatelles so that I could buy books and pay all kinds of teachers.
LADY BAUBLE:	I am not of your taste: if I were the mistress, in place of giving two guineas a month to my geography teacher, I would have the most beautiful things in the world brought from Paris; this would amuse me very much, instead of this man boring me to death; when I see him, I cannot stop yawning at every moment: he tells Mama, she scolds me, and that makes me hate the teacher and geography even more.
LADY SPIRITUAL:	Do you not like reading stories?
LADY BAUBLE:	No, honestly, my dear; still, it is necessary that I read, because Papa wants it: but when I am grown up; and can do what I want, I assure you that I will never read.[87]

Leprince de Beaumont hoped to inspire in girls a personal desire for books and learning. Child readers should clearly emulate Spiritual, but even the shallow Bauble was shown to be making her own choices about her time, education, money, and consumption.

Second, we can consider gendered ideologies in Weiße's *Der Kinderfreund* (written for an intended audience of girls and boys) through the character portraits Weiße offered of his fictional frame family. In the eighteenth century, as Nancy Armstrong has told us, "the difference between male and female was understood in terms of their respective qualities of mind."[88] Weiße's introduction of Charlotte (eleven), Karl (nine), Fritz (seven-and-a-half), and Luischen (five) taught their real-world counterparts that this started in childhood. Charlotte was presented as a little frivolous and flighty (female flaws), but Weiße also asserted that she had the capacity for serious learning but chose not to focus.[89]

Karl was the "opposite" of his sister because he was intellectual and serious, and "industrious beyond his years."[90] He also had a soft heart and was often brought to tears, a manly virtue during the sentimental German Enlightenment. Fritz, just like his sister, was described as hyperactive, though his hyperactivity was more physical than Charlotte's mental fickleness. In contrast to his older brother's bookishness, Fritz was apparently training himself for a more practical business career, interested as he was in mechanical things, travelogues, and drawing houses. His faults were the wrong kind of cleverness—for example, he was always able to find the biggest piece of cake and persuade his siblings that he suffered with the smallest slice. Finally, little Luischen was too young for most of her individual character to have emerged, according to Weiße. But she was described as having a good memory for stories and picture books—note that her primary characteristic had to do with literacy.[91]

In these amusing little portraits, the primary behavior marking a flighty bad girl or a serious good boy was how the child treated books. Charlotte flitted from subject to subject, while Karl never started a book without finishing it. While their flaws were more starkly gendered (flightiness and vanity for the girls, versus stubbornness and scheming for the boys), it seems that at this age the girls were actually not significantly limited in terms of education. They, like their brothers, were expected to demonstrate virtue through reading and sharing their stories. The difference is that they ultimately were educated for a different purpose. If Charlotte could conquer her faults, she would be "a very lovely person" with all the benefits of mind and body that God had given her.[92] But if Karl could conquer his faults, he would become a virtuous and learned man, one useful to the world.[93] Both served as models of new child subjects, but they presented futures divided by gender.

My third illustration comes from the short-lived but influential weekly *Für deutsche Mädchen*. The combination of stories, poems, and essays in this magazine aimed to teach girls how to behave in certain situations, such as how to choose a husband (The answer? For love, but someone you love who also happens to be invited to your parents' house—that is, socially appropriate.). But an equal goal was to cultivate the correct emotions in girls, to make them loving, compassionate, dedicated to parents and siblings, and, indeed, selfless. One example of these objectives united is an essay and dialogue titled "The Girl among Youths" in which the speakers held a very long conversation about how to choose the right husband. This section could easily have been read transgressively, for the thrill of hearing about dangerous, worldly men. The voice of wisdom in the piece takes the seemingly liberal position that girls should be encouraged to spend time with young men, rather than to imagine a vast gulf between them.[94] But along the way, Nitsch asserts a variety of misogynist ideas about girls' foolishness, delicacy, and vanity. While the essay depicts sites of sociability, it also advances reading (and specifically, reading fiction and periodicals) as a proper source of guidance for girls about the all-important marriage question.[95]

Finally, the fourth illustration is Wutka's *Encyklopädie für die weibliche Jugend,* which began with a preface that offered a familiar invocation of future motherhood as a reason to educate girls. The author was remarkable as a woman positioning herself within the pedagogical debates of the Enlightenment, and her preface is an intriguing critique of contemporary philosophy that excluded women.[96] But even more unusual is the story that the primary dialogue conveyed. In it, Emilie, twelve years old, found her friend Friderike, also twelve, in dramatic distress. Friderike had overheard two men describing her as a "plague of society," who should be left uneducated. She said that she did not want to read anymore or study anymore; she wanted to throw all her books and maps into the fire, and, if it were possible, her schoolmaster, too. Emilie's solution was to form a schooling society (*Unterrichtsgesellschaft*) with several of their other young friends and Emilie's "teacher, friend, and dear second mother," Auguste, as their leader.[97] The rest of the volume portrayed their lessons: reading aloud to each other from Bible stories and classical myths and asking questions of their teacher.

The religious moralizing and cultivation of separate spheres that informed their lessons was not so radical. But the story itself, which was peopled with bright, lively characters and unfolded with small moments of drama, offered contradictory opportunities to its young readership in the late Enlightenment. In its rejection of the unnamed men's judgment, this story, ideal for reading aloud or acting out, suggests the importance of girls' own choices and community formation. I suggest that despite the didactic nature of most publishing for girls during this period, such contradictions and ambivalences about girls' learning mattered to the reading experience of the target audience and the kinds of subjectivities that might emerge from literacy practices.

CONSEQUENCES OF GENDERED READING

Leprince de Beaumont's *Magasin des enfans* largely promoted a future for girls as conventional bourgeois wives and mothers. And yet, she also challenged those limits:

> What do [girls], some tell me, need to know about the difference between their souls and those of animals? They believe this truth and a thousand more on the word of other

people: they are not made for knowing anything else. Some say to me, you purport to make them logicians and philosophes; I respond to them, and *you* would have them be happy as automatons. Yes, Misters Tied-Down, I intend to pull them from this base ignorance to which you have condemned them. Certainly, I intend to make them logicians, geometers, and even philosophes. I want them to learn to think, to think rightly, in order to achieve a good life.[98]

How do we reconcile this fiery statement about the purpose of girls' education with the content of the periodical? Such expressions became less common by the middle of the nineteenth century in periodicals like Thekla von Gumpert's *Töchter-Album* (*Daughter's Album,* 1855). The specialization and expansion of children's literature had many happy outcomes, but one cost for girls was that their early reading began to be more and more focused on their future domestic responsibilities.[99] I concur with Grenz that the presentation of gendered norms in girls' books was blunter in the eighteenth century and more subtle (therefore insidious) in the nineteenth.[100] It is possible, though difficult to prove, that increased political censorship in German print culture during the rebellious 1790s may have contributed to this foreclosure of the more radical promises of revolutionary-era girls' literature.[101]

Understanding that girls' and boys' reading practices were scripted by gender is necessary for reconstructing the experiences of the new child subject. Beyond giving us a fuller picture of how these texts worked, a gender analysis of Enlightenment youth periodicals also supports my argument about children's reading practices more broadly. That pedagogues sought to craft a gendered subjectivity in young people through these periodicals demonstrates the growing relevance and utility of reading education during this period in which the restructuring of middle-class family life was so significant. Furthermore, the dialectics of girls' reading allowed actual readers to negotiate their gendered education in unpredictable ways.

CONCLUSION

Although the titles analyzed here are no longer widely read in the twenty-first century, Enlightenment youth periodicals have enjoyed a lasting legacy through their influence on golden age children's books that did become canonical. This influence is partly evident in parody, such as texts like *Struwwelpeter* (1845) that mocked the paragon child mode of storytelling. Even more, the early texts shaped children's literature through their cultivation of the modern, active child reader. Through transactional forms like the use of illustrations and forewords addressed to child readers, this new genre promoted a new kind of child subject. Authors endeavored to shape a class and age-specific audience, as well as to establish gendered expectations for readers. They were profoundly concerned with how an individual child reader would use their texts.

Did children have an Enlightenment?[102] Could they form autonomous reading selves? In practice, youth reading of periodicals could be highly mediated and supervised. Simply to gain access to these magazines, children needed parents and teachers. But the tension between this fact and new ideas about independent reading gave children an opening. In order to deal with the pedagogic double ideal in which they had caught themselves, periodical creators worked to make reading more attractive to children so that young readers would come willingly to their Enlightened education. Weiße, Nitsch, Leprince de Beaumont, Wutka, and others presented essays, fables, and Bible stories as a vehicle to moral action, not solely to stimulate the imagination. Nevertheless, the emphasis on capturing young readers' attention through amusement held unintended consequences. Just as agency and discipline are mutually constituted, these periodicals reveal a generative tension between learning and fun—and in that tension, the ideal modern child subject emerged. This entanglement of pleasure and pedagogy is central to the next chapter, which ventures into the forest of German fairy tales.

CHAPTER TWO

TELLING TALES

Folklore Transformed for
Middle-Class Child Readers

Once upon a time—or, more precisely, one day in autumn 1858—a little girl arrived at the home of Jacob and Wilhelm Grimm to pay a debt.[1] In those days, the Grimm brothers lived with Wilhelm's family in Berlin. They had already published the final edition of their collection *Kinder- und Hausmärchen* (*Children's and Household Tales,* hereafter *KHM*), and achieved semi-celebrity status for that work as well as for their other scholarly and political activities.[2] Carrying the *KHM* with her, "a pretty child with beautiful eyes," as Wilhelm described her in a letter to friend Anna von Arnswaldt, showed up at the house.[3] The girl read aloud the story of "The Clever Little Tailor" to Wilhelm (or to Jacob, according to the newspapers).[4] Its closing line, "And whoever does not believe me must pay me a Thaler," had been part of the *KHM* from its first publication; such features that evoked the oral, folk origins of fairy tales were preferred by the Grimms and sometimes invented to elaborate stories stylistically. When the child finished, she informed Grimm that because she did not believe it, she needed to pay but could not cover the entire sum. Instead, she gave him a *Groschen* (one-thirtieth of a *Thaler*) and promised to pay the rest later. According to Wilhelm's letter, at that point he offered to return the money, but the girl refused, instructing him, "Mama says one should not accept money as a gift." Then she left (or, according to the newspaper version, the Grimms ensured that she made it safely home), and this "Märchengroschen" tale was committed to Grimm scholarship and lore.[5]

Mediated as it was by Wilhelm Grimm, newspaper editors, and narrative conventions, what does this story really tell us about the girl herself? I will address the challenge of recovering fairy tale reading reception later in this chapter, but to begin I want to sketch some ways in which the Märchengroschen story encapsulates the modern child subject. First, this girl embodied the active child reader directly, by reading aloud from her own book, "well and with natural expression," as Grimm admiringly wrote. Simply by consuming the *KHM*, she was participating in the explosive development of children's literature in this era. Furthermore, the fact that Wilhelm Grimm found this girl and this story so charming itself depended on the transformation of childrearing in the Age of Revolutions, including growing adult interest in the "natural," interior workings of children's minds. This child engaged independently with what she read, so much so that she chose to reject it. And yet at the same time she obeyed its direction to the letter (an obedience that was underscored in Grimm's description of her "polite" manner). Or, put another way, because she didn't buy the story, she paid for it.

The story also illustrates the emergence of a particular child subjectivity through social class. Although Grimm only described her physical appearance to von Arnswaldt, the newspaper versions made a point of identifying her as "a little girl belonging to the upper classes."[6] More tellingly, her literacy and cash both attest to her membership in the bourgeois, educated child audience the Grimms sought to cultivate through revision of the *KHM* over the previous five decades. Despite explaining that she received "not much pocket money" (hence lacking the Thaler), she did possess her own coin purse and a concept of debt—as she promised to pay off this "skepticism penalty" in stages. And even though she reportedly traveled to the Grimms' house alone, her financial mores had been shaped by her family ("Mama says"). By the mid-nineteenth century, the *KHM* had remade an adult oral tradition into a book for young audiences and was dominating the fairy tale market. It was produced with an explicit class-based vision for a newly defined group of children with pocket money and serious reading responsibilities. As Ingeborg Weber-Kellermann asserts, "The victory march of the *Kinder- und Hausmärchen* could only succeed because the nurseries of bourgeois homes constituted a willing and enthusiastic circle of consumers."[7] The participation of middle-class German children was indispensable to the Grimms' publishing success.

While European historians have turned to fairy tales for evidence of cultural nationalism, the politics of gender and sexuality, historical linguistics, and various other inquiries, in this chapter I am primarily concerned with the family sociology that the modern child subject learned in fairy tales. By "family sociology," I mean the apprehension of class cultures and family practices as they intersected: how parent-child relationships, marriage and sexuality, proper age and gender roles, and the emotional life of families were understood and marked across class boundaries. The "self-conscious familialism" that Mary Jo Maynes has named as foundational to middle-class identity suffused the Grimms' project.[8] As fairy tales in general and the *KHM* in particular figured more and more prominently in the active child reader's world, what lessons did that reader learn about family life and class distinctions? In addition to using fairy tales to demonstrate how the new child subject was constituted in terms of class cultures, I also consider the peculiar qualities of this literary-oral hybrid genre in the context of nineteenth-century children's changing literacy practices. Through this analysis, I argue that the cultivation of class-based subjectivities in fairy tales rewritten for a youth audience furthered the development of modern childhood, which, although imagined and often discussed as a universal norm, was very much a class-specific project.

Like periodicals, schoolbooks, and children's writing, fairy tales worked as a pedagogic instrument. Examining fairy tales also brings to light particular aspects of children's socialization: the role of oral storytelling, the power of fantasy and imagination, the impact of popular publishing trends, and a new vision of proper childhood expressed through the conversion of an adult oral tradition to a literary genre specialized for young people. The Grimms' *KHM* constitutes a particularly rich corpus of data for the history of children's reading, not only because it later became one of the most influential collections of fairy tales in the world. Other fairy tale writers during the years around 1800 had begun to focus their attention on young audiences; a diverse range of folktales from various sources were accessible to bourgeois child readers. However, the Grimms were especially self-conscious about the ways in which their scholarly project transformed into a pedagogic one over the course of the early nineteenth century. Furthermore, the popularity of their text has ensured the preservation of seventeen separate editions published from 1812 to 1857 (seven of the main text, the *Große Ausgabe,* and ten of an abridged version, the *Kleine Ausgabe*). This, in addition to an 1810 manuscript of the *KHM* that was rediscovered at Ölenberg in the 1920s,[9] furnishes us with the means to examine precise changes in the fairy tales over time, and to investigate how the Grimms crafted their collection in response to changing didactic and aesthetic priorities.

The European fairy tale emerged from popular oral traditions as well as elite literature and was then transformed into children's literature. As the Grimms became more concerned with pedagogy over time, class and family became central to their revisions of the oral sources. Different editions of the *KHM* thus reveal adult perspectives on class cultures of reproduction, parenting, gender, marriage, and filial obedience. However, these tales may also be read against the grain for consideration of children's own experience of fairy tales.

ES WAR EINMAL: A BRIEF HISTORY OF FAIRY TALES

BEFORE THE GRIMMS

While middle-class child readers constituted a critical new audience for fairy tales in early nineteenth-century Europe, these stories were by no means invented for their benefit. The fairy tale forms popularized by the Grimms grew from both an abundant oral tradition and a long literary history. For two centuries, folklorists have worked to establish typologies and continue to debate the differences between oral folk tales, literary tales, wonder tales, fairy tales, legends, myths, fables, and other oral and literary relatives of these forms.[10] While these distinctions are not significant here, it does matter that the stories encountered by German child readers emerged from both an anonymous oral tradition of the European peasantry and a literary tradition circulating among elites throughout the early modern era. What was new about the Age of Revolutions was the establishment of an educated middle-class reading public ready for their own transformations of the fairy tale—transformations that targeted the child reader.

My approach to published fairy tales should not be taken as a dismissal of the power and intricacy of an enduring oral fairy tale tradition.[11] I concur with scholars such as Linda Dégh, Harvey Graff, and Walter Ong, who find orality and literacy coexisting and intersecting throughout the modern era in patterns more complex than a simple, teleological displacement of folklore with the printed word.[12] But because this book focuses on children's reading and writing, this chapter is centered on the publishing phenomenon of the *KHM*. To understand why the *KHM* formed part of the construction of the modern child subject, a brief survey of the landscape they entered and transformed is illuminating.

The fairy tales that German readers consumed in the early nineteenth century owed debts to commingled Middle Eastern, Italian, French, English, Celtic, Scandinavian, and Slavic traditions.[13] Particularly influential predecessors to the Grimms include Giovanni Francesco Straparola, Giambattista Basile, Madame d'Aulnoy, Charles Perrault, and Madame Leprince de Beaumont.[14] In addition to disseminating a paradigmatic version of "Beauty and the Beast" popular today,[15] Leprince de Beaumont used fairy tales in her magazine as a didactic instrument. "Some will say, we [already] have twelve volumes of fairy tales, our children can read those," Leprince de Beaumont wrote defensively in the foreword to her *Magasin des enfans,* thinking most likely of the work published by writers such as d'Aulnoy and Perrault. She also rejected the idea that fairy tales were "pernicious for children, for whom they are only suitable to inspire dangerous and false ideas." Instead, she claimed, "I find a way to make children understand, when they read 'Bluebeard,' the inconveniences of a marriage of interest; the dangers of curiosity, the misfortunes that can happen because of a little indulgence for the caprices of a spouse; the futility of lying to avoid chastisement."[16] Leprince de Beaumont articulated here two important and seemingly contradictory perspectives on fairy tales: first, that fairy tales needed to be carefully selected and shaped for children's peculiar needs; but, second, that the fairy tale was by nature a suitable vehicle for pedagogy and civilizing aims.[17]

Scholars agree that the late eighteenth century saw a significant shift in the forms and intended audiences of European fairy tales, as well as an explosion in publishing. Major writers of the Enlightenment and the Romantic era—the likes of Friedrich de la Motte Fouqué, Novalis, Ludwig Tieck, and the extraordinary E. T. A. Hoffmann—continued to experiment with fairy tale forms into the nineteenth century, including crafting metaphorical allegories with political commentary for adult readers.[18] This period also witnessed the first significant publications of fairy tales designed particularly for the child reader—thus furthering the modern reimagination of that reader traced in this book.

In late eighteenth and early nineteenth-century Europe, the term *fairy tale* could mean any of a diverse range of story forms that were widely popular among young readers.[19] Fairy tales appeared throughout Enlightenment youth periodicals, as in "Flörchens Geschichte: Ein Märchen" ("Little Flora's Story: A Fairy Tale") from a 1774 issue of the *Leipziger Wochenblatt für Kinder* (*Leipzig Weekly for Children*). They also showed up across book catalogues aimed at children and youth, as in the advertisements at the back of a 1795 edition of Sophie von La Roche's *Briefe an Lina als Mutter* (*Letters to Lina as a Mother*). La Roche's publishers recommended Ludwig Theobul Kosegarten's Cupid and Psyche story, one of the earliest known European fairy tale plots. The second edition of *Psyche: Ein Märchen des Altertums* (*Psyche: A Fairy Tale from Antiquity,* 1789) could be purchased for eight Groschen, a middling price compared with the other advertised volumes. A third example demonstrating the ubiquity of fairy tales in this era comes from the archival preservation of one young reader's collection from the 1810s and 1820s. Of the thirty-four volumes collected by Ferdinand Freiligrath in his youth, three are volumes of Christian Fürchtegott Gellert's fables.[20] These fables brought the elements of fantasy and amusement to Freiligrath's shelves, since most of his other texts were schoolbooks or dictionaries.

In the early 1790s, Benedikte Naubert anonymously published a collection titled the *Neue Volksmährchen der Deutschen* (*New Folktales of the Germans*); this claim to a long-standing oral tradition directly presaged the Grimms' nationalist project.[21] In 1809, Wilhelm Grimm discovered her identity and visited Naumburg to interview her, one year before the brothers completed the draft manuscript of the *KHM*. Astrid Münder has noted that, unlike less scrupulous men, Grimm kept the secret of Naubert's identity, beyond sharing it with his brother and two other important figures in German fairy tale collection—Achim von Arnim and Clemens Brentano.[22]

Von Arnim and Brentano were brothers-in-law and collaborators embedded in the literati of the German Enlightenment.[23] Brentano was a grandson of writer Sophie von La Roche and brother to Bettina (Elisabeth) Brentano-von Arnim, to whom the Grimms dedicated the *KHM* (see a discussion of Bettina Brentano-von Arnim's childhood letters in chapter four).[24] Von Arnim and Brentano moved in circles that included the Grimms, Hoffmann, and Joseph von Eichendorff; von Arnim and Bettina Brentano's daughter Gisela von Arnim also became a writer of fairy tales, and married Herman Grimm, one of Wilhelm Grimm's sons.[25] Together, Achim von Arnim and Clemens Brentano published what is generally recognized as the first collection of German folk songs, *Des Knaben Wunderhorn* (*The Boy's Magic Horn*, 1805 and 1808).[26] The romantic nationalism of *Des Knaben Wunderhorn* was a direct inspiration for the Grimms' fervor for collecting folklore "from the people." Scholars also owe a debt to Brentano for preserving among his papers the earliest extant manuscript of the *KHM*. In 1810, two years before the publication of the first volume, the Grimms sent an incomplete draft to Brentano for his feedback. Although he apparently never responded, this "Ölenberg manuscript" was discovered there in the 1920s, providing us with a starting point for the Grimms' practices.[27]

Of the Märchen collectors popular during the nineteenth century, the most similar to the Grimms were Wilhelm Hauff and Ludwig Bechstein, whose fairy tale books might also have appeared on the shelves of bildungsbürgerlich child readers in the early to mid-nineteenth century.[28] Bechstein's collections were marketed to young readers from the outset, but followed after the *KHM*. Any discussion of the fairy tale landscape in early nineteenth-century Europe would be incomplete without mentioning two final collections. The stories compiled in variations as One Thousand and One Nights (also known as the *Arabian Nights*) originated in the twelfth century, with different literary versions as early as the fifteenth century displaying Persian, Indian, Arabic, and Egyptian influences.[29] Antoine Galland's translation into French from one Arabic edition appeared between 1704 and 1717. The characters, settings, and style of his *Mille et une nuit* stories influenced the writing of European fairy tales for centuries to come, including the *KHM*.[30] The last influential nineteenth-century fairy tale writer I will mention here is someone who probably would have appreciated that place of honor: Hans Christian Andersen.[31] First published in 1835, Andersen's fairy tales were swiftly translated into German and grew in popularity throughout the late 1830s and 1840s.[32] In 1844, Andersen visited the Grimms in Berlin, expecting that they would know his fairy tales well. He left in humiliation when it became clear that Jacob Grimm had never heard of him. The happy ending to this story is that within two weeks Jacob read some of Andersen's tales and visited him in Copenhagen with apologies.[33] In truth, Andersen's tales were indeed widely read and took their place among the ubiquitous collections of fairy tales in bildungsbürgerlich nurseries. But perhaps the most significant, among the most popular, and certainly the most globally long-lasting of these treasured books were the Grimms' *Kinder- und Hausmärchen*.

KINDER- UND HAUSMÄRCHEN

The story of Jacob and Wilhelm Grimm can be situated within the European Enlightenment, from which they developed their intellectual and spiritual ideals, and within the Age of Revolutions, in which they came of age politically. Enlightened currents that surface in the *KHM* include ideas about the child and the moral effects of nature.[34] Political revolutions changed the course of the Grimms' lives. Jacob lost his first job, a wartime position with the Hessian War Commission, after the Treaty of Tilsit gave Napoleon control over Central Europe. After that, Jacob began working as the personal librarian for the new Westphalian King Jérôme—Napoleon's brother.[35] Later, both brothers actively participated in the liberal politics that led to the revolutions of 1848.

Before those experiences, the Grimms grew up in relatively provincial, middle-class circumstances. Jacob Grimm was born in 1785 and his brother Wilhelm a year later, both in Hanau.[36] Their father, Philipp Grimm, was a lawyer who married a city councilman's daughter, Dorothea Zimmer Grimm. Three brothers and a sister followed the older boys, who were educated in Kassel. Though the early death of their father in 1796 was a blow to the family's financial well-being, the boys were nevertheless able to study at the University of Marburg and in their adult working lives they moved in scholarly, bourgeois circles.[37] In 1825, Wilhelm married Dorothea Wild, one of several sisters who contributed tales to the *KHM*; Jacob never married.[38]

The brothers' primary scholarly interest was German philology, and it was through their exploration of old German customs and languages that they began working on folklore.[39] In fairy tales, they hoped to discover the common language and literature that defined a unified German identity. Through their various publications, the Grimms contributed to a growing interest of urban middle-class intellectuals in folk culture.

Both brothers were usually professionally employed in addition to their own research. This was once interrupted, when they were professors at the University of Göttingen in Hanover and the ultra-conservative Ernst August II came to the throne. After he revoked the Hanoverian constitution in 1837, the Grimms and five other liberal professors (the "Göttingen Seven") refused to take an oath of allegiance to what they saw as tyranny, and were expelled from Göttingen.[40] Hermann Rebel (among other scholars) draws a direct line between the political disenchantment of the Grimms and their cultural projects, writing, "Their goal was a new German and yet cosmopolitan culture that would allow them to transcend their own failed political revolutions by opening a world of education and spirit apart from politics and war."[41] Yet the Grimms had already been working on the fairy tale collection and other cultural-linguistic projects for three decades before the political failure in Göttingen. It may be argued that the Grimms retreated to their intellectual labors in parallel to the political reactions that followed 1848, but their early passion for German nationalism persisted in the ever more popular editions of the *KHM*.

Responding in part to the project of their friends von Arnim and Brentano, Jacob and Wilhelm Grimm began to collect stories from family friends, neighbors, assorted local informants, and literary sources at the beginning of the nineteenth century.[42] Later on, more and more tales were drawn from novels and newspapers popular with the bourgeois audience. Through published versions of the *KHM* from 1812 to 1857, they gradually revised the tales, working toward moral and stylistic unity. The preface to the first edition in 1812 begins with a melodramatic metaphor about the impending extinction of "the riches of German poetry in early times."[43] Like many German Romantics, the Grimms were committed to maintaining what they found to be natural, innocent, original German literature, and in this first edition of their collection, they claimed to have "endeavored to record these tales as purely as possible."[44] This perception of authenticity was essential to the Grimms' original goals of cultural preservation.

Georg Reimer published Volume I of the first edition in Berlin in 1812. Volume II followed in 1815 with an elaborated literary style but the same format.[45] The second edition, which saw the most dramatic shift in style from a scholarly to a popular voice, was prepared in 1819 and a volume of supplementary notes was published in 1822. In 1825 they created the *Kleine Ausgabe* (small edition), a selection of fifty tales produced with a keen eye on the book market. Altogether, between 1812 and 1857, seven *Große Ausgaben* and ten *Kleine Ausgaben* were edited and printed, with 211 tales making it into the final full edition.[46] Of this list, many tale types appear in more than one rendition, such as "Die sechs Schwäne" ("The Six Swans," 49), "Die zwölf Brüder" ("The Twelve Brothers," 9), and "Die sieben Raben" ("The Seven Ravens," 25) which each vary slightly from the same plot.

But it was not only the sources and style of the tales that changed across editions. The development of the *KHM* also reflected the Grimms' philosophical shift away from cultural preservation and toward the moral instruction of children. Their new mission was driven by the escalating concern (pedagogic and commercial) for child readers that is followed throughout this book.[47] The *Kleine Ausgabe,* for example, owed its existence to Wilhelm Grimm's attempt to capitalize on the success of English translations of their collection that had been marketed to parents and children. Furthermore, after the initial publication of their project, the Grimms began to reconceive of their mission not only as scholarly and nationalistic, but also explicitly pedagogic. As early as the second volume in 1815, the Grimms wrote, "Through our collection, we wanted not merely to serve the history of poetry and mythology; it was equally the intention that the poetry itself, which lives in it, take effect: that it give delight wherever it could delight, and also that it would become a proper *Erziehungsbuch* [educational book]."[48] Their vision of fairy tales as a vehicle for moral instruction—this Erziehungsbuch—illustrates the importance of molding the child subject for nineteenth-century Germans. This is evident both in the Grimms' assertion of the literacy practices of child readers as unique and in their allowance for pleasure and imagination as part of the educational experience. In the second edition of 1819, they retreated further from the untouched presentation of original stories, proclaiming in the preface that they had "carefully expunged every expression in this new edition not suitable for children."[49]

SCHOLARLY APPROACHES TO THE FAIRY TALE

While I take a sociohistorical approach in this book, fairy tales have been analyzed through a dizzying array of other interpretations. These include the taxonomical work of early folklorists;[50] psychoanalytic explanations that often ignore historical context;[51] Marxist scholarship;[52] structuralist interpretations;[53] feminist readings;[54] and prolific popular discussion.[55] One exchange in the *New York Review of Books* over Robert Darnton's *The Great Cat Massacre: And Other Episodes in French Cultural History,* illustrates some differences between these approaches.[56] A strand of critique came from psychoanalysts who understood fairy tales as most significantly concerned with supposedly universal human desires. In his reply, Darnton wrote, "To tell the truth I had a sneaking suspicion all along that a libidinal undercurrent flowed through the peasants' Mother Goose. I would go so far as to argue that the peasants had sex lives." A second criticism came from the Frankfurt School and folkloristics in the form of Jack Zipes's concern that Darnton had neglected earlier fairy tale research and gone too far in using particular tales from Grimm and Perrault to define German and French cultural differences. To Zipes, Darnton implied that this criticism could partly be dismissed as disciplinary defensiveness: "Instead of trying to monopolize Little Red Riding Hood for history, I think that everyone should have a crack at her, even [the psychoanalysts]."

What I have taken from both Darnton and Zipes is the aim of reading fairy tales not as a simple reflection of social reality, but as nevertheless bearing historical meaning and significance. I situate my analysis of the child reader's encounter with the family sociology of the *KHM* primarily within the socio-historical approach to fairy tales as "commentaries on the mores and customs of a particular society and the classes and groups within these societies."[57] This work acknowledges the oral traditions that have (re)shaped literary fairy tales, but also treats the *KHM* as a text arising from a specific historical moment and social context.[58] This analysis also draws on the close readings and excavations emerging from folkloristics in the mid- to late twentieth century.[59]

My primary method in this chapter traces changes over time through two sets of choices the Grimms made in the transformation of their collection for a child audience: selecting source material and editing tales across editions. The story with which the Grimms opened the *KHM* through every edition, "Der Froschkönig oder der eiserne Heinrich," ("The Frog King, or Iron Heinrich," 1), works well as an illustration of this method. One explanation for the Grimms' preference for "The Frog King" as their opener has to do with what they saw as the particularly German features of the tale. According to their notes of 1856, the story's origin was in Hesse, the state where the brothers were raised and the home of Dorothea Viehmann, the storyteller whom the Grimms virtually canonized as the iconic German peasant woman.[60] The first half of this tale is the "Frog Prince" story that is still familiar today, of a princess who is helped by and then marries a prince who had been enchanted as a frog. But the Grimms' version continues on to an epilogue (which was included from the 1810 manuscript version onward) describing the happy reconciliation of the frog king with "der treue Heinrich," his faithful servant. Maria Tatar has suggested that the inclusion of the second part of the story reflected virtues of fidelity and tradition that the Grimms understood as "quintessentially Germanic."[61]

What is particularly fascinating about the choice of this tale for the prime spot in the book is not just its nationalist overtones, but that over the course of editions the Grimms changed it from an erotically charged story to a moral lesson on vows, chastity, and companionate marriage. In the 1810 manuscript, the princess quickly takes the prince to bed as soon as he is no longer a slimy frog.[62] For the first published edition in 1812, the Grimms slightly changed this so that when the frog complains that he is tired and wants to lie down with her, she rejects him and it is only *after* he turns into a handsome young prince and is named as her "dear companion" that they "fell asleep together with pleasure."[63] By the 1857 edition, we find the princess violently throwing the frog at a wall when he suggests sharing a bed, eliminating any hint of impropriety. At the same time that eroticism was expurgated from the story, the Grimms turned it into a didactic message about marriage and the duties of a daughter. By adding lines such as, "Someone who has helped you when you were in need you should not hereafter scorn," the editors not only remarked on the importance of honoring promises.[64] They also emphasized the obedience due by a girl first to her father, and then to her husband. The princess must invite the frog to her bedroom out of loyalty to him as a companion and deference to her father's command. Furthermore, the Grimms implied that a proper marriage should be inspired by love rather than mercenary interest. The frog tells the princess, "Your clothes, your pearls and jewels, and your golden crown, those I do not want: but if you will love me and if I may be your companion and playmate," then help will be given.[65] Over time, the Grimms added several references to the prince as the princess's "dear companion" to highlight the supposed love between them. Of course, it doesn't hurt if the frog you happen to care for turns out to be a prince of equal rank! Companionate marriage was a romantic ideal rather than common practice in early nineteenth-century Europe. Regardless, by the time the Grimms had fully revised "The Frog King," the tale perfectly suited their purposes both as a faithfully Germanic story and as a didactic family lesson.

CLASS CULTURES OF FAMILY LIFE IN FAIRY TALES FOR CHILD READERS

The class cultures enacted in the fairy tales of the *Kinder- und Hausmärchen*—and shaped by the Grimm brothers across editions of their collection—were most evident in depictions of family relationships and everyday life. Peasants, merchants, and kings alike saw their destinies hinge on family ties and family practices. To be clear: that does not mean that the family sociology of fairy tales mapped directly onto real social class distinctions. As residues of a much older oral tradition, the status designations in these fairy tales drew from the vocabulary of estates (characters such as priests, nobles, or peasants), even while the Grimms experienced a new, less fixed system of social classes emerging around them. Nevertheless, social hierarchies constitute a core theme of the *KHM*. Through observing the family practices redefined and elaborated across editions of these stories, I reveal the Grimms' attempt to construct a particular subjectivity by situating child readers within social expectations of family relationships and bourgeois habitus.

PROPER CHILD BEHAVIOR

Like other pedagogic texts, the tales of the *KHM* contained guidelines for respectable child conduct and age roles. Yet the instability in gender, status, and age hierarchies stirred up by the Age of Revolutions meant that ideas about children's proper place were up for debate. Since the Grimms articulated their project as an Erziehungsbuch, it became a generative site for addressing these conflicts, including how children should behave within families. When instructing middle-class children how they should contribute to their households, the *KHM* celebrated industry, fidelity, cleverness, and humility, but above all filial obedience.

This issue is addressed so frequently in the Grimms' collection that it would seem that disrespectful, wayward children were a widespread social problem in early nineteenth-century Europe. Many tales revolved around rewarding children for obedience to parent figures or disciplining them for recalcitrance. Usually, obedience was demonstrated through hard work (by both girls and boys) or by acquiescence to marriage offers (by young women in particular).[66] There was, however, some potential for subversive readings of the more extreme tales about self-abnegating obedience or intractability punished, to be explored later.

Children's obedience already constituted a theme in the sources used for the *KHM*, but the transformations of one story, "Frau Trude" ("Mrs. Trude," 43), illustrate how the Grimms elaborated such lessons. Reading from the final edition, the tale begins, "Once upon a time there was a little girl who was willful and nosy, and whenever her parents told her something, she would not attend to them: how could this go well for her?"[67] The word *vorwitzig,* which I have translated here as "nosy," related particularly to children, and implied not just curiosity, but a careless manner. It captures a familiar pedagogic tension between disciplining unlicensed curiosity and promoting independent learning. In this case, the protagonist disobeys her parents in order to pursue her curiosity about the strange and wonderful things she has heard of a witch, Frau Trude, but discovers horrors at the witch's house; ultimately, she is turned into a log and thrown on the fire. Her gruesome end fits the crimes not only of disobedience but of choosing to leave her family.

After "Frau Trude" was introduced to the *KHM* in the third edition (1837), the Grimms made no significant changes to the tale in subsequent editions. However, some telling differences surface by comparing the didactic story written by the Grimms to the original literary source, a poem written by "Meier Teddy" at least as early as 1822.[68] The original poem launches directly into a dialogue between the little girl and the witch without the opening vocative address to child readers introduced by the Grimms to underscore the inevitability of a bad outcome for disobedient children. Furthermore, the poem invites more sympathy for the child in its initial verses, through her report that "my mother scolded me, my father beat me." And while the child's obstinance seems patently foolish given the danger she is warned about in the Grimms' version, Frau Trude initially comes off as more seductive and comforting in the original: "Your parents, little cousin, are sometimes stupid/ And they punished you, so do not weep about it."[69] The poem is weirder, leaving an impression more of the witch's mysterious power than of the girl's mistake. In addition to the fact that the Grimms stressed obedience in their reframing, their decision to seek out and add other stories on this theme in later editions of the collection supported their vision of the fairy tales as an Erziehungsbuch for child readers.

Through obedience, middle-class children could perform proper age roles in their families. Indeed, the very idea that a child had a job to do for the family that was not a contribution to the household economy but was rather satisfied through the industrious pursuit of education—this development demonstrates the emergence of a new child subjectivity as a bildungsbürgerlich invention of the era. Chapters four and five are replete with examples of young people performing their proper "work" of pursuing literacy through their letters and diaries.

IDEALIZED PARENT-CHILD RELATIONS

While children owed their parents obedience according to the *KHM,* the Grimms also used fairy tales to promote affection between parents and children. Adding sentiment to the exchange of authority and obedience, this evolving notion of parent-child love helped define new bourgeois domesticity. The cliché today of fearing a parent who is "not angry, just disappointed" is one result.

Although fathers and mothers alike were supposed to use love as a vehicle for instruction, essentialist beliefs about maternal attachment became ubiquitous in fairy tales by the middle of the nineteenth century. Rousseau's emphasis on the supposedly natural devotion of mothers was translated to the German context especially through the writing of Pestalozzi and Froebel. It was also evident even in basic stylistic choices the Grimms made as editors, such as in the first line of "Der Wolf und die sieben, jungen Geißlein" ("The Wolf and the Seven Young Kids," 5). By the 1843 edition, the tale opened with:

> Once upon a time there was an old goat who had seven young kids, and loved them just as any mother loves her children.[70]

But in the earliest recorded version, the 1810 manuscript, the story simply began as:

> Once upon a time there was a goat, who had seven young kids.

Here, there is no mention of a mother's natural love. The Grimms changed this gradually, with the first published version of 1812 reading:

> A goat had seven young, whom she truly loved and carefully guarded from the wolf.

By the 1819 edition, now explicitly targeting young readers, they had altered this to emphasize the naturalness of this mother's love:

> A goat had seven young kids, whom she loved well in a motherly way and carefully guarded from the wolf.

The final rendition extended this as an example of "any" good mother's love for her children.

The revision of "Hänsel und Gretel" ("Hansel and Gretel," 15) similarly attests to the Grimms' emphasis on parental love through their deliberate privileging of biological ties over other relationships. The story begins when a father abandons his children in the forest because of the family's poverty. In the 1810 manuscript version, the father's reluctance to abandon his children in the forest was much weaker, and the blame seemed more equitably shared by both parents. His wife still initiates the idea when food runs out, but he acquiesces without much discussion of his objections: "The husband didn't want to for a long time, but the wife gave him no peace until he finally agreed."[71] Note that the couple are referred to as "husband" and "wife." In the first published version of 1812, the wife was named as the children's mother. By 1819, the children's mother had been replaced with a wicked stepmother who was the clear antagonist. Furthermore, the Grimms continued to elaborate on the husband's resistance, writing him more lines to demonstrate his love for his children and reluctance in the face of his wife's cruel nagging. In the first published edition, the husband refuses her suggestion:

"I cannot bring my heart to lead my own dear children to the wild animals who would soon rip them to pieces in the woods."

"If you don't do it," said the woman, "then we will all have to die of hunger together." Then she gave him no peace until he said yes.[72]

But even that wasn't enough for the Grimms, and by the final edition this exchange was yet further expanded, with the ineffectual father getting an additional last word after his agreement:

"But the poor children still make me feel sorry."[73]

Throughout the Grimms' editing, stepmothers were presented as and even transformed into threats to the idealized family, while biological parents were celebrated.[74] It was categorically impossible for a birth mother to act in cruel or unloving ways toward her children. And to shore up patriarchal authority in a new sentimental era of family life, the Grimms elevated a father's love and affection for his children.

PROPER GENDER ROLES

Intersecting with age hierarchies, proper gender roles appear as a concern throughout the *KHM*—not just for adults, but also for children, and even for animals (as allegory). The changing gender order during the years around 1800 impacted how Europeans across classes (albeit in different ways) understood relations between husbands and wives, managed children's work and education, divided labor within households, and essentialized expectations of motherhood versus fatherhood. As Maynes notes, it was the families of civil servants, as "the first middle-class male careerists in Central Europe," who led the way on establishing this new domestic ideology; that category included the Grimms, given Jacob's positions with the Hessian War Commission and as court librarian. The prescription of gender norms in the *KHM* was most concerned with how girls and women should behave within the family. Fairy tale characters faced gender-asymmetrical expectations of fidelity, self-sacrifice, silence, and loving support.

Throughout the fairy tale corpus, young readers were given models of how to perform household work according to a prescribed gender order. In "Sneewittchen" ("Snow White," 53), the goodness and virtue of the heroine is signified by her willingness to "cook, make the beds, wash, sew and knit, and . . . keep everything orderly and clean" for the dwarfs.[75] The stylistic tinkering undertaken by the Grimms between the version they recorded of this tale for the 1810 manuscript and the first published edition underscored the importance of Snow White's household work by turning one descriptive sentence into a full paragraph contract between the dwarfs and the girl.

A trope of child siblings playing house after parental abandonment or magical enchantment repeats throughout the *KHM* as a blueprint for how households should be organized in adulthood. For example, in the final version of "The Twelve Brothers":

> The eleven [older brothers] went into the forest, caught game, deer, birds, and pigeons so they would have something to eat, and the sister and Benjamin [the youngest brother] took care that it was prepared. She sought wood for cooking and herbs for the vegetables, and put the pots on the fire, so that the meal was always ready when the eleven came home. She also kept the little cottage in order and covered the little beds in nice white and clean [sheets], and the brothers were always satisfied and lived with her in great harmony.[76]

The description of daily work is more than just ornamentation in these fairy tales. Notice how each step and detail in this example is spelled out, even in a fantasy. While this is not labor that bildungsbürgerlich child readers would likely undertake themselves, the story assigns particular household tasks to the sister much in the way that middle-class girls would be expected eventually to supervise servants' work. In the 1812 version, the Grimms only write that "one of the brothers" had to stay home to perform the household chores, without reference to his age; their revision assigned these tasks to the youngest boy. When their sister arrives in the forest, she takes over most of the duties, but the fact that Benjamin, the child, also stays home actually underscores the association of "men's work" out in the world with full, masculine maturity.

Even some animal fables addressed the gendered division of household labor. The message of "Von dem Mäuschen, Vögelchen und der Bratwurst" ("The Mouse, the Bird, and the Sausage," 23) is particularly provocative. The title characters begin to keep house together with clearly defined roles: the bird provides for the household by heading out into the world, the mouse undertakes the heavier household work, and the sausage does the cooking. Life continues swimmingly until the bird decides he is being treated unfairly by this arrangement, and demands an exchange of responsibilities. Upsetting the household order ends in disaster, with the sausage eaten by a strange dog, the mouse burnt up in a cooking pot, and the bird drowned in a well. In an annotation to this tale, the Grimms discussed sources: they cited a satirical poem by Johann Michael Moscherosch(1642), but made a point of observing, "But the fairy tale still lives on in the oral tradition, although with different circumstances; namely, it is told only with the mouse and the sausage, without the bird; that one must cook this week, the second the other [week]."[77] The three characters instead come from the literary version by Moscherosch that the Grimms preferred.

If we consider this tale as an allegory for the gendered division of labor, the Grimms' preference for a more complex version of the tale, even though it meant selecting a literary rather than an oral source, suddenly makes sense. The story of animals splitting household labor simply by taking turns looks quite different from a tale that suggests catastrophe will befall all who try to perform work outside their naturally prescribed roles. Hans-Jörg Uther points out that for Moscherosch, the three characters "embody the three estates which should ensure through [their] subordination that the state continues to exist."[78] This is undermined, as Moscherosch states directly, "when one is no longer content to be in his estate."[79] The power of this social commentary, Uther suggests, was weakened or entirely absent in the Grimms' version. But what if the implications of the story extended not only to estate hierarchies but also to gender hierarchies? Just as in other status markers, such as dress, some distinctions of estate from before the eighteenth century were overshadowed by distinctions of gender in the nineteenth century. I suggest that the Grimms co-opted Moscherosch's allegory about being content in one's place two centuries later to hint at concerns about gender spheres and the division of labor within families.

CLASS CULTURES OF FAMILY FORMATION

The preoccupation of the *KHM* with problems of why and whom to marry reflects turbulence around family formation during the Age of Revolutions. It also contributed to the family sociology encountered by the modern child subject in fairy tales. Coming from a politics of bourgeois domesticity, the Grimms criticized marriages based solely on interest and promoted instead the companionate marriage ideal of love accompanying financial considerations.[80] Although cross-class marriages were common in the *KHM*, such alliances were not intended to serve as a literal model for child readers. Exogamy in the *KHM* does not promote radical social change, but, rather, indulges a bourgeois fantasy. The young diarists whose stories I tell in chapter five might have dreamed of romance, but they still married within their own class.

Some tales included in the *KHM* suggested choosing a spouse by determining who would be a responsible provider or an industrious contributor to the household economy.[81] But marriages primarily or exclusively of interest were increasingly cast in the *KHM* as negative, mercenary, and, more often than not, déclassé. In "Die Räuberbrautigam" ("The Robber Bridegroom," 40), a miller promises his daughter to the first rich man who comes along. For the second edition in 1819, the Grimms added the line, "but the girl did not love him the way a bride should love her bridegroom," and another phrase in 1837, "nor did she trust him."[82] Stressing love's absence—and suggesting that it was unnatural—ratcheted up the villainy of the miller and the robber bridegroom because the marriage had been contracted between the father and husband without the daughter's affection secured. The new importance of love was also underscored through the depiction of heartless, violent peasant marriages mocked by the Grimms.[83]

The companionate marriage most celebrated in the *KHM* combined affection (often inspired by feminine beauty) with financial prudence. The Grimms selected additional tales to publish in later editions that highlighted such matches. For example, a tailor in "Die Geschenke des kleinen Volkes" ("The Gifts of the Little Folk," 182) asks for only enough gold from the fairies he meets to satisfy his domestic dreams: "'Now I will become a master [tailor], marry my cozy little item (as he called his sweetheart) and be a happy man.'"[84] He is identified as a virtuous man not only by his lack of greed but also by his eagerness to settle down in responsible matrimony with a loving wife. This tale was only added to the collection for the sixth edition of 1850. Similarly, in "Die Nixe im Teich" ("The Nixie in the Pond," 181), a huntsman's apprentice falls in love with a "beautiful and truehearted maiden" in the village. To his good fortune, "when his lord perceived this, he gave him a small house; the two of them held a wedding, lived peacefully and happily and loved each other wholeheartedly."[85] Added to the *KHM* for the fifth edition in 1843, the tale presents affection safely within the bounds of a traditional, prudent union.

THE "KINDERWUNSCH"

New visions of parent-child relations and marriage came together in the focus on reproduction as part of the family sociology of the *KHM*. The desire to have a child, *der Kinderwunsch*, already drove the narrative in many of the tales chosen by the Grimms, and as the brothers edited their collection, they further highlighted the importance of childbirth. This theme itself predates the *KHM*, but the Grimms translated it into a modern paradigm of valuing an individual child for emotional connection rather than economic potential. Fairy tales literally realize the "pricelessness" of children (to borrow Viviana Zelizer's useful formulation), a key marker of Western modernity.[86] Fairy tale characters pay enormous, impossible costs to acquire children, enacting the idealization of a sentimental parent-child relationship as emotionally priceless in the European middle classes.

Across tales, it is axiomatic that a childless couple must want a son or daughter. Birth is positioned as a precious event, something that the Grimms heightened across the editions by choosing different sources and refining the tales through editing. Children are compared to "all the treasures of the world" in several tales.[87] This may seem to run counter to another common fairy tale theme, that of child abandonment. As with other ambiguities in the *KHM*, one explanation is that the collection is caught in a transition between viewing the child as another mouth to feed (for some) and as emotionally priceless (for others). In tales of child abandonment, the wickedness of the villains is in fact heightened by their disposal of what the Grimms deemed as a precious gift.

The Kinderwunsch theme manifested in the opening of many tales. "Rapunzel" and "Sneewittchen" are examples of well-known tales whose plots in the Grimms' versions are driven by intense longing for a child, contrary to the emphasis on romance in versions familiar today. Infertility is sometimes presented as a moral failing, as in "Das Eselein" ("The Donkey," 144). The Kinderwunsch also produced the fairy tale plot of strange adoptions, in which couples are so desperate for children that they accept a child "only the size of a thumb" or a baby found in a bird's nest.[88] As for the closing of tales recorded and revised by the Grimms, the culmination of romantic love was hardly the most common conclusion. In fact, after the hero rescued the heroine (or vice versa), the tale usually continued past the marriage to a birth. Although "fairy tale" later became synonymous with "love story," it was reproduction and childbirth that pervaded the *KHM*.

While the urgency of child-bearing was already a prominent theme in the fairy tales from first publication, the Grimms emphasized it through their editing choices. For example, the 1812 version of "Die Nelke" ("The Carnation," 76) is a courtly love tale, but has been transformed into a Kinderwunsch plot by 1819. The first version of the tale opens with a king who refuses to marry until one day he falls in love at first sight through the window. The result of this union is introduced through a passing phrase: "after the lapse of a year she bore a prince."[89] For the 1819 revision, the Grimms replaced the entire opening love story with a paragraph describing the childless queen's prayers to God for a son or daughter. To heighten the drama they inserted the phrase, "our Lord had prevented her from bearing any children."[90]

To instruct young readers, the Grimms also emphasized the Kinderwunsch over time in "Die Goldkinder" ("The Gold-Children," 85) and "Hans mein Igel" ("Hans My Hedgehog," 108). In "The Gold-Children," a poor man hooks a golden fish three times. In exchange for freedom, the magic fish gives him various treasures, including two golden children. The fish promises these gifts directly in the earliest edition.[91] But for the 1819 revision, the Grimms made more of these miracles through a delayed, more elaborate sequence:

> "Listen," spoke the fish, "I see that I will probably keep falling into your hands. Take me home with you and chop me into six pieces. Give two of them to your wife to eat, two to your horse, and plant two in the soil, and then you will receive blessings from them." The man took the fish home and did as he had told him. And it came to pass that from the two pieces that had been planted in the soil, two golden lilies grew up, and that the horse had two golden foals, and the fisher's wife bore two children who were entirely golden.[92]

These additions made the golden babies' arrival more special. In "Hans mein Igel" a childless farmer is mocked by his friends and wishes for even a hedgehog child out of exasperation. In 1815, the first line simply read "There was a rich farmer who had no children with his wife."[93] But this was elaborated for the 1850 and subsequent editions as, "There was once a farmer who had money and property enough, but as rich as he was, there was still something missing for his happiness: he had no children with his wife."[94] Through this kind of revision, childlessness was marked not only as a character trait but emphasized as emotionally painful or even unnatural. Longing for and prizing individual children was a key virtue in the new sentimental ideology of the modern family and a lesson delivered for even very young readers through the family sociology of the *KHM*.

FAIRY TALES IN PRACTICE

Certain features of the *KHM*, largely inherited from the oral tradition, made fairy tales particularly useful to the agency of the modern child reader. I have argued that in their attention to audience and deliberate crafting of family sociology, the Grimms reshaped their collection over time in ways that furthered the construction of modern childhood. But the revolution in reading fairy tales did not come only from adult folklorists. Whether from the transactional dimension of parents reading to children or from children telling and retelling their own stories, the oral, protean nature of even a published collection like the *KHM* matters for considering its effects on reader response.

The Märchengroschen story with which this chapter began illustrates some challenges of historicizing real children's reading. Wilhelm Grimm himself anticipated doubts about the entire account, telling von Arnswaldt, "One might believe it is invented, but it is true."[95] The child's name is unknown as is where she lived. Had she read the tale before, and would she read the book over again? Was she alone while reading or in the company of adults or other children?

We cannot even be certain that she enjoyed the fairy tale.[96] Differences in the versions of this story across sources reflect the illegibility of her actual reading practices and response, even to the critical point of what caused her to doubt the tale's truth. While Grimm says only that she disbelieved the whole tale, in the newspapers she was quoted as saying, "I do not believe the story because a tailor will never marry a princess."[97] Was this mere journalistic embellishment? In other words, determining the impact of any book on a historical reader is challenging, but reader response theory and other approaches have shown us that it is not impossible to use evidence from texts to think about their audiences.[98] In theorizing the responses of young readers to the *KHM*, I draw on the characteristics of the European fairy tale tradition that invited children to develop their own interpretations and adaptations.

ADAPTABLE FEATURES

The plasticity of the fairy tale form made these stories open to endless retellings and divergent interpretations by readers. We can see this in the diversity of adaptations produced from canonical tales such as "Rothkäppchen" ("Little Red Riding Hood," 26), to take one example. As Jack Zipes and Alan Dundes have shown, the recognizable core of this story has appeared in many guises, and has been subjected to varying critical lenses.[99] Many German children who read the *KHM* likely also encountered Perrault's version, if not other poetic renditions by Tieck or Eduard Mörike. But they also could access a varied oral tradition of *Rotkäppchen* stories.[100] Comparing differences in the recorded versions, even simply between Perrault and Grimm, reveals the inherent variability of the tale and therefore some of the choices children had in their own telling, retelling, misremembering, and reinvention of Red Riding Hood. The moral of the story could be altered or amplified; the titular character's power to rescue herself from the wolf could be celebrated or not; the ending could be triumphant or tragic; and colorful details about the wolf, the girl, the grandmother, and the setting could be endlessly embellished. Although the Grimms' editing in a sense attempted to fix such details and control the reader's vision, these potential variations demand that we take into account the role of imagination as children learned and grew up with these tales.

Children themselves could choose which stories to revisit in their reading and which to skip, which stories to tell over and over—and to whom. As David Hopkin writes in his study of nineteenth-century French folklore, "Storytelling is an inherently social activity."[101] The embellishments and even the central message of a tale transform in its retelling depending on the intended audience. Children selecting and telling or writing stories to please a teacher, to entertain younger siblings, to amuse their parents, to impress their schoolmates—these audiences each suggest a different purpose and potential for deliberate refashioning.

When compared with the *Erzählungen*, or moralistic stories, included in the periodicals that I discussed in chapter one, fairy tales reveal a different proxy for child storytellers. Youth periodical stories often featured adults impersonating children. An adult author might model diary writing or correspondence through a fictional child's first-person example. Such stories were generally lengthy and overly sophisticated, with erudite, polished prose. In the fairy tales, by contrast, while the settings were less realistic than those of youth periodicals, the Grimms modeled a kind of non-linear, unpolished, repetitive storytelling that in fact better reflects children's reality as tellers and consumers of stories. This was especially apparent in the earlier editions of the *KHM,* before the prose was rewritten and stylized, but it holds true in many tales of the 1857 edition as well. For example, the 1857 version of "Der Gescheite Hans" ("Clever Hans," 32) is entirely composed in a choppy dialogue style reminiscent of a young narrator's "and then he says . . . and then she says . . ." style:

> Hans's mother says, "Where are you going, Hans?" Hans answers: "to Gretel's."—"Fare well, Hans."—"Fare all right, good-bye mother."—Hans comes to Gretel's: "Good day, Gretel."—"Good day, Hans: what good things are you bringing me?"—"Bringing nothing, give [me] something." Gretel gives Hans a needle, Hans says: "Goodbye, Gretel."— "Goodbye, Hans."—Hans takes the needle and sticks it in a hay wagon and goes home behind it. "Good evening, mother."—"Good evening, Hans, where have you been?"—"At Gretel's."—"What did you bring her?"—"Brought nothing, was given [something]."— "What did she give you?"—"Gave a needle."—"Where do you have the needle, Hans?"— "Stuck in the hay wagon."—"That was stupid, [you] should have stuck it in a sleeve."[102]

The rest of the story continues in this fashion. Other examples throughout the *KHM* mirror the fragmented, repetitive mode of many child storytellers. The variety and flexibility of fairy tales has always offered audiences the opportunity to participate in their retelling. New to the Grimms' project was their refashioning of these tales to target child readers.

MEMETIC FEATURES

Fairy tales are also memetic. Here, I am in part following work by Jack Zipes that applies Richard Dawkins's sociobiological theory of memetics to explain the transmission and popularity of fairy tales.[103] Zipes describes the fairy tale meme as "a cultural artifact that acts as a cultural replicator or cultural adaptor that manages to inhabit our brains. It becomes so memorable and relevant that we store it and pass it on to others."[104] I use the term in a looser sense to describe the interchangeable tropes, stock characters, set phrases and idioms, and other characteristics of fairy tales that make them familiar and easy to remember.[105] As they revised, the Grimms incorporated more of these memetic features into their collection. They also added extra endings to originally shorter tales (for example, the punishment of the villain, or a detailed description of the wedding), endings that look remarkably similar across different stories. For example, three stories end with a similar account of the villain being dragged behind horses inside a barrel filled with boiling oil or nails. It was already true in the case of "Die zwölf Brüder" and "Die Gänsemagd" ("The Goose Girl," 89) but the Grimms added the punishment to "Die drei Männlein im Walde" ("The Three Little Men in the Wood" 13), while the evildoers in the 1812 version had simply been left out for wild animals to eat. Repetitive endings made it possible for readers to anticipate where the story was going, and engage actively in the transactional experience of reading.

Objects or encounters arriving in "threes," the use of rhyming verse, and predictable actions from familiar character types allowed child listeners or readers to predict the plot. Consider the dwarfs returning home to find Snow White in their cottage:

> The first spoke: "Who has been sitting on my little chair?"
> The second: "Who has been eating off my little plate?"
> The third: "Who has been taking from my roll?"
> The fourth: "Who has been eating from my vegetables?"
> The fifth: "Who has been jabbing with my little fork?"
> The sixth: "Who has been cutting with my little knife?"
> The seventh: "Who has been drinking from my little cup?"[106]

Whether by joining in with this rhythm or simply guessing what came next, children could participate in the telling or reading of a story, despite the odd and fantastic logic of fairy tale land.

Another memetic feature in the *KHM* was the Grimms' addition of explicit morals to gloss some tales, in the style of a fable. Sometimes these were straightforward, such as the closing proverb *eile mit weile* ("haste makes waste") at the end of "Der Nagel" ("The Nail," 184).[107] The Grimms often explicitly commented on the virtues or flaws of particular character choices. But does that mean that readers internalized these morals? It seems reasonable to suppose that some readers simply skipped over such moments, or ignored them as part of the fairy tale formula rather than seeing them as a lesson to be intentionally absorbed. In other cases, the use of a moral served the playful spirit of fairy tales, in addition to a didactic purpose. This happens in "Der kluge Knecht" ("The Clever Servant," 162), one of the many tales of foolish and disobedient servants, which closes with this address to the reader: "Take an example from this: do not distress yourself about your master and his orders, do instead whatever comes to mind and whatever you feel like. Then you will proceed just as wisely as clever Hans."[108] The subtext still aims toward recommending obedience, but it could also be read as part of a sarcastic joke about this stock character of a silly peasant.

This memetic nature of both literary and oral traditions facilitated children's reconstruction of fairy tales, making it easy for young people to retell their own versions later. Many writers have attributed their own literary imaginations to early experiences with storytelling. At this same time in Russia, for example, Alexander Vel'tman recollected: "[Uncle Boris] was moreover a great shoe-maker and an amazing storyteller. To watch over a lively boy and sew shoes at the same time would have been impossible; therefore, sitting at the bench, he deftly tied me to himself with a long tale, little considering that over time, I too would become a storyteller."[109] Becoming a professional author in adulthood was not the only way for children to make these stories their own. They might share the book with others, retell the tales, or read them in the company of siblings and friends.

TRANSGRESSIVE FEATURES

The supposed Erziehungsbuch of the *KHM* was rife with moral transgressions. Even when not encouraged by an ironic or sarcastic tone, subversive readings of fairy tale messages were not only possible but invited by some plots. How was a reasonable child supposed to interpret stories such as the odd religious tale, "Marienkind" ("The Virgin Mary's Child," 3)? In it, the Virgin Mary, who stands in for a philanthropic patron, rescues the daughter of a woodcutter from poverty.[110] The little girl grows up in heaven with the Virgin Mary, but inevitably succumbs to the temptation to open a forbidden door (revealing the Holy Trinity). When her crime is discovered, the Virgin Mary expels her from heaven: "You have not listened to me, and you have lied at that, you are no longer worthy to be in Heaven."[111] The obedience this child owed her parent figure founders on curiosity and pride. Even after being abandoned, the girl refuses to confess. Only at the final hour, after a series of events that almost cause her to burn at the stake, does she change her mind. As the Grimms told it, "When she was lashed to a stake and the fire began to burn all around her, then the hard ice of pride melted, and her heart was moved by remorse."[112] But is the virtue of unquestioning obedience the only possible message to take from this story? Even compared with other cruel fairy tale episodes, the extreme punishment inflicted on this child seems ludicrously out of proportion and cruelly delivered, undermining the very authority promoted on the surface of the tale.

Obedience was painted as a virtuous choice in fairy tales even when the adult demanding a child's obedience was wicked. In "Die drei Männlein im Walde," the envious and cruel stepmother forces her stepdaughter to look for strawberries in winter while wearing a paper dress:

> "Dear lord!" said the girl. "Strawberries do not grow in winter, the ground is frozen, and snow has covered everything. And why should I go in a paper dress? It is so cold outdoors that my breath freezes: The wind will blow right through the dress, and the thorns will tear it off my body." "Do you still want to answer back to me?" the stepmother said. . . . she thought, "She will freeze to death outside and starve, and will never more come before my eyes." Now the girl was obedient, so she put on the paper dress and went out with the little basket.[113]

This protagonist is rewarded for her blind obedience. When she encounters some odd gnomes in the forest, she immediately begins to do whatever they tell her. That tractability earns her three gifts from the gnomes: beauty, gold, and a king for a husband. But were child readers likely or even expected to respond in the same way to obedience stories featuring loving parents versus cruel or ridiculous ones? Did despotic parental behavior undermine the respect owed these figures enough to produce seditious reading responses?

One of the strangest tales in this group of extreme obedience plots is "Das eigensinnige Kind" ("The Obstinate Child," 117), a story totaling less than 125 words. It tells of a son who dies of disobedience, after which his little arm refuses to stay in his grave until his mother hits it with a rod—"and then the child had peace under the earth for the first time."[114] What effects could reading this horror story have had on child readers' self-perception and their relationships with adults? Were stories of fantastically stubborn or submissive children and repressive or firm parents intended, to quote Jane Austen, "to recommend parental tyranny, or reward filial disobedience"?[115] Shining a light on such aspects of the text produces a range of unexpected readings. Are these most extreme tales intended to provoke subversive or resistant readings by children? And in that case, can we still call such responses subversive? In the Age of Revolutions, as new forms of political subjectivity were being imagined and tested, what does the child's obedience to authority mean for broader rights discourse? The adults who promoted these tales may have themselves been conflicted about the value and pleasure of reading such moments, in their departure from the more conventional moral "messages."

Another kind of subversive reading provoked by these fairy tales is the use of transgressive humor as an antidote to the politics of bourgeois respectability. The humor of fairy tales invited the child reader's laughter more directly than did other genres examined in this book, especially on sexual and scatological themes. What moral message of the *KHM* was a child supposed to derive from the donkey in "Tischchen deck dich, Goldesel, und Knüppe aus dem Sack" ("The Magic Table, the Golden Donkey, and the Club in the Sack," 36) who spits out gold pieces in front and behind? Or consider this moment in "Daumesdick":

> "Lift me down. It's necessary." "Just stay up there," said the man on whose head he sat. "I don't mind it, the birds also sometimes drop something on me." "No," said Thumbling. "I also know what is appropriate: just quickly lift me down from here."[116]

Perhaps a child's enjoyment of this earthy humor should not be considered subversive, prompted as it was by the text itself. But such material did sabotage the cultivation of a refined bourgeois sensibility.

A further possibility for transgressive readings lay in the role of magic and fantasy, in the strange, miraculous happenings of fairy tale land. What part did that essential and mysterious element of imagination play in shaping child readers' responses to the *KHM*? Did reading fairy tales offer young readers an escape from realism into a world of magical fortune-finding and Cinderella stories? Today fantasy is strongly associated with young audiences, even though children's imaginative play can be prosaic or mundane, and children themselves skeptical literary adventurers. The fairy tale sits at the intersection of more directly didactic forms (like Enlightenment periodicals) and later literature for young people that prioritized imagination and delight. Rosemary Jackson has argued that fantasy is inherently subversive because it "traces the unsaid and the unseen of culture: that which has been silenced, made invisible, covered over and made 'absent.'"[117] But she also calls for contextualizing the production of fantasy within its social reality. The Grimms' deliberate rendering of folk culture for bildungsbürgerlich readers helped constitute class cultures through fantastic escape into the lives of others. The *KHM* purported to show German children their own distant past, affirming that they were moving through a modern middle-class society.

Eighteenth- and nineteenth-century pedagogues increasingly worked toward not only instruction but also amusement. We could see this cynically as a ploy for child readers' attention. But another way to understand the entertainment of fantasy is that these tales simply offered child readers pleasure. They are fun to read. I suggest that it is possible to seek, as Jackson writes, "to understand what might be going on under the cover of this pleasure" and to remember at the same time our own formative and present encounters with fairy tales—subversive, mysterious, funny, romantic, frightening, or magical as they might be.[118]

CONCLUSION

Wilhelm Grimm and the anonymous Berliner girl who opened this chapter met over a century and a half ago. The Grimm brothers had not set out to make their name synonymous with the trappings of an idealized childhood, but by the time of this encounter with a doubting yet faithful young reader, their collection had indeed become ubiquitous on middle-class family shelves. Why was this Märchengroschen story recorded and published at that moment, and why has it repeatedly circulated in the years since their meeting? At first, it fed the emergent desire of a mid-nineteenth century reading public for sentimental accounts of earnest children behaving in what adults perceived as emotionally "childlike" yet intellectually precocious ways. Later, the ascendance of the Grimms for both scholars and following generations raised on the fairy tales of the *KHM* ensured that the Märchengroschen story would continue to be repeated.

The development of the fairy tale genre as a powerful engine of children's book publishing, one that continues to dominate the market today, fueled the development of modern childhood in the Age of Revolutions. Folklorists and literary fairy tale writers, including the Grimms, appropriated an adult oral tradition and literary genre in order to remake these stories in a specialized form for a bildungsbürgerlich child audience. At the same time, ambiguities and contradictions persisted in the messages for child readers—readers who might be enchanted or skeptical, compliant or defiant. This chapter has considered fairy tales as a written form of middle-class domestic fiction. However, a living oral tradition has thrived on big screens, through urban legends, and in children's rooms alongside the written word and helps us see why fairy tales still matter for understanding childhood. (And whoever does not believe me at this point should pay me a Thaler—or at least a Groschen).

Among the genres examined in this study, fairy tales appear the most concerned with pleasure and entertainment. Yet they also served as a teaching tool for the instruction of family and class norms. The next chapter will address the role of children's amusement in a highly didactic genre, as I explore the terrain of geography schoolbooks.

CHAPTER THREE

READING THE WORLD
German Children's Place in Geographic Education

While the ostensible purpose of twelve-year-old Luise Vorwerk's journey with her family from Hamburg to Paris in May 1842 was to advance her merchant father's business, the travel diary that Luise kept reveals another aim of the family's trip. Each day, she recorded her observations of the places, people, and industry she encountered, documenting not only those experiences but also her education in such matters.

> On the Prussian border we were supposed to be inspected, but a coin that Father pressed in the hand of the wife of the customs official eased things. . . . One already hears the Westphalian dialect here, which I noticed very much. At the post in the village of Hamm, we met a former Prussian officer who had been in Hamburg at the time of the siege.[1] The beautifully cultivated scenery began after [reaching] Unna. One village followed the other, and prominent smokestacks everywhere indicated many factories. . . . Cologne is a fortress, tightly built, with old high houses and very many churches, from which the unfinished towers of the famous cathedral protrude. . . . The hireling who accompanied us showed us a place where, according to the superstition of the Catholic inhabitants of Cologne, the Three Kings landed and rested under the trees.[2]

The pages of this travel journal are filled thus with dutiful observations of well-known sights such as the cathedral of Cologne or the Tuileries in Paris, demonstrations of industrialist class interests through approving attention to factories or the railway, and Luise's own reflections about differences in customs or language. Her instruction in geography and history that year consisted not in rote repetition of facts about rivers, but in active preparation for life as a critical thinker and bourgeois subject. The writing of this diary, as well as its later preservation, suggest unprecedented adult attention to the worldviews of young people.

As with periodicals and fairy tales, a new geographic education for children was just emerging in the years around 1800. Students in the eighteenth century still trudged through a purely descriptive approach to geography in rigid, memorization-driven instruction. By the middle of the nineteenth century, however, developments in pedagogic philosophy met discursive shifts in geographic epistemology in the fashioning of a modern approach to geographic education. The discipline became recognized as a social science concerned with the dynamic relationship between humans and nature, which demanded an active, problem-based pedagogy. My examination of geographic textbooks and schooling during this period has turned up a number of distinctive features: growing concern for child readers' amusement, an association of learning about the world with the family and the home, the orientation of children in space as explorers and armchair travelers, an emphasis on map-reading and the use of atlases in schools, increasingly gender-segregated reading, and the influence of German Romantic nationalism and colonial ambitions. Such seemingly unrelated characteristics and changes could be explained by a shift in geographic epistemology—or historical conditions concerning race and world networks—or economic or technological changes. Beyond all these possible explanations, I argue that the story of geography is even more the story of the modern child subject emerging in ideology and practice.

This chapter uses the case of geographic schoolbooks and instructional practices to investigate changes in German ideas about learning, with a particular interest in the part that reading played in those changing ideas. How was the world shaped and embodied for children in these texts—especially the imagined spaces and social categorizations of Deutschland, Europe, and the world? What role did race, religion, nationalism, revolutionary politics, and the colonial imagination play in geographic education, and how did those political categories intersect and shift into the nineteenth century? How were expectations about what boys and girls should learn of the world gendered? How did the forms of geographic schoolbooks change over this period, and what might that indicate about changes in children's reading experiences? How did schoolbook-reading position children in local, national, and global orientations through active reading?

An introduction to the genre of geographic schoolbooks reviews texts from the late eighteenth century through the middle of the nineteenth century before the chapter splits into two parts: the *practices* and the *content* of children's geographic education. I first explore how authors of geographic schoolbooks imagined their young readers as well as how they would use the books. I then turn to the content to show how children were located in the world through their education and the shape of that world.

INTRODUCTION TO THE GENRE

GEOGRAPHIC EPISTEMOLOGY IN THE SCHOOLROOM

Changing geographic epistemology at the end of the Enlightenment accompanied the development of the nation state, imperialism, and other forms of state power, and shaped nascent ethnological discourse in Europe (see table 1 for a summary of these transformations).[3] Alongside the expansion of geography as an academic discipline, geography instruction become a formalized part of school curricula, incorporated alongside the classics, mathematics, and religion.[4] Though pedagogical opinions varied on the ideal proportion of children's education that should be devoted to experience and exploration, cartography and atlases, or teachers' lectures, the reading of books was most consistently prized as a path to geographic knowledge. Geography textbook author Georg Christian Raff declared in the 1776 opening address to his child audience that "children learn twice as much if they also read what their teacher says."[5] In his foreword to the same book, Johann Georg Heinrich Feder argued that children need books to improve their attentiveness and entertain them. But the part that reading should play in children's study of geography was fraught, as Feder revealed in the same passage: "On the first journey around the world, for example, perhaps

TABLE 1. Summary of changes in European geographic epistemology

Geography, mid-eighteenth century	Geography, mid-nineteenth century
descriptive	explanatory
topical classification of knowledge	scientific system of knowledge
geography divided in three parts: mathematical, natural, political	geography forms a connection between the natural and the social worlds
the earth is a static arrangement of discrete objects	the earth and man change through a dynamic relationship
geographic knowledge is advanced through logic and reason	geographic knowledge is advanced through empiricism and observation
the study of geography requires the memorization of facts	the study of geography depends on the subject's own experience

nothing more can be observed than that we live in this land and other people speak our language, [whereas] in that land [live] black people, great apes, elephants, etc., from that land comes coffee and sugar, this or that sort of wine popular with students, from here the first potatoes came, from that country or city comes a famous person, and so on. For this no particular textbook is needed."[6] In Feder's model, the earliest-formed notions of space, the world, its peoples and nature were built not from literacy but on culturally transmitted "common wisdom" such as tales German families might tell about "the land of black people, apes, and elephants" (in Feder's widely shared racist definition). Certainly, the transformations of geographic thought during the years around 1800 reached children by a number of routes, not only through schoolbooks.

Factors that contributed to upheavals in geographic thought in this era included the map-scrambling Napoleonic Wars, the expansion of colonial knowledge production, scientific advancements in geology and paleontology, and intensifying travel activities in a world of improved roads, ships, and postal networks.[7] Instrument-aided empiricism was another development that brought about discursive shifts in geographic education. Historians Charles Withers and David Livingstone have pointed out that expanding knowledge about distant lands provoked questions of truth and credibility for eighteenth-century audiences.[8] Despite the continued popularity of travel narratives as a source of knowledge production about the world beyond Europe, measurement and empirical analysis were becoming more useful for geographers. In a study of the German geographic imagination around 1800, Chenxi Tang traces how the move toward measurement-based science overwhelmed the topical approach to geographic study with endless data.[9] A method beyond categorization and memorization was now required, and the question of reliable evidence became increasingly important in schoolbooks for children.

One sentence from an 1812 manual-cum-schoolbook for teaching geography neatly illustrates these changes. As a disciple of Pestalozzi, Johann Henning was particularly committed to modern pedagogic ideals in his *Leitfaden beim methodischen Unterricht in der Geographie* (*Handbook of a Methodical Instruction in Geography*). His goal was "to raise geography out of the doom of an empty nomenclature, to bring its material into an incommutable order set by nature itself, to base [the study of] life in all parts of the earth on the configuration and proportions of its nature, and to convert all this into an object of independent observation for youth."[10] Moving toward method and away from topical classification, tailoring information to students' age, attempting to unite the natural world and the human world, and emphasizing individual experience and observation—all these moves marked a new geographic pedagogy developing in the years around 1800.

Table 2 summarizes changes in the approach, authorship, and readership of geography and world history schoolbooks from the middle of the eighteenth century to the middle of the nineteenth century. About half the approximately one hundred geography texts surveyed for this chapter were published before 1800 and half after, many in multiple volumes and editions. Most of the schoolbooks range from three hundred to five hundred pages, but there is significant variation in the page and type size. The corpus includes geography texts, world history narratives, atlases, and some natural science schoolbooks published in various regions of Central Europe. Despite the narrowing of geography as a professional discipline by the end of the eighteenth century, the borders between these fields were not so fixed in children's education. School atlases also increased in number and technological sophistication over this period. The work of famous cartographers such as Adolf Stieler was reformatted and marketed to a youth audience. Together with the maps, charts, and occasional illustrations in other texts, these atlases illustrate the visual dimension of children's geographic education.

Authors of schoolbooks around 1800 in Europe were almost universally men. However, women writers contributed to young people's geographic education through their publication of travel narratives, fiction, and periodicals, as well as

TABLE 2. Summary of changes in geographic textbooks

Geographic textbooks, mid-eighteenth century	Geographic textbooks, mid-nineteenth century
a miscellaneous set of statements	a coherent science informed by laws
a series of questions with answers, for memorization and recitation	narrative essays and problem sets with answers
author's expertise derives from university-based scholarly credentials	author's expertise derives from secondary-level pedagogic experience
written without age-specified readership	written for the particular needs of children
reader is assumed to be a young man	reader's gender is an explicit concern
readers are members of a small, elite class	readers are members of a growing middle-class reading public
"school" books are used in a wide range of domestic and institutional settings	schoolbooks are increasingly intended for formal classrooms
atlases are luxury items used primarily by adults for scientific purposes	the school atlas emerges as a key segment of the book market for young readers

pedagogical philosophy. One interesting feature of eighteenth-century school-books is their insistence on title pages and advertisements of the authors' and cartographers' scientific credentials in history, poetry, philosophy, or classics. Over time, the Enlightenment idealization of intellectual authority gave way to more frequent claims to expertise from pedagogical experience.

Who were the readers of geographic schoolbooks? While most of these books were intended for secondary-level education, some were specifically designed for younger children. For example, Luise Hölder's illustrated *Kleine Weltgeschichte* (*Short World History*), written as a dialogue between a mother and her children, was intended for ages six to twelve according to its subtitle.[11] The readers' youth can also be seen through the simplicity of language, as in the case of Raff's text. He promised to rescue small children from their lowly status as "ABC students" through the reading of basic geography.[12] Some longer and more advanced texts were abridged and rewritten for younger readers, such as Johann Cannabich's *Kleine Schulgeographie* (*Short School Geography*), adapted for the lower and middle grades from his *Lehrbuch der Geographie* (*Geography Reader*).[13] Yet, as with periodicals, age is one of the arenas in which the explicit intentions of textbook writers did not necessarily match children's reading in practice. Johann Matthias Schröckh admitted this himself in a 1774 world history textbook that was designed for children between approximately ten and fifteen years old: "I say 'approximately,' because ability, curiosity, and other characteristics or needs can move these limits forward or backward. This decision belongs to the schoolmaster alone."[14] Friedrich Nösselt noted in his *Lehrbuch der Weltgeschichte für Töchterschulen* (*World History Reader for Girls' Schools*) that "a teacher of stratified [multiple grade] classes will easily be able to select the more interesting [parts] for [little] children."[15] Though he aimed these texts at a secondary level (*Töchterschulen*), in the preface he noted his "pleasure that even the smallest girls gladly visit his history lessons," and suggested ways in which teachers could modify the book for younger audiences.[16] In practice, contingencies of book access, school placement, family birth order, and household resources probably determined children's age-graded use of such texts as much as did individual ability and curiosity.

While it remained true into the nineteenth century that schoolbook readers ranged widely in age, the audience of geographic schoolbooks changed more throughout the period in terms of class and gender. Geographic schoolbooks were initially available only to a small, elite class. Moving into the nineteenth century, publishers began to target an expanding middle-class reading public. While the default child reader was imagined to be male, a significant number of geographic schoolbooks were explicitly produced for girls and girls' schools.

Other texts directly addressed both boys and girls, such as Heinrich Rockstroh's *Erzählungen aus der älteren und mittleren Geschichte (Stories from Ancient and Medieval History)* for "junge Leser und Leserinnen" (young male and female readers) or Karl Stein's *Allgemeine Weltgeschichte (General World History)* "for the use of sons and daughters of the educated classes."[17]

These books were used in a variety of settings: Gymnasien and Realschulen (secondary schools); Volksschulen (primary schools); military schools; and at home, with or without private tutors. One common method for using schoolbooks in home instruction, with either a parent or tutor supervising, was for students to copy out notes on their reading. For example, a collection of family documents archived in Hannover contains a set of school exercise books kept by brothers Carl and Adolph von Lüneburg between 1816 and 1821.[18] The subjects were "Geography of Europe" (which also included notes on a general introduction to the study of geography), "History of England," "History of German Leagues," and various essays. Each notebook held between ten and thirty pages of notes or direct transcription of textbooks, and some of the boys' writing was glossed with corrections from a teacher. There is also evidence of self-correction, and places and dates were circled and marked in margins throughout the geography and history notes.

Geographic schoolbooks varied from short subdivided sections to long essays to lists of questions and answers. Early examples like the 1770 *Vermehrtes Geographisches Handbüchlein für die zarte Jugend (Expanded Geography Handbook for Gentle Children)* covered similar terrain to later textbooks, but the organization was strikingly different. Rather than a methodical introduction to terms or an accounting of a journey across continents, this little book offered a hodgepodge of trivia, including a list of historically important cities, a section on coinage, a list of the seven wonders of the world, and a comparison of Russian and Portuguese melons.[19] Such a motley collection lent itself to the catechetical model of reading and recitation rather than reading for interpretation or comparison. Later geography textbooks were more narrative and organized into methodical sections, as in Josef Annegarn's lengthy *Handbuch der Geographie für die Jugend (Handbook of Geography for Youth*, 1834). (See Appendix B for the table of contents from Annegarn's volume as a typical example.)

Some schoolbooks, such as Friedrich Franz's *Lehrbuch der Länder- und Völkerkunde (Reader of Lands and Peoples)*, were printed with large margins that allowed for an occasional gloss or description of the neighboring paragraph.[20] Student notebooks preserved in private collections often followed this model too, with teachers' comments and corrections scrawled in the margins. The form allowed readers to retrieve information from the book in a non-linear fashion.[21]

Many schoolbooks were printed with a closing index of terms, peoples, and especially places. This element indicates that publishers also did not expect students to begin at the beginning and read until the end in a direct path. Rather, the index allowed child readers to privilege certain kinds of information, focus on certain places in the world, return to sections that attracted them or were emphasized by teachers, and neglect material not relevant to their own idiosyncratic navigation of the text.

CHANGING GEOGRAPHIC LITERACY PRACTICES

IMAGINING CHILD READERS

Schoolbook forewords and prefaces provide a useful window into the transformations of geographic pedagogy because authors needed to justify publication (and updated editions) by explaining what their texts offered child readers that was new and different from established scientific literature. For example, Heinrich Rockstroh suggested his *Erzählungen aus der älteren und mittleren Geschichte* was a necessary addition to the existing field of textbooks because it "serve[d] as a preliminary or first instruction in world history, and so therefore [should act] as such only for a young age."[22] He established the market for his book by tapping into the Age of Revolution's new understanding of childhood as a special stage of life requiring attention to children's particular learning needs.

Often forewords and prefaces were addressed directly to teachers and/or parents; some were written to an aristocratic patron; and a few to children. The tone could veer widely from preface to main text, as with Rockstroh, who presented his chosen periodization of ancient history within the book itself as an objective and natural breakdown of time. By contrast, in the preface, he exerted himself to justify this particular chronology to an adult audience, undermining that easy authority of his own text. Yet authors could not control whether child readers examined those pages intended for adult audiences.

In 1812, Pestalozzi disciple Johann Henning charged primary school teachers to develop geography instruction that was not only driven by the needs of the school, "but also especially by the nature and the peculiar requirements of elementary school students."[23] Henning's approach prefigured what we might call "student-centered" education today, which had become a hegemonic ideal for educators of bildungsbürgerlich children by the end of this period (albeit not a universal practice). By 1850, when August Lüben published his *Leitfaden zu einem methodischen Unterricht in der Geographie für Bürgerschulen* (*Guide to a Methodical Instruction in Geography for City Schools*), he asserted in the preface that "the material [was] arranged and handled with respect to the gradual development of the child's spirit."[24] The idea that children's reading should be specialized for their age was so well established at that point that Lüben could take it as axiomatic.

One consequence of this emphasis on age-graded reading was that authors began advocating a more interactive, more flexible kind of instruction. The tone of prefaces grew increasingly sentimental over the period, with authors addressing "dear children." In the preface to the first edition of Schröckh's schoolbook, which updated an older text that had been focused on the consumption and retention of information, he identified critical thinking as an aim of classroom instruction as well as the memorization of content: "But teachers who are not used to treating children as mere machines understand better than I need to tell them that the powers of reflection in their students can and must be raised early and sharpened, so that all they learn does not remain a mere burden of rote memorization."[25] Lüben, writing that it was "natural, appropriate to the child's educational path," suggested that the lists of cities and population numbers in his text not be memorized, but rather serve as a sense of approximate context.[26] Beyond memory and repetition, the modern child was encouraged to think independently.

VISUAL LEARNING

Visual sources, including maps, atlases, and illustrations, offer another way to examine children's learning practices and interventions in their own geographic education. Picturing places has likely always served as an important component of imaginative learning about the world, but as technologies developed to disseminate printed representations, these materials became essential to children's geographic education. As Tang writes, cartography in the years around 1800 hoped "to make the vast territory of [an individual's] country, indeed the entire world, into an oriented space by imparting to him a specific kind of spatial judgment."[27] This spatial judgment was a critical aim of children's geographic education. Schröckh, for example, lamented a lack of maps in his world history book: "The student must always know and see into which part of the world history is taking him. This will also keep his eyes busy with a certain activity: and everyone knows how useful it is for youths always to have their much more active imaginations entertained, alongside their sprouting intellects."[28] It is striking that Schröckh should claim it as a well-known fact (yet necessary to name) in 1774 that children should be active participants in an education that aimed to capture their imagination. Although luxurious atlases were reserved for the ownership of only the most privileged children in the early nineteenth century, Volksschule classrooms began to feature maps on the walls and globes on teachers' desks. Increased access to visual ways of learning about the world was not simply a result of technological advances, but also reflected a growing appreciation for geographic thinking as a critical component of children's education.

Approximately ten percent of the geography and world history schoolbooks I examined included maps, usually on larger sheets that folded out from the back of the volume. More books may have originally contained maps, as the fragile folding paper would have been easy to lose over the centuries. Books that did not include their own maps were often intended to be used with accompanying atlases. The 1851 edition of Cannabich's *Kleine Schulgeographie* advertised on its title page discounts on a school atlas from the same printer.[29]

Henning believed interaction with maps was the most important element of his geographic teaching method. The exercise he advocated above all others was asking students to copy "parts of the earth's surface, as depicted by maps onto slate or paper."[30] This suggested more than passively regarding a teacher's map at the front of the room, but rather a moment of active engagement and creation. Henning thought maps were important not only because of the geographic information they conveyed, but even more so because the visual stimulation of figuring out a map was entertaining. "This framework of learning on the map is in no way tedious and boring for children, but rather a very pleasant activity, because it consists not merely of dry memorization, but also of the comprehension of the map's picture and the relative positions of places, and of imaginative play . . . anyone who has observed the child's nature will give me my due, that children require the clearest, most vivid descriptions, and that nothing is more boring to them than the types of description that appear after the names of cities in geography textbooks."[31] Henning went on to say that maps served learning better than recitation because the fun of playing with maps would make children better retain geographic facts. These recommendations depended on new ideas about children's needs and capacity.

However, maps were not simply toys, but also essential instruments of the establishment of a particular world view for children. As Mark Monmonier has written, "To present a useful and truthful picture, an accurate map must tell white lies. Because most map users willingly tolerate white lies on maps, it's not difficult for maps also to tell more serious lies."[32] Take Adam Gaspari's notation on the scale for maps accompanying his geography text: "In order to have the same scale everywhere, the scale of Russia, being the largest European kingdom, has been set as the base. But since Switzerland, the Netherlands, Germany and Italy turned out to be too small for their peculiar features to be noticeable, so the scale of Russia was taken five times for the first two and doubled for the latter two . . . The map of Europe based on the scale of Russia would have extended far beyond the fixed size, so its scale is only half as large."[33] In other words, Western European countries like Switzerland and the Netherlands deserved closer attention than Russia, at least for bildungsbürgerlich children.

The use of maps supported the sentimentalization of the modern child's education. In an adaptation of Mungo Park's travel narrative framed by a family dialogue that will be discussed further below, Christian Schulz sets the scene by observing that "Friedrich had to take the maps to hand here, so that he could indicate to his siblings any of the various places, regions, mountains, rivers, etc. that were mentioned" (figure 6).[34] Map reading here was presented as a family activity, and essential to placing tales of adventure in their geographic context. But the book also came with a real fold-out map that child readers could themselves use to reenact this journey of sentiments.

Atlases introduced many bourgeois children to maps. Student atlases had been produced in the eighteenth century, but the real publishing explosion came in the 1820s and 1830s as atlases were created specifically with children in mind.[35] Perhaps the most widely disseminated was a school edition of Adolf Stieler's famous atlas, a *Schul-Atlas über alle Theile der Erde* (*School Atlas on All Parts of the Earth*), published in dozens of editions throughout the early nineteenth century.[36] It included pages on the planets and mathematical geography, plates for particular European countries, details of the German states, and assorted maps of Asia, India, Africa, North America, Central America, and South America. Atlases are inherently participatory books, inviting a child reader to follow borders and locate places, translate legend symbols and interpret levels of representation, and make tracings and their own depictions of charts and maps. And atlases could be read or played with by children for any number of purposes outside official geography instruction.

FIGURE 6. Fold-out map at the back of *Mungo Park's Reise in Afrika* (*Mungo Park's Journey in Africa*), 1805. Euro 18 46110, Cotsen Children's Library, Department of Special Collections, Princeton University Library.

Cartography always involves choices, but a youth audience highlights the explicit didactic or political nature of the choices that were made with children in mind. Of thirty maps in Karl Weiland's *Compendiöser allgemeiner Atlas der ganzen Erde* (*Compendious General Atlas of the Whole World*, 1833), twenty-one depict regions of Europe (including Russia and Turkey).[37] Legends on the European maps recorded symbols to mark cities, market towns, forts, rivers, and mountains. Universities were marked in Hannover and Brandenburg, while religious houses were included in the Swiss legend. The map of France devoted significant space to an elaborate, colorful grid of French military divisions and departments, intended to be mentally attached to visual representations by the reading German child. Meanwhile, in the seven pages devoted to Asia, Africa, and the Americas, the legend was suddenly reduced to simply marking scale and European possessions. Place names were labeled directly on the map, but there was no longer a legend to identify cities or villages. More surprisingly, the map of India, China, and Afghanistan marked the scale not only in geographic miles but also in the Indian measurement *Koss* and the Chinese *Li*. It may be that these units of measurement were included simply as an exotic ornamentation, but it also facilitated young capitalists' education in international trade.

In addition to textbook maps and school atlases, illustrations added an important component of children's developing view of the world. Earlier books rarely included pictures beyond the occasional frontispiece engraving, but as technology changed, more color plates were printed, especially in biography galleries, travel narratives, and adventure fiction; this was part of the process by which children's books became associated with illustration in the twentieth century. The pages of Johann Christoph Heckel's *Atlas für die Jugend: und alle Liebhaber der Geographie* (*Atlas for Youth and All Enthusiasts of Geography*, 1776) opened with a frontispiece typical of the period (figure 7). A seated man (tutor or father) holds a book in one hand and points at a large map spread out on the table with the other; three boys actively lean forward around the table, peering at the map.[38] As the title and this picture indicate, the atlas was meant to inspire curiosity and participatory learning. The modern child subject could explore freely (within boundaries).

Although some publishers could not afford full-page illustrations, most books at least included some kind of ornamentation around the text of title pages or chapter openings. Even these simple drawings aimed to shape children's worldview. For example, at first glance the flowery borders around illustrations in Carl Grumbach's *Die Reisemappe* (*The Voyage Files*) seem inconsequential, but a child who valued this book might have spent time looking more closely (figure 8). The borders featured non-European animals, birds, and lush plants

FIGURE 7. Frontispiece of Johann Heckel, *Atlas für die Jugend,* 1791. Euro 18 18833, Cotsen Children's Library, Department of Special Collections, Princeton University Library

twining around the central illustration, all evoking an exotic landscape for the child's imagination while simultaneously dehumanizing the Indigenous peoples of Africa, Asia, and the Americas as further curious flora and fauna. Grumbach's text attached most of its thirty illustrations to stories of Africans, Asians, and Native Americans (even though the book included sections on European peoples). The orientalist gaze was offered early to young European readers.

FIGURE 8. Illustration from Carl Grumbach, *Die Reisemappe*, 1828. Euro 18 46233, Cotsen Children's Library, Department of Special Collections, Princeton University Library.

Visual elements could serve as an alternative path through a book's narrative, open to further interpretation or unlicensed use. Luise Hölder's richly illustrated *Kleine Weltgeschichte,* presented in the form of a dialogue between a mother and her children, makes this apparent. The book's content was quite conventional: the first volume covered the creation of the world to the birth of Christ while the second volume tackled Attila the Hun through Napoleon.

Seite 223.

Und Romulus befahl den Raub der Sabinerinnen zu vollziehen.

FIGURE 9. "And Romulus ordered [them] to carry out the Rape of the Sabine women." Luise Hölder, *Kleine Weltgeschichte,* 1823. Euro 18 13368, Cotsen Children's Library, Department of Special Collections, Princeton University Library.

But the most surprising element of this text comes in the illustrations. Rather than depicting the subjects of the narrative with typical classical imagery, these showed children themselves dressed up as the historical figures and brandishing odd bits of props to act out the scene. One caption explained the ringleader's plan as he directed his siblings and pets in play-acting Noah's Ark: "Come, Miekchen, said Dietrich. We are the sons of Noah; these here are his animals, and you are our sister."[39] One plate even depicted a crowd of little children performing the abduction of the Sabine women (figure 9). The dramatic action of the story was used as an exciting draw for young readers rather than forbidden as a salacious episode.

While these illustrations reflect adult desires about how children should play and learn, or even a nostalgic, sentimental gaze, the fact that these pictures guided young readers through the text means we also need to think about how children understood the illustrations. If we consider the power of imagination and imitation in other settings, it is plausible that a child reader in the early nineteenth century would have participated in this kind of historical play. The participation of young people in their own learning and meaning-making about the world was key to the construction of the modern child subject during the Age of Revolutions.

AMUSEMENT

The obligation to amuse child readers grew in importance as the memorization-recitation model waned. In books targeted at young readers, entertaining stories to describe peoples and places were common (as is evident in titles such as Johann Voit's *Schule des Vergnügens für kleine Kinder (School of Pleasure for Little Children*, 1803).[40] But even for older readers, some dose of pleasure grew increasingly indispensable in nineteenth-century schoolbooks.

As part of the development of modern childrearing practices for a modern child subject, eighteenth-century German pedagogues began to advocate an education that was more flexible, child-directed, and even "cozy."[41] To be sure, Enlightenment textbooks still articulated a moral didacticism, but these authors saw themselves as making a break with the dry and rigid model of the past. They believed a more successful learning process would require greater warmth and interactivity in geographic education, as Cannabich wrote in his short geography, "Finally, I have limited myself to introducing the countries and places not only through a mere dry nomenclature, but rather have endeavored to present concrete characteristics to the beginner, and thereby facilitate his memory for retaining the necessary names and numbers."[42] Feder argued that if children read geography with more pleasure they would better retain the information.[43] He also exemplified a new era in geographic education that was specifically produced with bourgeois children in mind.[44]

Schröckh's successful adaptation between 1774 and 1816 of a textbook originally published by Hilmar Curas in 1723 demonstrates this shift and the modernization of pedagogy. Curas was concerned with how best to aid the memorization of the history he had prepared and the ethical implications of its content, without much attention to the age-specific needs of his readers. But Schröckh's text, *Lehrbuch der allgemeine Weltgeschichte* (*Reader of General World History*), was explicitly redesigned for a child audience, and, to that end, at least nominally emphasized the need for students to develop their own powers of critical thinking alongside learning the content.[45] He was furthermore concerned that young readers experience the study of geography as pleasurable rather than onerous.

Of course, children were meant to be amused only as far as this facilitated their attention and knowledge.[46] In 1806, Adam Gaspari defended the dryness of his *Lehrbuch der Erdbeschreibung* (*Geography Reader*), writing, "I know that children love to hear about of the customs and ways of life of these [places], but I do not know of what use a rambling description of these [topics] would be, other than for pleasure, and time is too precious for that."[47] At the same time that he made this assertion about children's supposedly natural tastes, he refused to please them. By 1828, the pressure to amuse child readers was pervasive enough that Grumbach resisted it by arguing that the purpose of his *Die Reisemappe* "cannot and should not consist [only] in that: to regale the reader in a pleasantly diverting way."[48] Educational entertainment could be a danger, as Henning learned when he tried to incorporate the pleasures of learning from nature into his teaching: "Several times a week I went with my students into the open air in order to show them certain soil formations or other natural conditions of the surrounding area; but soon I saw that it was impossible to constrain the attention of 20–30 boys outdoors."[49] Yet geographic instruction began to incorporate elements of children's pleasure reading into the nineteenth century.

The new charge to amuse children in their geographic education produced some intriguing experiments, including songs, adventure stories, and even games. One example is a board game from around 1800 called *Die Reise von Prag nach Wien: Ein geographisches Spiel für die Jugend* (*The Journey from Prague to Vienna: A Geography Game for Youth*).[50] The playing board shows a map with small sketches of people, carriages, natural features, and so on, illustrating possible encounters and catastrophes of traveling on the road. The map ranges from Trieste on the Italian Peninsula in the south to Lübeck in the north; from Düsseldorf in the west to Pressburg (now Bratislava, Slovakia) in the east. The instructions in the version held by the Cotsen Children's Library at Princeton University are on a separate sheet of paper, in French. Because Germany was a major center for the production of toys intended for audiences across Europe, game rules were usually printed in French, German, English, and sometimes Italian.[51] A fold-out version of this game with instructions (in German, but otherwise identical to the French version) was also included at the back of a youth periodical published in Nuremberg in 1805.[52]

Each player takes a job as doctor, cartwright, customs inspector, or postilion. Participants advance around the board using colored wax to mark the players, dice, and playing pieces that are gained or lost with success in the game. Various dangers menace the traveling players, such as being imprisoned in a tower or lost in the Thuringian forest. If a player loses all his funds, the instructions suggest that the player make up a circumstance in which he has been forced to beg, and that a convincing story could be rewarded by the other players returning half his wealth. On arrival at each city, the players must answer geography questions about their destination or forfeit playing pieces for wrong answers. The instructions call for the child best acquainted with geography to be appointed Director, with a note that turns as Director should be shared if several want the role. A rule about what happens if the Director mistakes a geographic fact implies that this was indeed intended to be played with peers rather than a parent or tutor.

This game vividly illustrates the fusion of geographic instruction with a new approach to socializing children that elevated amusement alongside learning. Indeed, children's geographic education was a primary motive for the expansion of board game production at the end of the eighteenth century.[53] Perhaps even more starkly than geographic schoolbooks, this game reveals the possibilities of children's agency through their education. As Mary Flanagan writes, "Because they primarily exist as rule systems, games are particularly ripe for subversive practices. A hallmark of games is that they are structured by their rule sets, and every game has its 'cheats'—even play itself, pushing at the boundaries of a game system, could be said to involve a kind of subversion."[54] *Die Reise von Prag nach Wien* invited children's active engagement and creative invention, but it could not control precisely how real game players would interpret, modify, or ignore the rules. Geographic schoolbooks were not so obviously entertaining as games like this one. However, from the late eighteenth century, even textbook authors became increasingly concerned with capturing pleasure and amusement in the geographic education of young people.

Gender presumptions inflected authors' imaginations of child readers. Age intersected with gender as new ideas about children's education in general brought girls' education in particular to the fore. The rise of schoolbooks published for girl readers and the gender norms delivered by these texts further reveal how geographic education was specialized for this new audience of young readers. Elizabeth Segel has observed that "one of the most obvious ways gender influences our experience as readers is when it determines what books are made available to us."[55] German girls around 1800 read books marketed for their brothers and male classmates, as girls have long done. But those books that were produced specifically for girls afford the opportunity to see explicit ways in which students' reading experience was gendered. Titles include Wilhelm Fornet's *Allgemeine Weltgeschichte für Töchter gebildeter Stände: Ein Leitfaden zum Gebrauche in Schulen und zum Selbst-Unterrichte* (*World History for Daughters of the Educated Classes, for Use in Schools and by Self-Instruction*, 1840) and a *Weltgeschichte für Töchterschulen und zum Privatunterricht: Mit besonderer Beziehung auf das weibliche Geschlecht* (*World History for Girls' Schools and Private Instruction: With Special Reference to the Female Sex*) by Christian Oeser that appeared in 1843 and then was revised by Christian Gotthold Neudecker for publication in 1848.[56] Nösselt wrote a particularly successful series of geography and world history schoolbooks from the 1820s to the 1840s; I have taken Nösselt's texts as an example of how gender shaped geographic instruction.

Nösselt started his career at the Maria-Magdalenen Gymnasium in Breslau (now Wrocław, Poland), and eventually founded a secondary school for girls, which became the Augusta Schule. He later published a version of his geography and world history texts for *Bürgerschulen*, but began by writing for girls. Nösselt's textbooks were published for use either at home or at one of the growing number of girls' secondary schools.[57] At the same time that many aspects of children's education were becoming freer and more flexible, the gender division of educational spaces, texts, and even disciplines was becoming more defined. Just as more and more girls were pursuing an education that included situating them in a global market and culture, those girls' own practical exploration of that world was circumscribed, and gender-bounded texts for children proliferated.[58] As maternalist feminists would do later in the century, Nösselt used the same gender ideology emerging from the Enlightenment that excluded women from active public participation in the world to argue that girls should be educated in geography and world events. By teaching girls about the past and the nature of other nations in the world, he hoped to impress upon them the importance of "an excellent paternal world order."[59] And yet at times, he seemed to equivocate about what his female audience required that was different from boys' education: he suggested that teachers of girls should emphasize "the beauty of magnanimity and the damnability of vice and weakness," but he also allowed that "much of what boys learn, girls must also know."[60]

Selection was crucial to how world history and geography were gendered in their presentation to young female students. Nösselt claims to have delayed publication "in order to gain richer experience in the style of lecturing and in the selection of facts themselves."[61] He encouraged the classical education of girls in ancient history, even if they did not read Latin and Greek.[62] Surprisingly, Nösselt also kept his text current to within a few years of publication: He added France's July Revolution of 1830 to the 1835 edition and discussed the upheavals of 1848 in the 1850 publication. Far from restricting girls' education to private, domestic concerns, Nösselt brought contemporary political conflicts and shifting national borders to their attention. This fact seems to contradict Nösselt's insistence in his prefaces that "above all . . . history must be presented to girls from the 'homey' side."[63]

Nösselt's struggles with choosing what to include had unexpected consequences. Nösselt stated, as though it were obvious, his preference to limit stories of war. His ideal world history for girls resembles mainstream history and geography education today with its emphasis on narrative over the memorization of dates, names, and places. In the early nineteenth-century context, however, Nösselt reserved this modern method of instruction particularly for a female audience whose Bildung would be, he suggested, heightened by that which appeals to their hearts.[64] Similarly, Neudecker wrote in the introduction to his history book for girls: "A history for girls depends therefore not as much on critical truth and completeness, as rather on the connection of the narrative with life, and especially with the lives of women."[65] This emphasis on experience over declared scientific truth rings of twentieth-century progressive education, although it was restricted to girls' reading in this case.

On the surface, Nösselt accepted and promulgated familiar gendered divisions of social roles, writing that geographic texts for girls should focus on virtues and domestic issues, not military conquest, and that boys should focus on memorizing details of various wars. And yet, rather than using gender difference to justify the neglect of female education, Nösselt built his career on publishing for girls. His writing sidestepped that debate, taking it as a given that middle-class and upper-class girls should be educated. The proliferation of geographic schoolbooks aimed at girls offers a window to a fundamental contradiction in the expansion of educational opportunities for young women during the late Enlightenment: even as more and more girls were given access to previously closed institutions, the gender stratification of spheres, moral systems, categories of knowledge, and educational purposes became more and more rigid.[66]

TEACHERS' CONTRIBUTIONS

When it comes to the part that teachers played in children's interactions with geographic texts, the books themselves offer descriptions or exhortations of practice. For example, Raff told his readers, "But it is not good for you, dear children! if we explain to you everything that is in this book at once and in one way, right at the first read-through. You should read it even more often still, and maybe two, three, or six times through. Your teacher will always tell you something new, but your teacher only does that when he sees that you understand, and that you are quite diligent."[67] Perhaps it is unsurprising that Raff thought his own work was worth rereading, but this comment suggests that children were expected to seek understanding through reading before their teachers weighed in—and, more interesting still, that many children were *not* diligent about their reading. Nösselt wrote that "the individuality of the teacher of course does a great deal" to shape students' attraction to history and their understanding of world figures.[68] He encouraged teachers to lecture according to their own research beyond the text.[69] Schröckh noted that teachers have great freedom to navigate his text and its questions as best suited their purposes, but this was just as true for his child readers.[70]

That expectations of teachers' participation varied makes sense, given the great range of educational environments in the late eighteenth and early nineteenth centuries. Gaspari wrote that he had "taken into consideration those whose entire geographic education is restricted to a single course, e.g. in *Bürgerschulen,* where no scholars, no people of superb knowledge are to be formed."[71] One task for an author was to judge how much ancillary material to include to explain the text for children, the adults reading with them, or both. Lüben proposed that his *Leitfaden* could be used for self-teaching, but noted that a teacher would supplant the need for the written exercises he included.

As far as Henning was concerned, young geography students could not necessarily rely on the adults in their lives to guide their reading. "Many wished for a book that could be at hand for parents and teachers if they wanted to acquaint their pupils with the homeland. I envisioned all the children who are seated on the school bench, and come away from it into professional life; I thought of the parents and teachers, who themselves have no knowledge of their country, and therefore also do not know how to guide their pupils toward it."[72] In this light, reading was especially essential for the new bildungsbürgerlich child (and future professional).

Because Henning's book served as both manual and textbook, it was particularly rich in insights into practices. He gave very specific instructions about where the globe should sit in a classroom (the north wall), how maps should be used (so that all children could see), and how the schoolroom should be laid out to best facilitate learning (by imagining the walls and floor mapped onto global features like the poles and the equator).[73] He also included a set of written exercises at the back of the volume, remarking, "Only sustained, varied practice gives diversified skill, so here many and varied exercises must also be employed if the student is to orientate himself with ease and confidence within the current political boundaries on the earth's surface."[74] A list of questions followed, asking which rivers were part of which states, where their borders lay, and so on. Most of the questions were concerned with European geography, even though a significant portion of the text was devoted to other parts of the world. It suggests that even though descriptions of non-European places were included, in practice students probably spent most of their time on geography closer to home as the material deemed actually necessary for German youth to know.

Henning connected geographic study to creative, autonomous learning. However, he suggested that young children should focus on mastering the specifics of geography before moving to a higher level. "One studies only in order to master a new field and a new creative power. The exercise encourages the autonomous activity of the student . . . [But for young children in geography,] it is not so much that the mental powers should be exercised, as that the young, aspiring spirit should be introduced to this scientific field."[75] Pestalozzi disciples such as Henning may have been more radical than other teachers in their professed aims to emancipate learners from oppressive, rote, authoritarian schooling, but even Henning desired to dole out information in small measures to some students who seemed beyond his control.

Children themselves could seize opportunities in the texts and in their broader education to redefine the meaning of geographic learning from the abstract productions of adults. Even the seemingly rigid question–answer recitation format, which was becoming less common in this period, could be altered in practice by children skipping some sections, lingering on others, or modifying answers. But this was changing, too: by converting Curas's 1723 recitation-based history to a volume of prose chapters divided into short sections, Schröckh suggested that studying the world and its history was in fact better served by more open-ended and narrative content receptive to children's agency. "Some teachers . . . would in all comfort hear recitations of memorized answers at such a lecture; but very seldom be assured that the same is understood by their students, and in fact subject them to a kind of torture, which quite reduces their desire for history. So it is my intention therefore that they should first be told the story: sometimes shorter, sometimes more extensively, sometimes also in somewhat different words than are used in the book."[76] While Schröckh spoke here to the flexibility of teachers, the same principles applied for children's selective reading.

An intriguing comment on child development and the teacher-student relationship comes from the introduction to Gaspari's *Lehrbuch der Erdbeschreibung*, in which he meditated on the questions children might ask within their geography lessons, writing, "we must distinguish an inopportune curiosity from a sincere drive for learning . . . Children ask questions often and wonderingly, especially the lively ones; if their question is a mere invention, they themselves hardly expect an answer, and then the question is not even worthy of response."[77] He did concede that children also sometimes ask questions reflecting on what they have already learned, and then deserve an answer. But his cranky advice to teachers to ignore obvious or irrelevant questions suggests that children often did bring their own curiosity, mischief, and confusion to geography lessons.

Even the authors of these texts, as much value as they placed on reading, were nervous about students' interactions with books. The mysterious relationship between an individual reader and a book, even supposedly straightforward geography texts, posed a number of threats against which children must be guarded. Rockstroh warned against reading without thinking, and other authors impressed on adults the importance of not letting children wander through their interpretations of the world by handling a book without a guide.[78] The pedagogic double ideal surfaced again here, as children were supposed to demonstrate their self-control by interacting independently with texts and yet somehow emerge with uniformly dictated conclusions.

ALTERING TEXTS

Textbooks allow us to trace developments in the pedagogy of geographic education and, in turn, some likely ways in which reading changed children's geographic learning. Yet what do we know about what children really did during and in response to this instruction? To find out, I have turned to more direct evidence of how young people used their schoolbooks in practice, such as examples of geographic texts that have been altered in various ways. These alterations, including readers' notes, marginalia, and other writing in books, show simultaneously the agency of child readers and the directive, governing aspects of their education.

Marginal writing in geography and world history schoolbooks allows a glimpse into geographic education as it was experienced by particular, if often anonymous, individuals. The marginalia I have found in young people's text-books range from doodles and signature practicing to underlining and other incidental marks to lengthy reading notes scrawled in the margins, on endpapers, and even between lines of text. Marginalia in schoolbooks mark the choices that children made about what knowledge mattered or, in some cases, should be modified. I identify here a range of those possible consequences for how we can understand children's geographic reading.

Marginalia have only relatively recently become important to studies of reading, largely because of the challenges involved in tracking anonymous scribbles and deciphering the mysterious relationship between individual reader and text.[79] Marginal writing in books is a rich but untapped source for the history of childhood. Heather Jackson has suggested that children's margina-lia reveals fundamental truths about reading in general "in a particularly raw state."[80] I suggest that we should extend Jackson's analysis of the "assertions" wrought by filling blank spaces in a book to seeing youth marginalia as a form of student agency.

In the *longue durée* history of marginalia, writing in books has not necessarily been a transgressive act. Today, as William Sherman notes, the book trade refers to texts without any user annotation as "honest" books.[81] But Stephen Orgel describes the development of our contemporary fetishizing of clean books as "one of the strangest phenomena of modern bibliophilic and curatorial psy-chology."[82] Sherman suggests that the prohibition against writing in books may have derived somehow from the civilizing process of the eighteenth century. However, I argue that for children at least, the encouragement of marginal annotations in schoolbooks was directly linked to mastering the text during the Enlightenment.

Marginalia in German geography and world history schoolbooks often indicated simultaneously the annotator's deference to normative reading prac-tices in geographic education alongside the potential for reading autonomy. Sometimes the phrases recorded in the margins simply provide a summary of the passage being glossed. This kind of annotation could aid both memory and comprehension, as the reader created a sort of index to the text to make it easier to read the chapters out of order or skim for needed information. Both goals show the young reader exerting control over the learning process. On several occasions, we see evidence of the student's individual interpretation of the provided knowledge through the creation of little representative schema in the margins marking genealogies or mapping conceptual relationships. But this potentially self-directed marking could also simply underscore what was considered important historical or geographic information by the teacher.

To illustrate the range of possibilities, I have chosen three examples of alterations made by readers to three different geographic texts. First, sometime after it was purchased for or by its young owner, a particular copy of Friedrich Nösselt's *Kleine Geographie (Short Geography)* received an interesting addition (figure 10).[83] A student sewed eight pages of notepaper into the back of the book and covered these sheets with working notes and scribbles. Notwithstanding an initial thrill of seeing a "real child reader" in evidence, these pages could prove rather disappointing for historians, as the writer was mostly concerned

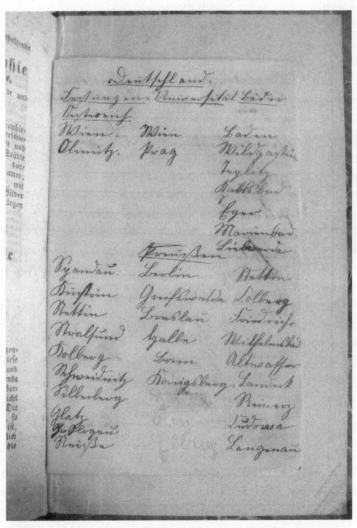

FIGURE 10. Notes sewn into the back of Friedrich Nösselt, *Kleine Geographie,* 1857. Georg-Eckert-Institut für Schulbuchforschung.

with practicing names of cities, rivers, mountains, and so on in the same dry, contextless manner as the textbook itself. There are perhaps no grand insights about the nature of space or global relations to be won here, but in the very fact of its existence—the written exercise of a single student interacting with and modifying the geographic knowledge conveyed by a textbook—these pages point to the key role that geography education played in a particular kind of learning experience. Whether these notes were taken by a private pupil, or as a study tool in preparation for more traditional methods of instruction at a girls' secondary school, the otherwise voiceless student has literally marked the book with her own reading outside the intended use.

In the second example, the anonymous owner of Paul Nitsch's *Kurzer Entwurf der alten Geographie* (*Short Outline of Ancient Geography*) wrote marginal comments and emendations on about seventy pages (about a quarter of the total).[84] The notes were made in two different pens, most in German *Handschrift,* but some in Latin script. The annotator also made liberal use of crossing out and underlining within the text, and seems to have made some marks to indicate how far reading or studying had advanced. But it is the changes to the geographic information that are most fascinating. The writer frequently wrote in different versions of place names—for example, underlining "Mauretanian" and writing "Numidien" in its place—or changed the spelling—as in altering "Messania" to "Messenia".[85] Other terms also received a pen stroke, such as "Kaiser" replaced with "König" before the name of Tullus Hostilius. Was such a change simply a matter of definition, a preference for the Germanic term, or a genuine correction of an anachronism, as, after all, Tullus (r. 673–642 BCE) really was a king of Rome, not an emperor? It is also possible that the student chose to translate to a more familiar term, or was instructed to make this change by a teacher. The endpapers of this book also do not disappoint, as there, in addition to the usual practicing of letters and signature, the reader had written a wobbly list of fourteen books to be read or purchased with numbers (probably representing prices), such as Ovid, *Robinson Crusoe*, and an atlas. This was all followed up by a large sketch of a man with a mustache on the back cover (figure 11).

The third example, a particularly well-scribbled volume of *Lehrbuch der allgemeine Weltgeschichte*, is part of a series by Johann Matthias Schröckh.[86] The book was printed with plenty of space on both sides of the text and frequent section headings in the margins that listed the topic and located the passage chronologically. This format may have directly elicited marginalia—at least, it seems far more inviting to marginal writing than the crowded pages of the original Hilmar Curas text.

The marginalia in the 1774 edition of Schröckh's *Reader* are longer and more narrative than the writing in Nitsch's text, perhaps reflecting a difference between Nitsch's more encyclopedic style of listing geography and Schröckh's discursive world history. Some notes seem to be framed as answers to the questions with which Schröckh began each section, but many of the marginal marks are numbers. Schröckh's revision of the Curas original especially revised the

FIGURE 11. Scribbles and doodles on the back board of Paul Nitsch, *Kurzer Entwurf der alten Geographie,* 1792. Georg-Eckert-Institut für Schulbuchforschung.

periodization and emphasized chronology, so perhaps the glossing of dates by the annotator reflects that focus on temporality. Most of the notes were in pen, though some were pencil—both from the same hand. The placement of the notes was quite respectable, almost prim: most were written neatly in margins, although some were squeezed between lines. In addition, the reader added some underlining, and X's after sentences, perhaps to mark progress in the text. Occasionally printed letters, words, and dates were altered. Finally, toward the end of the book the reader's attention seems to have wandered enough to include a little abstract doodling.

In this case, the reader produced five basic types of marginalia: 1) noting key terms from the text; 2) summarizing or condensing information in the adjacent passage; 3) expanding the adjacent passage by adding information from some other source, such as a teacher's instruction; 4) modifying the text, even in minor ways; and 5), creating schema for representing the information through scribbles in the margins. These forms of marginal writing were likely intended either to aid memory, to aid comprehension, to practice writing, or—the most intriguing yet elusive possibility—as expressions of mischief, inattention, disobedience, confusion, or simply incorrect reading.

Consider, for example, the first instance, which came next to a discussion of human innovations in the Fertile Crescent. The student here wrote several Old Testament names: Jubal, Cain, and Hanoch. The purpose seems to have been to ensure memorization of details the student would be expected to recite. This kind of annotation was probably understood as not only acceptable but standard practice, and yet it does reflect the technological change and widening literacy at the end of the eighteenth century that allowed children to use books in this way. Since the first of those names, "Jubal," was written three times, each a slightly different way, I surmise a secondary purpose for this kind of annotation: using any random paper to practice forming letters. This type is a step removed from the more sanctioned simple note-taking—that sort of writing practice was probably supposed to happen on slates or scrap paper like used envelopes, to judge from other archival collections.

Changes or additions to the text are the most exciting type of student annotation. Where these were substantial—that is, more significant than filling in the missing "d" and "t" in the misprinted word "deutschen"—there was still a wide range of possible interpretations. Did edits express political disagreements? Were some changes made by the instruction of a teacher? Was it a mistake, or a geographic or historical fact about which there was disagreement? Or could some of the changes be made simply to play with the book? In at least one example, the addition of information to the text seems to have been made to aid comprehension. In a passage on ancient Greek geography, the reader inserted an almost imperceptible set of parentheses around several clauses. The sentence, a typically lengthy German extravagance, reads "Early on, the Pelasgians, whose living spaces were too constricted, also penetrated Greece proper, (of which nearly the whole people of Græcus, a leader from the Pelasgian house, obtained the area) and as far as Thessaly."[87] The annotator added the parentheses before "of which" and after "occupied the area," which I believe was intended to make the meaning clearer, connecting "Greece proper" to "as far as Thessaly."

Gleaning meaning from a pair of penciled parentheses may seem a little petty. Why are these irregular, often pedestrian, sometimes indecipherable marks in one book interesting? The types and purposes of marginalia I have identified all speak to child readers participating actively in their education. Although these examples are offered as illustrations, future research may provide further answers about young readers' annotating practices and the material relationship between child and book through a systematic investigation of text alterations across volumes.

CHANGING GEOGRAPHIC PERSPECTIVES

LOCATING CHILDREN IN THE WORLD

A World in Revolution

The political conflicts and border upheavals of the revolutionary age entered children's media astonishingly quickly. In the childhood library of the poet Ferdinand Freiligrath, his copy of the *Nouveau dictionnaire de poche français-allemand et allemand-français* (*New Pocket Dictionary: French-German and German-French,* 1802) not only promised to explain all the weights and measures of the new republic, but also discussed in the preface how the French Revolution had changed the language (noting that the dictionary had marked each new word with the abbreviation "n.c." for "new creation").[88] For two examples of how German versions of vocabulary previously borrowed from French had recently been nationalized (or "purified"), the preface offered "artillery" (*die Artillerie*) and "bayonet" (*das Bajonnet*).

In 1820, the subtitle of Cannabich's *Lehrbuch der Geographie* proudly marked the book as being up to date "after the newest peace treaties."[89] Then in 1851, the same author noted in the preface to the seventeenth edition of his *Kleine Schulgeographie* that the print of the current edition was begun while the Dresden Conference on the new establishment of the German Confederation had made its beginning, and we generally expected a speedy final result of the same. Months passed, however, without such appearing, and as the printing of this new edition was meanwhile disseminated in Germany: it was then paused, in hopes that something might soon become known in regard to the German Confederation. Although this hope was not realized and has not yet come to realization, still the further printing of the current edition could not be postponed any longer, because the earlier was completely sold out.[90]

Beyond the boastful marketing ploy to justify further editions, this note also demonstrates the sense that children's geographic education should address current affairs.

The World at Home

The incorporation of bourgeois domesticity in children's geographic education reflected a broader development in geographic epistemology. German schoolbooks owed a debt to Rousseau for the intertwining of sentimental approaches to the family and geographic education, as Tang has written: "The river in the child's village conveys his longings and dreams. In proposing to take the child's intimate spatial experiences of his home and hometown as the starting point of geography lessons, Rousseau fundamentally reconceived the nature of geographic knowledge."[91] Children's orientation in space, as shaped by their reading of schoolbooks, started in the most local way, with the middle-class family home. This is displayed in many volumes via the common frontispiece theme that depicted children with either a father or both parents, learning the world in a domestic setting.

Henning particularly emphasized early childhood in the family home as a crucial time for the introduction of geography by parents. Although he encouraged early childhood education to be "free, observational . . . [and] lively," suggesting that it would be directed by children's curiosity, he also demanded much of parents, asserting that instruction should be "at least always directed by a solid plan and overseen [as part of] the life of parents and tutor with their children in nature. One must name everything that children see in field and forest and meadow for them, and if they forget it, start anew. . . . Accustom them to considering a subject often and at length and from different angles with diligence, as well as comparing it with other things already discovered."[92] The responsibility Henning placed on the parents for cultivating a spirit of geographic discovery—particularly on mothers—followed Pestalozzi's approach to early childhood education, and prefigured Friedrich Fröbel's development of kindergarten.

One striking text from 1805 offers a particularly effective illustration of the relationship between bourgeois domesticity and the geographic orientation of young German readers. It is a translation and adaptation (by Christian Schulz) of Scottish explorer Mungo Park's travel narrative. This version of *Mungo Park's Reise in Afrika* was published just after Park's second expedition in Africa disappeared.[93] Schulz's text served many of the same purposes for German children that Park's original narrative did for British readers, "[making] it possible for expansionist-minded Europeans to imagine themselves as a welcome and positive force," as Kate Ferguson Marsters suggests.[94] But in the course of his "translation," Schulz heavily revised the original English text for a German audience (most notably by stressing an anti-slavery message).

What is even more unusual is that Schulz chose to set the story inside a frame narrative of family dialogue, the result of a winter evening's conversation between Herr Ehrenwerth and his children. The opening paragraph of the introduction is full of familiar imperialist imagery about the interior of "darkest Africa," but the second paragraph elaborates the family setting, presenting "an affectionate father of very respectable character, [with] industrious and well-constituted children. He loved them immensely and it was his greatest pleasure to see them in their circle."[95] Schulz writes that this father devoted several hours each night to his children's education, after finishing his own business of the day. For their part, "his obedient children, who strove for nothing more than to please their parents, took just as much pleasure from seeing this good father in their midst ... He also no doubt told them a little story as a good reward, but not of witches, ghosts, and goblins, but rather from the real world ... They listened to this with undivided attention, because in this manner they learned some things, and always grew cleverer, better and more sensible."[96] Three aspects of this description, a model intended for imitation by the real child readers holding the volume, bear particular attention: First, we can see once again the sentimentalization of discipline that characterized changing ideas about bourgeois children's education through this era. Obedience and affection were bound together. Second, Schulz actively sought to amuse children while they learned, though he guards against the fanciful frivolities of "witches, ghosts, and goblins." Third, this framing scene of the focused child listeners underscores pedagogues' newly intense interest in capturing children's attention, as well as the moral aspect of Bildung.

Following this introduction, the main part of the book unfolds as Luise, ten, Friedrich, nine, and Wilhelm, eight, ask questions of their father while he relates the story of the Mungo Park expedition, with frequent references to geography. A sample exchange:

LUISE: But has there not already long been—I am thinking here of Colonada's treasures—trade with the coasts of Africa?

EHRENWERTH: You're right, my daughter, the most famous European trading nations, in particular the English, have had their trading posts on the coasts as well as at the mouths and shores of great rivers, such as the Gambia, but no-one has ever dared to penetrate deeper into the interior. Only men such as our Mungo Park could dare such an undertaking.[97]

Note here that even if her geographic knowledge and tone seem closer to that of the author than a typical ten-year-old, Luise's active participation is crucial to the dialogical method. In addition to deploying the common metaphor of European penetration into the interior of Africa, her father's reply also invites identification with the adventurer, "our Mungo Park."[98]

The depiction of the father's teaching and storytelling resonated with new geographic education ideals. Schulz describes how gladly Ehrenwerth conducted his children's education, writing, "He loved very much to take a walk on fine summer days with his family in the open fields, or a foray into the dense forest or in the lovely gardens. Here he introduced them to the surrounding objects in large and small."[99] Notice the emphasis (with echoes of Rousseau) on the power of individual observation and experience and nature. Schulz offered an idealistic model for how his child readers should themselves interact with parent educators, in which "all were allowed to interrupt their father's story with items they did not understand, or about which they wanted a closer explanation."[100] Although he certainly expected children's attention to be closely focused on the geography and history they were learning, this vision included a relative degree of self-direction for children as learners. Schulz also explicitly promoted the utility of storytelling as a pedagogic instrument, describing the pleasure of a geographically fired imagination: "Since there was always something to marvel at, to hope, to fear, to abhor, or to ask, while their vivid imagination was constantly busy with new items."[101] Buying books like this adaptation of Mungo Park's narrative would not only fill young readers' minds with knowledge but also inspire their attention and imagination.

However cloying or unrealistic this depiction of the best of fathers and most obedient of children may seem, what is conspicuous about this text is how geographic learning is bound to familial love: "They had become so used to his affectionate handling that it became the most powerful impulse for them to make themselves—through excellent, good, moral behavior and constant hard work—ever more and more worthy of [their father's] love and approbation."[102] Learning, including the study of geography and faraway places, was thus located in the family home.

Children as Explorers

The modern orientation of children in space as discoverers and the elevation of the individual student's experience might at first glance seem to contradict this primacy of the domestic sphere. But pedagogues exerted effort to reconcile mastery of the world with their emphasis on home and family. Children were the quintessential armchair travelers, "armchair geographers," in fact, since this subjectivity was developed and expressed through reading.[103] The model of the child reader as explorer was made possible by framing geographic knowledge in homeyness. This occurred through young people's consumption of the personal narratives of geographers, natural scientists, explorers, and fictional adventure stories (for example, the wildly popular Robinson Crusoe derivatives, including pedagogue Campe's *Robinson der Jüngere* [*Robinson the Younger*]).[104]

Enthusiasm for exploration and discovery was part of schoolbooks as well, as in Raff's description of the sights and senses brought by a journey through the world with his geography textbook: "Another time, we might lead you to a merchant or in a spice shop.–Now we visit artists and craftsmen with you. And finally you will also hear whether there is a king, or a prince, or a magistrate in a certain country.... Sometimes we take a walk, ride on a cart or in a carriage, hear the birds sing, look at the fields, and work in the gardens, etc. Now we go home cheerful, enjoy ourselves, and read our books once again."[105] The last sentence of that passage is particularly telling: after the sensory tour that Raff promises the study of geography will afford, the child will return home to read—cheerfully. The link between literacy and exploration was thus reinforced. In a similar vein, though not as fancifully painted, Carl Grumbach wrote that he wanted to present to "boys and girls" not only conventional descriptions of lands and peoples, but also "remarkable discoveries from travels and authentic events ... [and] some of the peculiar concepts and opinions, conventions and gestures of foreign (but not always wild) peoples!"[106] He stressed the authority of individual experience and observation for generating geographic knowledge in a way that would dispose child readers to imagine themselves as travelers and geographers.

Schulz's adaptation of Mungo Park's narrative provides a good example of how these two different pedagogic aims were reconciled in the model of the armchair geographer. While the German translation framed Park's narrative in a domestic setting, the story itself celebrates the "heroic" geographer's exploration. Mungo Park's intent in publishing the narrative of his journey was to provide "an ocular demonstration" that the Niger River flowed east. Park as "sentimental traveler" was emphasized in Schulz's edition, since he set that promotion of individual experience and the romance of exploration inside a family drama for young Germans.

The reading child subject as imagined explorer was one manifestation of discursive shifts in geographic epistemology around 1800 that redirected attention to the value of individual experience, local perspectives, and empirical observation. The local was conceived as a foundation for the geographic imagination of broader units such as "Germany," "Europe," and the world, and the knowing subject's local experience and understanding of space was at the root of all geographic knowledge. Ordinary spatial knowledge of "the real thing" (subjective experience) began to take prominence over the rational or mathematical determination of space.[107] So, for example, Feder explained that the best way for very young children to approach so large a field of knowledge as geography was to focus on the basic understanding of a few terms: "sites, villages, and countries, rivers, lakes, and mountains . . . the position of these parts of our earth's surface."[108] This was cast in opposition to the practice of memorizing lists of place names and statistics. For children themselves, their earliest understanding of words like "mountain," "river," or "country" could then refer to places from their own local experience.

Henning asserted that it was natural for children's geographic education to begin with their local environment: "Each observation and understanding that he gains [within immediate horizons] will be for him the foundation, the positioning point, the means of clarification, in short the sense (the organ) for all similar findings that he receives through reports from eyewitnesses."[109] The ideal approach to geographic knowledge was instinctual for children, as long as teachers did not let external understanding from books interfere—asserted Henning in a geography *book,* intended for children to read. This kind of paradox was common during the construction of modern childhood. The elevation of individual experience—as with the incorporation of the family—reveals the part that sentiment and subjectivity played in the evolution of a geographic education especially for children.

COLONIZING IMAGINATION

Division of the Globe

From this location in the world, what did children learn? Tang identifies three defining characteristics of the modern German geographic imagination: the asymmetrical division of the globe into Europe and a vast "elsewhere," the classification of Europe by nation-states with well-defined territories, and the conception of the world as a collection of "spatially delimited ethnic cultures."[110] Josef Annegarn's 1834 *Handbuch der Geographie für die Jugend* documents this asymmetry, with chapters on North Africa organized around ancient cities, chapters on European geography subdivided by contemporary political states, and much of Africa, Asia, and Australia listed as collections of islands and peoples.[111] The world of geographic schoolbooks in the years around 1800 was shaped by German nationalism and colonial desire. Pedagogues demonstrated sincere faith in the power of literacy as an instrument to shape model citizens and naturalize global relationships based on power. Geographic schoolbooks delivered a vision of European cultural hegemony in the world for child readers.

European Nations

Central Europe's protean political borders in the early nineteenth century exposed the choices that schoolbook authors had to make to write a geography text, as Robert Schneider acknowledged in his 1840 reader, *Deutsche Vaterlandskunde, oder das Land der Deutschen mit seinen Gebirgen, Gewässern, Gesteinen, Pflanzen, Thieren und Menschen* (*German Fatherland Science, or the Land of the Germans, with its Mountains, Waters, Rocks, Plants, Animals, and People*): "I have tried to pursue a clear picture of the whole, which is otherwise so difficult to survey, at the same time always considering physical and ethnographic relationships; I have sought therefore a natural ordering which is otherwise difficult in the case of politically fragmented Germany."[112] And yet, when it came to the body of the text that children read, Schneider presented the geographic features as fixed and natural, rather than as the result of human action and interpretation.

That the jigsaw puzzle of German kingdoms, duchies, principalities, and other states making up the former Holy Roman Empire was in so much flux during the years around 1800 does not mean that a larger notion of "Germany" did not exist. Indeed, books like these were a key instrument for such imagining of the German nation. Geography textbooks offered a strong sense of *Deutschland* as a particular territory as early as 1770 in the section "Of each European State, especially and to wit of Germany, where we live" from the *Vermehrtes Geographisches Handbüchlein*. In this case, that included Austria, Bavaria, Swabia, Franconia, the Upper Rhine Plain, the Lower Rhine, Upper Saxony, Lower Saxony, Westphalia, and Bohemia.[113] Schneider included the Netherlands and Switzerland in his 1840 reader, acknowledging that these nations, "do not belong to the German Confederation, but rather to the German nation."[114]

How was this imagined German nation characterized for child readers? Schneider opened *Deutsche Vaterlandskunde* with population statistics, but moved on quickly to the subject of language. He simultaneously defined German nationalism through a shared language (characterized as "pliable, deep, rich, and producing masterpieces in every form") and lavished page space on differences of dialect across the regions.[115] The longest section, on the character of the quintessential German man, was typically nationalist and romantic: "The

German character is identified by depth and sincerity of temperament, by a deep, inward, more introspective than demonstrative life; by hard work, perseverance, thoroughness, constancy, loyalty, morality; by great mental agility in all directions and in all areas of knowledge; by ingenuity, keen intellect, great versatility, great geniality, governed imagination."[116] The section closed with a description of famous intellectuals and universities before moving on to the next section on the German economy, agriculture, weights, and measures. Thus the practical information necessary for a future middle-class professional to know was attached to the promotion of a romantic and patriotic vision of German-ness.

The emphasis on a new middle-class conception of the home as well as a local, individual experience as part of children's geographic education collided with political rhetoric in geography schoolbooks through the construction of *Heimat,* the romantic ideology of German nationalism.[117] Cannabich argued that students in German schools needed to receive more detailed information on Germany as the center of their geographic study simply because they were German.[118] When Johann Joachim Schwaben translated Leprince de Beaumont's *Magasin des enfans* (see chapter one), he made a special point in his notes on the adaptation that he had greatly expanded the sections on geography. He insisted that German readers would need more details on German geography, "since all [students] must be made familiar with their fatherland first."[119] Henning quoted Pestalozzi at the beginning of his text: "One who does not know his homeland, that which he sees, how will he come to know strange places, which he doesn't see?"[120] The use of questions invited children to reflect on their own experience in order to understand geographic knowledge.

Cultures of the World

German children were oriented in a world divided by the intellectual "progress" of European nations and the "backwards" nature of ethnic cultures in the rest of the globe. Non-Europeans were further classified into pseudo-scientific categories that advanced the spread of racialist thought from the Enlightenment into the nineteenth century. The geographic imagination of German schoolbook authors around 1800 inflected their depiction of societies in Asia, Africa, and the Americas and also determined which parts of the globe would be included in standard geography textbooks. While in the twenty-first century divisions of power are often marked between the global North and global South, it was the European perception of difference between the Occident and Orient that preoccupied authors around 1800.[121] By figuring places and peoples outside Europe as bodily objects both unknown and desirable, the colonial fantasy promoted in children's geographic education contributed to orienting young people as imaginary explorers. Reading was thus an instrument of furthering racist colonial knowledge production and also an avenue to individual curiosity about the world, both dimensions of modern education.

Henning's 1812 geography text provided typical descriptions of that world. African countries were most often defined by natural features (coasts, rivers, and so forth), while Asian countries were identified by ethnic cultures, and European countries by political entities and noble families. The native peoples of the Americas were treated as "heathens, who mostly engage in war, hunting and fishing," rather than as political groups or nations.[122] Civilization was marked, literally, by cities, with lists of urban centers in Europe provided.[123]

Grumbach's sections on non-European peoples in his *Die Reisemappe* illustrate the typically racialist and embodied portrayals of geography instruction. He introduced Sierra Leone with descriptions of the men's "good limbs" and "flat noses" and the women's "pendulous breasts" and supposed physical strength.[124] Gender was central to colonial desire in schoolbooks like Grumbach's. For example, most of the section "About the Arabs" is devoted to an Englishman's travel narrative, a long description of a (certainly invented) "harem" in a room covered in beautiful rugs:[125]

> [His wife's] female slaves, women of all nationalities as well of all colors, surrounded her. The lady stood up to welcome us, but [I] could not judge her beauty because of a long veil covering her face, and many cumbersome clothes covering her whole figure. From chin to waist, she was literally encased in gems. . . . An old Persian woman who was among the company soon took off her veil, but the Persians and Arabs retained their cocoons no matter how much I begged them to grant me a glimpse of their faces. They examined my clothes very curiously, and invited me to take a bath, which I refused.[126]

The study of Arab society, politics, culture, and history was all filtered through this provocative, fabricated encounter of a white man with exoticized women's bodies.

Another example of race and gender intersecting in forming racialist classifications is the series of geography and world history textbooks for girls discussed earlier in this chapter. Friedrich Nösselt devoted a significant number of pages to discussing the "natural" ferocity of Arabs compared to the "softer force" of European truth.[127] Christendom was rendered the gentler, feminine pole of conflicts in the Mediterranean. As Susanne Zantop writes about the latent German colonial fantasy of the eighteenth century, "the 'manliness' with which African nations defended their lands precluded their feminization and the generation of sexually appropriate fantasies."[128] The physical arrangement of Nösselt's text underscored this difference for young readers when he directly juxtaposed a "neutral" explanation of Islam as a religion to the history of conflicts between Spain and the Arab world.[129]

The Age of Revolutions witnessed the transition from biblical notions of race to a "natural philosophy" approach led by Johann Friedrich Blumenbach, Johann Gottfried Herder, David Hume, Immanuel Kant, Jean-Baptiste Lamarck, Georges-Louis Leclerc, Carl Linnaeus, Michel de Montaigne, and others.[130] Many of these thinkers were interested in reviving Aristotle's notion of a "Great Chain of Being" that connected—in an ordered hierarchy of superior and inferior creatures—all humans and animals on the earth.[131] The galleries of foreign peoples that filled geographic textbooks for the expanding reading audience of young people show the part that the newly intense focus on instruction and childrearing played in how science was disseminated. Children's education was a central conduit for popularizing new scientific conceptualizations of human beings, simplifying these ideas and transforming them into the powerful pseudo-scientific categorizations they became in the later nineteenth century.

In the 1790 textbook *Lehrbuch der Länder- und Völkerkunde* (*Reader of Lands and Peoples*) by Friedrich Franz, the main characteristics assigned to China were fertility and ancient traditions, while a major section of the chapters on Africa was devoted to the "Color of the Population." Franz wrote that "in the small corner of [the African continent], from which wisdom spread its light in ancient times to distant countries, even the weakest spark of scientific enlightenment has been extinguished."[132] Geographic schoolbooks taught that peoples of the world could be evaluated and ranked by their proximity to the perfection of white European (elite men) in an unbroken chain. Imagining racial differences in this way was a critical component in forming the modern self—and it unfolded through the instruction and socialization of children. On the eve of the Darwinian transformation, readers were primed by their education to receive a new set of ideas about race, inheritance, and human society.

Reflecting on a childhood of the 1840s, one German writer painted a humble but cozy picture of his self-taught great-grandfather and grandmother reading to one another by the light of a gas lamp. Most often, they read from a large volume titled *The Hakawati,* or, *The Storyteller in Asia, Africa, Turkey, Arabia, Persia, and India*, written by "Christianus Kretzschmann, who was from Germania," and printed by "Wilhelmus Candidus." The memoirist wrote that "this book contained a number of meaningful oriental tales, which were not found in any other collection. [Grandmother's] ... favorite tale was the fable of Sitara; later it also became mine, because it treated the geography and the ethnology of our earth and its inhabitants purely ethically."[133] Taken by itself, the passage reflects some features of the modern German imagination of the world, such as the importance of reading and storytelling in childhood memories or the romance of the German colonial fantasy. But the source of this anecdote is more intriguing still.

The author was Karl May, whose travel and adventure novels not only dominated the youth and mass market reading of the late nineteenth century, but continue to circulate in Germany in the twenty-first century. As astute readers may have guessed, this entire account is fiction. No such book seems to exist.[134] The supposed author's name, "Christianus Kretzchmann," invokes May's paternal grandmother, Christiane Kretzschmar, while Candidus ("white" in Latin) references his mother's maiden name (Weise, the same in German). May's family legacy is thus coded in this imaginary book, a self that is constituted by reading.[135] May's personal myth of his first literary encounter with the world, chosen to open the story of his life, also tells us a story about how German children were expected to learn about the world in a new educational regime developing in the early nineteenth century. It was characterized by the European desire for the exotic, the cultivation of individual imagination, a subjectivity formed through stories about faraway places, and the centrality of geographic orientation to early childhood literacy.

CONCLUSION

In 1776, Georg Christian Raff addressed child readers directly in the introduction to his geography text, advertising all they would learn if they read the book. Otherwise, he asked, "do you prefer to remain ignorant, like those children who in their eighth year still believed that behind the mountains and forests the world has an end?"[136] Schoolbook authors and other adults in charge of children's instruction during this era believed that geographic education could be personally transformative for middle-class young people. Even though they worried about the possible dangers of individual children's unguided encounters with books, they understood reading to be an essential path to knowledge about the world.

This chapter has treated geographic education as a window into the socialization of children through reading. Changes in geography and world history schoolbooks drove the development of the modern child subject. New approaches to learning are evident in authors' ideas about their child readers, including the new imperative to amuse and to provide an increasingly gender-specialized education, as well as aspects of the texts themselves, including visual media and readers' alterations of books. The content of new geographic schoolbooks in this period located child readers in the world through an emphasis on the home and elevation of reading as exploration and conveyed a specific vision of the world that had been remade at the end of the European Enlightenment.

Geography is the discipline of knowing the world. Developments in how that epistemology was conveyed to children through the turn of the nineteenth century set the stage for modern schooling and the age of adventure stories at the end of the century. Feeding nationalisms, stimulating colonial desire, and raising respectable middle-class citizens who could carry their armchair geography into business, cultural pursuits, and the education of the next generation—the new geographic education offered to support each of these aims.

A century on from the developments charted in this chapter, the progressive American educator Lucy Sprague Mitchell explored the complex relationship between education and children's sense of their own location in the world in her book *The Young Geographers*. She recounted asking a group of twelve-year-olds to place many imaginary nations on the physical map of Europe in such a way "that they could live alongside of one another with least friction."[137] After they were finished arranging countries according to coal deposits and river currents and railroads, the students were given a contemporary political map of the continent. This greatly dismayed them, prompting such questions as, "How can Russia get out to the sea? She'll certainly try to," and "Don't France, Belgium, the Netherlands and Germany need to guard their boundaries every minute? There's no sense to their boundaries!"[138] Mitchell's students, who were foiled in their search for "rational" (that is, environmental) explanations for national borders, carried these political and economic problems of geography into their subsequent study of European history. Detailing a sense of adventure she saw in these young geographers, Mitchell concluded that children "can and do think in geographic terms" as they make discoveries of social relations.[139]

I offer this story as an example of the legacies bildungsbürgerlich families and writers established for modern geographic education. They were at the leading edge of transformations that brought amusement, problem-solving, and exploration into what had been didactic, expert-driven instructional models. Mitchell's stories of children's curiosity, even from a different context, express the potential for young learners' own agency to follow instructions, pay attention, get bored, fantasize, strive to understand, question, ignore, map—in short, for children to make their own meanings about the world. In the remaining chapters of this book, I turn to direct evidence of nineteenth-century German children writing their way to meaning through letters and diaries.

CHAPTER FOUR

WRITING HOME

Letters as a Social Practice

On a snowy day in October 1850, Peter Paulsen wrote to his young son at home in Schleswig. He thanked the boy, also named Peter, for writing while they were apart: "Your letter gave me great pleasure. Each word shows how you love me: proof of this love that you are diligent, orderly, and obedient to your good mother, through which you give me the greatest joy."[1] This direct articulation of the purpose of letter-writing was a typical feature of German children's correspondence throughout the early nineteenth century, but the father's brief message is noteworthy for the succinctness with which it synthesizes developing pedagogic ideals about sentiment, self-discipline, and writing. The exchange demonstrates how the Enlightenment idealization of self-control in children evolved into the sentimental frame of the mid-nineteenth century: this paradigm was satisfied not only by writing loving letters to one's father, but by being disciplined and obedient to one's mother. This particular note was attached to a longer letter for Peter Paulsen's wife, along with individual letters addressed to his other children. The fact that he deliberately wrote a letter for each child to claim as his or her own underscores how seriously bildungsbürgerlich parents took children's literacy education.

How did this kind of letter writing, evident mostly in elite family archives of the mid-eighteenth century, become a common practice for a middle-class educator's family by 1850?[2] The letters children wrote themselves offer some answers about how this practice spread over the century. In this chapter, I argue that the social literacy practice of children's letter writing allowed young people to participate in constructing the modern child subject.[3]

While I have thus far focused primarily on texts that children consumed, I now turn my attention to texts that children themselves produced, addressing writing as pedagogy, writing as social literacy, and writing as self-formation. The genre of correspondence, like youth periodicals, fairy tales, and geographic schoolbooks, brought children into the construction of a new middle class and new ideas about children's learning. Writing and reading have become tethered together in modern education. For many children in the late eighteenth and early nineteenth centuries, their reading informed their writing skills. This could range from direct copying—especially in the common practice of transcribing school essays—to imaginative writing that emulated literature. Reading strengthened writers, and writing could make readers more critical. Representations of child writers also proliferated in the texts that children read. Depictions of children preparing their own plays to perform could inspire the same in readers, diary-keeping paragons and diligent letter writers demonstrated ideal practices in stories, and archetypes of virtue and wickedness often displayed those qualities through writing diligence (or the lack of it). The common use of epistolary and diary forms in texts written for children modeled and explicitly instructed children how to organize their own thoughts and express them in genre-appropriate ways. Finally, children used their own diaries, letters, and other writing to record and comment on their reading. Writing provided the means to critique or even parody texts children read.

Writing was used by teachers and parents as a discipline that promoted self-control, time-keeping, and obedience to conventions and adult authorities. But that discipline was still a mechanism that children themselves could deploy: for humor, for resistance, in imitation, to develop a voice, for self-fashioning and self-expression, or to negotiate family relationships. Children's participation helped construct modern education even while they were governed by those practices, and the rich evidence of children's writing surveyed in this study offers a window into the agency of literacy, which is often difficult to view by other means.

Despite increasing attention to children's voices across historical sources, few studies have been devoted to thorough investigations of children's letter writing as a practice.[4] Why have texts produced by children often been treated by historians as passing illustrations, secondary to more authoritative records? Three explanations seem likely: First, the challenge of locating sources has discouraged rigorous analysis of children's letters. Second, children's writing of any era can appear simple and formulaic, and adult letters have largely been read as social tools while disregarding children's letters as experiments derivative of adult correspondence.[5] Third, children's letters have been mistakenly assumed to hold merely antiquarian interest, rather than offering evidence relevant to complex social history questions. Yet we miss something important about the part literacy played in transformations of middle-class childhood in Europe if we overlook children's letter writing or use it only superficially.

My analysis makes the case for children's correspondence as a valuable historical source, countering each of these objections: First, not only was letter writing a ubiquitous practice in middle-class German children's lives, but this study has unearthed a broad range of these letters in family archives. Second, letters document the pedagogic exercises in which children and adults engaged, constituting a set of communicative practices worthy of investigation distinct from the adult genre. Third, much more than ephemeral objects, letters served as a key instrument for the social development of children.[6]

Letters record the participation of bourgeois children in household affairs, kinship networks, and cultural spheres connected through school friends and parents' acquaintances from very young ages. Approaching children's writing as a social literacy practice has a double meaning: on the one hand, it marks letter writing as a path toward social literacy (that is, the development of children's ability to "read" their social world and follow class- and gender-based scripts), and on the other hand, it underscores the social context of letter writing as one of several reading and writing practices in which children engaged. These letters show children practicing adult conventions and asserting their important place in the family by reporting on household news, money management, and other practical concerns; demonstrating their bourgeois accomplishments and sentimental education; cultivating associations that would be important in adulthood; and engaging in relational autonomy through a number of different vertical and horizontal relationships. Children's letters document a lifelong process in the making of middle-class culture and the forging of social ties. If the eighteenth century was indeed, as Habermas names it, "the century of the letter," and if German philosophers were on to something when they claimed their historical moment as "the pedagogical century," perhaps it is no accident that the genre of letter writing became so central to the education of middle-class German children during the Age of Revolutions.[7]

This chapter draws on hundreds of letters that formed children's correspondence with their parents, other relatives, teachers and friends, written mostly between the 1780s and 1850s. The letters come from eight archives and some published sources, representing several regions of what is now Germany, especially Berlin and Brandenburg, Schleswig, Lower Saxony, Lippe, Württemberg, and Bavaria. The archives were selected both for geographic range and for collections likely to hold extensive family and personal papers. I have collected as many children's letters as I could find, with a central focus on letters written by bourgeois children before late adolescence. Additionally, the archival documents are supplemented with children's letters (primarily from families notable in arts or politics) published by F. E. Mencken as *Dein dich zärtlich liebender Sohn: Kinderbriefe aus sechs Jahrhunderten* (1965). In many cases, only one or two letters from a particular child writer are extant, and both sides of correspondence were only available for a few families. As other epistolary research has shown, it is rarely possible to reconstruct a complete corpus of any individual's correspondence.[8] For the purposes of this chapter, I have selected letters to cite that reveal exemplary traits characteristic of the genre.

The set includes letters written by approximately 125 children from fifty middle- and upper-class families, two-thirds boys and one-third girls.[9] The writers range from five years old through to late adolescence, although my focus is on the years between ages six and fourteen. Most of these letters were written in German, with some in French and a few in Italian or English. Most were short (one to two pages) and carefully composed, though some examples were more draft-like and mistake-ridden. Although many were sent through the post, that was not necessarily the case for letters written for a special occasion to someone who lived in the same household.[10]

Why have any children's letters been preserved? The growing significance of children's correspondence in the social life of the family is reflected in the very archiving practices that led to the conservation of letters like these. One file from the von Neurath family archive, for example, spans fifty-seven years, the collection beginning with letters Charlotte (née von Erath) wrote to her parents as a child herself in 1799 and concluding with letters from her own grandchildren in the 1840s.[11] These letters were gathered together under Charlotte's name as a record of her most important connections. Families who included children's correspondence among their records usually exhibited an awareness of posterity and conviction in the importance of their own legacy, including documenting the education of children. Still, the letters that were saved and eventually deposited in archival collections represent only a small portion of all the letter writing children undertook as part of their social literacy education. Furthermore, polished letters were more likely to be preserved than imperfect drafts.

Tracking the conventions and typical subjects of correspondence helps us understand children's letter writing as a genre. Letter writing was also a pedagogic exercise, which can be seen in the preoccupation with the medium that filled children's letters. Both bourgeois children and adults used letter writing as a social instrument, as becomes clear when we focus on questions of audience and the relationships constructed and articulated by correspondence.

THE GENRE OF CHILDREN'S LETTER WRITING

Just as correspondence is a genre with particular conventions and expectations, the letters of children from bildungsbürgerlich families of the eighteenth and nineteenth centuries formed their own particular sub-genre. Guidelines for salutations and valedictions, modes of address, bounded self-expression, and common inquiries governed correspondence. Learning those conventions was an essential part of engaging in the social literacy practice of letter writing. Children's letters also differed materially from the physical characteristics of correspondence between adults, and by the subjects of children's writing.

Letters have been studied historically for evidence of events and relationships, analyzed rhetorically as tools of communication, and inserted in debates about friendship, love, conversation, subjectivity, and class development. Historians of letter writing in modern Europe have often focused on the dimension of gender in both the production of and discourse around correspondence.[12] Ruth-Ellen Joeres has argued that letter writing began to take on the characteristics of new gender stereotypes in the later eighteenth century, depicted as "sentimental, naive, unsophisticated, and so on."[13] While acknowledging that much of the discourse about women's education invoked the child as a symbol of immaturity, I extend this insight about the relationship between social categories and the development of the genre to age. See, for example, Joeres's observation about women's subjectivity in letter writing as "highly constructed, even circular in its argumentation: letters reflect women because women, as constructed, are 'natural.' But both letters and women also need to be 'trained,' that is, shaped and properly formed."[14] This contradiction resonates strongly with the pedagogic double ideal faced by child letter writers in the Age of Revolutions.

Some of the letters I gathered in this study were written by young people who were already taking their place in adult worlds. They may have been writing home from school, as did fifteen-year-old Eugen von Seeger in long letters at the beginning of the nineteenth century, or preparing to exercise aristocratic power, as in the eighteenth-century correspondence between tutors and the young princes of the Schleswig ducal house.[15] These writers resemble the sixteenth-century youths examined in Steven Ozment's study, *Three Behaim Boys: Growing Up in Early Modern Germany* (1990). But for the most part, the letters I analyze here, examples of what Konstantin Dierks calls "the familiar letter," were composed by children whose age and education marked them as distinctly different from their adult readers.[16] One example of a particularly novice writer was Emil Herder, who at age five wrote to his father: "dear father! Come home soon, and be fond of me, and tell me about the chamois [antelope] and there [then] I want to climb on you again. and I ulso want to [say I] love you, and if you com, bring some of the nice appricotts with you. Your faithful brother Emil."[17] (Although German orthography was not then standardized, I have tried to render what were clearly mistakes or idiosyncratic spellings in my translations.) In addition to the confusion of the letter's closing and mechanical errors, the run-on logic of this brief note was fairly common in young children's letters—and reminiscent of the additive rhetoric of some fairy tales discussed in chapter two.

As young as he was, Emil still wrote a letter that exhibited some of the key correspondence conventions of this period: the opening salutation and closing phrase, as well as typical expressions of admiration and affection. Contrary to the distinction some current educators make between teaching formulas such as address forms and stock phrases versus "the business of actually saying something," Emil's use of these conventions said much about the successful discipline of his education.[18] Children's deployment and refashioning of adult style in the letter genre documents the history of instruction in literacy and social mores. Another key convention for children's letters was the transmission of greetings from household members in one place to all the potential readers of the letter: when seven-year-old Heinrich Lehmann reached the end of his short, five-sentence note to his mother in 1859, he realized he had left something out and closed: "I have forgotten to offer greetings to you. Papa loves you."[19] Salutations and valedictions, which articulated the relationship between letter writer and recipient, were among the most important of these genre conventions. The tone of these oft-repeated phrases moved from respectful obedience at the beginning of the period to more sentimental language in the mid-nineteenth century, as seen in the growing popularity of the signature, *dein dich liebende* ("your you-loving . . ."). The connection between Bildung and sentiment in letter writing was marked explicitly in these moments, as when nine-year-old Princess Caroline ended an 1806 letter to her father, "If you find this letter good, it will greatly please—Your Caroline."[20]

Beyond these rhetorical conventions, the genre of children's letter writing was also defined by what the letters looked like and what young people wrote about. Children's letters as artifacts provide evidence that writing was an active literacy practice for young people, one that required them to make choices, exhibit judgment and taste, and connect to their readers. How a letter looked mattered to the adults supervising and receiving them, and to many of the writers: people often thanked each other for beautifully written letters (acknowledging the letter as a crafted object as well as a vehicle for elegant expressions), or apologized for flaws. Unsurprisingly, many young letter writers penciled in faint lines to guide their *belles lettres*. There was significant variation in the quality and expertise of the handwriting. Some letters I have examined were obviously created by novice writers, with large, shaky letters. But others demonstrated their authors' elite educations with lovely hands and the right letters for the right purpose. Some child writers would switch to the appropriate alphabets for French or Latin words, and even changed the spelling of their own names between languages. Children made more spelling mistakes than is at first apparent from the letters that tended to be saved. One preserved example is this closing in a brief letter by a seven-year-old boy: "meny greetings to al and remein as healthy az we have lifft yu. I am your lovin son."[21] (That boy was Otto von Bismarck.)

Most of the letters I have examined were posted, with some envelopes archived. Using the postal system for family letters was another way for modern children to assert their independence and savvy, as when ten-year-old August Graf von Platen wrote from the cadet school in Munich to his mother with a postscript: "P.S. On Sunday I carried this letter to the post myself."[22] Because cheap postage was not introduced until the middle of the nineteenth century, we can see the social value elite families placed on these seemingly formulaic little letters.[23] Others were clearly hand-delivered (the letter from Caroline mentioned above was inside an envelope simply marked "To Papa"). Parents and children did not need to be separated by physical distance in order to cultivate the art of correspondence, further evidence that the use of letters for a pedagogic and social purpose transcended communicating information.

Typical subjects for children's letters of this period included travel (as a common impetus for letter writing), the weather, expressions of religious faith, and health. The three most common topics of children's letters demonstrate how letter writing connected young people with some of the same social networks and concerns that preoccupied adult correspondence: 1) holidays, 2) money and other practical issues, and 3) reports on family or other members of the household.

The turn of a new year and birthdays of a parent or grandparent were common catalysts for a child to write. As eight-year-old Carl Heinrich Pathe wrote on New Year's Day 1832, "Much beloved parents! Today belongs to the most important days of the year. Who would want to avoid it, not to get an overview of the past year?"[24] And what was the best way to mark important family celebrations and relationships? According to many of the children who composed such notes, by writing a letter. Most birthday letters celebrated adults, rather than children. One funny exception was Wilhelm Herder's letter about his own birthday, in which he reported to his father about both his increased cleverness and all the presents he had received. Notably, the haul included paper, ink, and quills from several of his siblings—essential instruments of the modern child reader and writer.[25]

Older children and those away at school often expressed their need for money, clothes, books, or other items. Carl Seeger, for instance, wrote at age ten in 1783 to his father to ask for money so that he could tip the musicians at a wedding he was shortly to attend.[26] Other children wrote of money and goods in thank you notes, as when six-year-old Gabriele von Humboldt expressed her gratitude to her father in 1808 for a necklace that made her feel "like a lady."[27] Some bore still more grown-up responsibility: eleven-year-old Dorothea von Schlözer reported in 1782 to her traveling father that a tutor wanted to change money with him, and that another household member asked for silk hose from Innsbruck. She also asked that he send wages to all the servants.[28] The juxtaposition of these examples reveals a time of transition: while some young people assumed adult responsibilities early, others were given opportunities to play or practice at the financial and epistolary duties of the bourgeoisie.

Finally, children's letters were full of news and queries about other relatives and members of the household, an explicitly social subject. Ten-year-old Gustav Weise wrote to his father that his toddler brother had gotten four new teeth in 1849; seven-year-old Luise Herder told her father about a new word game her mother had invented (one that she could play with her younger brother) in 1788.[29] Six-year-old Conrad Meyer was sillier about his sister in an 1831 letter, reporting that she smiled like an angel and lapped milk like a kitten.[30] But these reports on the family were hardly all concerned with silliness and games. In fact, young children often had to write on the occasion of a parent or sibling's death.

At age fourteen Gustav Weise sent a letter to his father about the death of his baby brother Alfred, writing, "as you will have learned . . . our good little Alfred died last Friday." After writing several lines about the baby, his sudden illness, and the burial arrangements, the second half of Gustav's letter was preoccupied with excuses and apologies for not having written better and longer letters in recent weeks, in response to his father's apparent reprimand: "But you must understand that I only came to begin [letter writing] in the evenings after 10:00, since we have had so much to do during the day. Also I still did not have a proper pen for writing and I was very tired . . . But I want to arrange it so that I will write longer and better letters in the future and that you will no longer be able to complain about it."[31] After all this, Gustav closed the letter by observing that his father would have much to tell on his return. Those conversations will, of course, always remain unknown to us. Was Gustav simply invoking the usual convention, that his father had been away and would have stories to report from his travels? Or did the young writer seek comfort from Hermann's expected return? When he did reach home, did Hermann continue to reprimand his son for supposed failings as a correspondent? Letters like this, their creation and preservation, are extraordinary. Yet they are also frustrating, offering us fragmented glimpses into family life without other sources to explain silences. The question of what we can and cannot know from the historical record echoes a more profound question of what letters themselves could and could not accomplish. Despite these silences, children's correspondence still provides a rich record of family life and social networks.

LETTER WRITING AS PEDAGOGIC EXERCISE

Novice writers learned to write letters by emulating adult models and corresponding with parents and teachers. Despite this pedagogic context, children's correspondence was not merely derivative of the adult genre. The pedagogic function of children's letter writing entailed a distinct set of practices. Letters were used by children to practice a number of different skills and demonstrate their knowledge of topics from political geography to religious doctrine. But by far the most common pedagogic purpose of letter writing was the development of young people's social literacy, their capacity to "read" their social world and navigate family and business relationships.[32] The education of young people in correspondence is evident through direct instruction from the letters themselves and from widely circulated manuals, the genre's many self-references as a medium, and letters as a demonstration of educational accomplishment.

How did children learn to write letters? In addition to home or school-based instruction in correspondence, letter manuals circulated widely in this era, with some of the most popular titles emerging from German publishers.[33] These served as both advice books and collections of models that children and other students of letter-writing might copy. They offered prepared salutations and valedictions, lines of verse for holiday celebrations, address forms, and guidelines for appropriate subjects. Many manuals, especially those targeting children, stretched beyond mere rhetorical guidance in the art of letter-writing to offer general conduct advice relevant to education in social literacy: how to relate to various individuals, how to communicate with an ideal style, how to articulate desires and emotions in a socially appropriate manner, and how to use letters in business.[34] For example, a quarter of the opening rules in the 1830 manual *Children's Letters for Use at School and at Home* were devoted to instructing children how they should relate to correspondents of varying social rank: children should "be polite and courteous in letters to everyone, but especially to such people who are higher than you."[35] By attempting to cover all the situations in which a child might need to write a letter, authors of letter manuals actually extended the purposes of children's correspondence.

Another source of letter-writing instruction came from the popularity of the epistolary form in fiction written for children, where the use of letters allowed for a certain kind of self-construction that aptly served the goals of Enlightenment pedagogues, but also served the practical purpose of modeling the style and idioms of educated correspondence.[36] Youth periodicals borrowed the extremely popular convention of epistolary tales from eighteenth century adult novels (prime examples including Samuel Richardson's 1740 *Pamela* and 1759 *Clarissa,* which were translated quickly into German).[37] That literary style in turn owed its dissemination to what Thomas Beebee calls "the letter's heterogeneous social uses."[38] In Christian Felix Weiße's *Der Kinderfreund* (*The Children's Friend;* see additional discussion in chapter two), Charlotte wrote letters to a friend living on a country estate. In these elaborate letters, which were serialized across the run of the weekly periodical, the girls debated questions about the human experience and shared their personal faults with one another, modeling the kinds of social ties and modes of expression that would serve these readers as adults. In the sequel, *Briefwechsel der Familie des Kinderfreundes* (*Correspondence of the Family of the Children's Friend,* 1792), Weiße decided to abandon other forms and narrate it entirely through letters. While the rhetoric of these fictional young writers was implausibly sophisticated, the use of the epistolary form underscores letters' importance to educating the active child reader and writer. Epistolary fiction reminds us of the multivalent nature of correspondence: a letter read by historians always has at least three participants—writer, recipient, historian—and children's letters of the nineteenth century often involved many more readers.

Returning to the real-life audience of these stories: most children's letters that have been preserved in archives are exceptionally tidy—still within the range of a young writer's ability, but with few orthographic or linguistic mistakes. However, because the children of the Schleswig-Holstein-Sonderburg-Augustenburg house belonged to a family secure in the perception of their own historical importance, even draft versions of the young family members' practice letters were preserved.[39] Some of the changes may be the result of self-correction, as when Prince Fritz took three tries to form the word "letter": "Ich will dir einen bru Briew Brief schreiben" ("I want to write you a letter"). Crossed-out words and scribbled-in additions also indicate the likely practice of a child writer preparing a draft that was corrected by an adult and then recopied by the child. In some cases, spelling mistakes in the first version were numbered, and the next page showed the student rewriting the marked words in order: *Wuns* to *Wunsch* (wish) or *sate* to *sagte* (said).

Children's letter-writing was usually supervised in some fashion, as we can see from exceptions such as nine-year-old Else von Arnim bragging that she wrote one all by herself: "Adieu, my good father, I also pray always for you, that you remain happy and healthy. I have written this letter entirely alone, Mother has not added a single word."[40] In most cases, a parent or teacher reviewed letters composed by children, often critiquing them. Ten-year-old Conrad Meyer's mother told him that his earlier efforts were not worth the postage to mail them before he produced one worthy letter to his father in 1835.[41]

Whatever the degree of adult involvement in correspondence instruction, child writers rarely learned to compose letters in isolation. Sibling collaboration was a common aspect of education in correspondence, again shaping the genre through social interaction even when letters were purely for practice and never sent to their imagined recipients. The set of letters written to Johann August Ernst von Alvensleben by his children and grandchildren includes several examples of the same letter, word for word, copied by younger siblings. For example, eight-year-old Adelheid wrote the following in French to her father on his birthday in 1801: "I congratulate you on your birthday and I hope that you will continue to live a long and happy life and I beg you to accept this little gift [probably an attached drawing]. Forgive [me] that I cannot write longer, I do not yet know enough French to write you more. I am, my dear father, your Adelaïde."[42] Her brother Albrecht ("Albert"), seventeen months younger, wrote the very same letter that day, with a few additional errors of spelling and letter formation. In this case the duplicated content of the letter, likely based in part on a model, was apparently less important than the form (to demonstrate skill, or at least developing skill) and the act of writing (to reinforce major family relationships).

In some instances, these documents provide evidence of the letters that were not written. At age ten, Gustav Weise started a letter to his father with the following half-apology: "You must not take it amiss that I did not write to you with Lottchen [his older sister Charlotte], but I think that my letter which I am writing to you now will please you just as much Lottchen's letter."[43] Other letters between Gustav and his father repeat this demand for more frequent or longer letters, with Gustav writing both to convey his educational progress to his absent father and to fulfill the social obligation of sharing household affairs with the traveling businessman.

Gustav and Hermann Weise's exchanges about the failings of the boy's correspondence also demonstrate one of the most common ways letter writing conventions were taught, through continual discussion of the medium itself within letters. Like video chats or cell phone calls of the twenty-first century, in which many minutes are preoccupied with frustrations about the connection, comments on the video frame and sound quality, or marveling at the technology's capabilities, children's letters were full of reflections on the practice of writing. Dorothea Schlözer noted to her friend in 1785 that she had written such a long letter that she had hurt her finger.[44] Other children could not generate enough content to fill a letter without resorting to talking about the medium, as when nine-year-old Heinrich Lehmann concluded a letter to his father: "Now I will write nothing further to you, because I do not know what I should write."[45] A particularly funny example of this comes from the later well-known writer Bettina Brentano, who filled an entire letter at age eleven to her sister Kunigunde with explanations of why she could not write her a letter: "You asked me all sorts of [questions] in your letter, but I cannot answer all of them, partly because the post is going out soon, and also because I have lost the letter, and I do not have any more time left to look for it. Content yourself therefore until the next time. Then I want to answer everything that you write to me. Only this news can I tell you, that Marie Sophie [another sister] is angry with you because you have still not written to her."[46] Letters about letters like this one exerted a social purpose as well as a pedagogic one, even without much news or particular content. Bettina used correspondence to negotiate relationships with these two sisters and others whether or not she had specific information to communicate. Princess Caroline's New Year's card for her father in 1806 was a similar sort of non-letter, composed mostly to forestall him asking why she had not written like her brother: "I am writing you . . . because I do not want that you should ask as last year: why I have not written you [a letter], because Christian did write one to you."[47] But this could go both ways, as when Adelbert Herder used a short letter in 1788 to reproach his traveling father for not writing often enough.[48] The ubiquity of letter writing as a subject in letters—apologizing for one's letter or acknowledging, requesting, or critiquing others' letters—is evidence of the centrality of social relationships to letter writing as an educational practice for bildungsbürgerlich children.

Another social-pedagogic use of letters had to do with demonstrating educational accomplishments. Letters were a mechanism for reporting on progress in school to distant parents, as when ten-year-old Carl Seeger informed his father that he was reading books diligently, though it was surely a coincidence that the announcement came just before he asked for money.[49] Or, letters could be used to pass on external judgments of educational achievement, as when August von Tschirschnitz and others enclosed their report cards inside letters to absent parents. (For the record, August secured a 1b, "quite good," in

Comportment for the Easter to Michaelmas term of 1841, but only managed a 3b, "very mediocre," in Arithmetic and Writing.)[50]

Young writers could also demonstrate their educational achievement through the letter as a gift or token. In an 1813 birthday note, Heinrich Wilhelm Weise promised his father to be more industrious, to keep his books in order, to walk on the street in an orderly fashion, and so on.[51] His birthday present constituted a vow to perform all the duties of a self-controlled child of the Enlightenment. The presents the Alvensleben children composed for their (grand)father's birthdays took the form of Latin odes, essays, and drawings to exhibit the skills they were acquiring, as well as notes written in the foreign languages they were studying. This demonstration of their affection through the display of their Bildung was something the children worked at, as in Ludolphe's missive around 1824, whose elegant Latin script indicates that he must have drafted and practiced it earlier.[52] But far from requiring perfection, Johann von Alvensleben saved plenty of "flawed" papers from the children: a poem with provisional stress marks only partly erased, a drawing from Auguste that she wanted to get back after the birthday so she could correct some faults, and the French letters quoted above by letter writers who did not really yet know French.

Indeed, the "childish" mistakes marking a letter as supposedly more natural began to be prized in notes intended to display a young person's Bildung in the nineteenth century.[53] Young Jacob Burckhardt wrote greetings to his grandmother that his mother originally glossed by noting that five-year-old Jacob had made "this beautiful letter" for her with the help of his tutor. Then she was disabused of this and encouraged to add a corrective: "No! Just now he says: Herr Munzinger guided his hand to the position for *beautiful* [letters] and the *untidy* [parts] he wrote *alone.*"[54] While this can be interpreted as an overly scrupulous little boy acknowledging his debts and faults, at the same time he was exerting ownership over the mistakes through this correction. Furthermore, his mother seemed proud both of the resulting imperfect letter and of his precision regarding the tutor's assistance. The significant place of children's correspondence in the social life of the bildungsbürgerlich family is reflected in the very archiving practices that led to the preservation of letters like these.

Jacob Burckhardt would become an influential historian with theories of the past that cut against the Rankean grain dominating European historiography in the later nineteenth century. He also followed a revealing political path. This child-centered education and celebration of his individual subjectivity produced an adult who turned away from the family business of theology. He lent some limited support to his liberal German friends in the 1848 revolution, but then retreated from at least the nationalist elements of nineteenth-century

European liberalism after the failure of that revolution.[55] The emphasis on literacy and bourgeois culture he gained in his youth remained with him even as his political subjectivity shifted later in life.

Understanding why families treasured mistakes in letter writing, which adults determined to be "childlike," depends on changing definitions of how a modern child should "naturally" behave and feel. Letters constituted a useful tool for educating the emotions of young writers, and for teaching children how to articulate feeling in a socially useful way. This is evident in the opening example of this chapter, when Peter Paulsen told his son that the letter the boy had written was proof of his love—through his diligence, obedience, and education. This framework for the emotions of childhood asserted that children's tempers, consciences, and feelings for others (especially their parents) should be expressed in a natural and heartfelt manner, but also be mediated by moral reading and writing. As Willemijn Ruberg observes, "A child was free to write as he or she wished (confidingly, naturally, individually), as long as this remained within the bounds of what was deemed proper."[56] The writer Matthias Claudius published his six-year-old son Fritz's letter in 1795 as a paragon of child-like style, probably because of Fritz's disorganized but repeated expressions of love that gave the letter a sense of spontaneity and demonstrated his successful instruction in sentimentalism.[57] In a similar vein, after six-year-old Andreas Heusler signed and dated an 1840 letter to his father, he added a self-deprecating postscript to describe the note as being "not much but from the heart."[58] Recognizing the use to which adults put these conventions and expressions of filial love does not mean that each instance was simply a thoughtless acquiescence to adult expectations. Nine-year-old Adelbert Herder's longing for his absent father makes a poignant impression in his refashioning of closing formulas for this 1788 letter: "live well think always on us, because we have always thought about you in the evening as [when] I lay with Mother on the sofa and closed my eyes, I have always seen you. live a thousand thousand times well."[59]

LETTER WRITING AS SOCIAL INSTRUMENT

Children's letters have often been mined by historians for biographic information, or presented as ephemeral objects of antiquarian interest. In fact, for the writers and recipients, letter writing exerted a very important social purpose, including self-development through social ties. As Habermas has written, nineteenth-century letters and diaries "were experiments with the subjectivity discovered in the close relationships of the conjugal family."[60] This section demonstrates how children used letters as a means of learning sociability, building relationships within (primarily) kinship networks, and cultivating socially situated selves. Children's primary correspondents were their parents, but letters written to grandparents and other relatives have also been preserved, as well as correspondence with teachers, family servants, and peers (especially siblings).

What do these letters reveal about child writers' awareness of their readers? The previously mentioned practice of conveying greetings indicates the readership of a child's letter beyond the immediate recipient. For example, eight-year-old Annette von Droste-Hülshoff included kisses from all her family to her grandmother in a short note of 1805, but then realized she had left someone out: "I had almost forgotten the good grandpa, kiss him for me."[61] Similarly, fourteen-year-old Ferdinand Freiligrath added a postscript to his 1824 birthday note for an aunt: "Father and Mother, as well as my siblings, also send their good wishes to you; they would have done this themselves, but they are prevented by their business, [and] they will nevertheless have their compliments to pay to you themselves next Sunday."[62] Letter writing was rarely a solitary endeavor for children. On both the sending and receiving end, correspondence brought children's compositional skills to the attention of adults in their lives as letters were shared and commented on. One example of this practice was noted in an 1831 diary entry of sixteen-year-old Anna Krahmer, in which she described the embarrassment of her sister reading aloud a letter from Anna's love interest, Heinrich, in front of a small group playing cards at home. Anna was mortified in that case that her friends and family heard Heinrich dismiss her affection for him in the letter, but sharing letters aloud was not an unusual custom in itself.[63]

Prevalent as letter writing was in young people's lives, it also appeared regularly on the pages of the diaries they kept. Correspondence—letters received, letters sent, letters expected—was a ubiquitous subject in diaries because it was a facet of daily life, the primary focus of children's personal journals. Young writers also used their diaries to record impatience when waiting for letters, family news that had arrived in letters, and the use of letters to request books or money. On a separate occasion, for example, Anna Krahmer wrote self-critically of her excitement when a letter for the family arrived from Heinrich.[64] The social power of correspondence was reinforced by Anna turning to her diary to record her feelings and self-reflection in response to this letter. In another diary, seventeen-year-old Emil Schneider recorded (in French) his expectation of hearing from a friend, writing, "Philipp has not yet responded to my letter . . . but patience, I do not yet despair of his friendship."[65] In a later entry, he noted finally receiving the awaited correspondence from Philipp: "This evening, when I came home, I discovered a letter from Philipp, in which he wrote to me that he had indeed been here yesterday but had not found time to visit me. Nevertheless the letter is witty and shows that he is in good spirits and cheerful."[66] Here, letter writing was a substitute for a visit and conversation, a means of supporting social connections. Furthermore, while Emil sought to interpret his friend's emotions from the language of the letter, he simultaneously evaluated the quality of his peer's style—supporting the development of his own compositional skills.

As is evident in these diary entries, the relationships children cultivated through the practice of letter writing were not limited to the most common connection, that of parent and child. They also kept up communications through a broader kinship network of grandparents, aunts and uncles, cousins, and close family friends. Henriette and Lisette Pathe, for example, sent an elaborate note of congratulations to their uncle on the occasion of his wedding.[67] More unusually, the Herder children regularly corresponded with their father's valet while he was traveling.[68] In one particularly poignant example crossing outside the immediate family, Fritz Schnizlein wrote to the mother of his classmate August to tell her how unhappy August (age twelve) was at military school, reporting, "Your August cries a great deal daily because he is not with you. He may become very sick about it, it would be better if he were with you. Overall it is no longer good for him here."[69] He begged August's mother to bring her son home. Although she did not, Schnizlein's training in formal and intimate correspondence was critical in facilitating his petition.

By far the most common correspondents for children after their parents were siblings. In 1797, twelve-year-old Bettina Brentano lectured her older sister Sophie on the diligent practice of letter writing: "I was not yet angry with you because I thought the same, that you had not [written], not because you did not love me anymore, but rather because the little Sophie had been a little too lazy."[70] She demanded stories of amusing balls and more regular correspondence from her sister. With significant age differences between some siblings, letters could serve a similar pedagogic and social purpose as with parents. Eight-year-old Eduard Mörike wrote letters in order to report on his progress at school to his brother, such as the following: "I am quite happy to answer your questions. In Latin I have come so far that I can conjugate 'tueor.' We do not do much arithmetic in class. School is going quite well for me. August is beginning to know his ABCs. August and I think of you often."[71] Again, this note underscored the use of education to affirm family bonds. Often, siblings played a part in each other's writing practices not as correspondents but instead by collaborating on a letter. For example, Auguste, Christian, Sophie, Emilie, and Robert Roller all wrote a little note of appreciation in 1808 to their mother, "who so tenderly cares for us." The card was apparently in Christian's hand (the oldest), but it was signed by each of them with differing levels of writing skill.[72] Sibling collaboration could be as simple as the example of a note on special stationery from Sophie von Brüsselle to her father, which concludes with an extra line of greeting written in by her brother Felix to co-opt his sister's letter.[73]

Letter writing served as a technology of the self for young writers.[74] In the active model of self-formation emerging in European thought by 1800, letters simultaneously demonstrated children's instruction in the conventions of educated correspondence and also offered a mechanism for children to exert agency over their own self-expression by crafting a written persona with tastes, habits, and attitudes. Crucially, this activity centered on a socially situated self, that is, a subjectivity located within and formed by the relationships that structured a bourgeois child's life. Dena Goodman argues that we must consider the self-fashioning work of letters as a social project, with "an understanding of autonomy that begins from the premise that all people are socially embedded and that selves are formed not against relationships with others but in the context of them."[75] The self-surveillance and self-formation facilitated by letter writing furthered the development of children's social literacy and the networks that would be critical to their bourgeois activities in the future, including politics, business, and family formation.

Children's correspondence records a variety of projects undertaken for self-improvement. Consider, for example, this passage from a New Year's letter written by Caroline Dorothea Pathe at age ten: "I have often troubled you, beloved parents, through childish carelessness. But in the new year I vow to be a new person. Through diligence and good conduct, I want to reflect the value of your love always."[76] Caroline's vow partly reflects a common convention of holiday letters, but this passage also demonstrates her engagement in self-examination for her parents' benefit. Letters often show children engaging in this kind of self-surveillance, a practice that, as Philippe Lejeune argues, aimed at "the construction of a subject who becomes autonomous only by taking responsibility for his own subjection."[77] Particularly intriguing in this example is Caroline's presentation of herself as inherently flawed because of her youth ("childish carelessness"). Children's efforts to write well were concerned both with satisfying pedagogic imperatives and with crafting and performing adult selves through social exchanges. This took the form not only of explicit resolutions but also of the smallest details, as when Princess Caroline turned a spelling mistake—misspelling *das* ("the") with an extra *s* ("that")—into a decorative flower mid-sentence in a letter for her father.[78] Correspondence allowed the child writer to strive for self-betterment through acts of editing, and to inhabit a socially situated self.

In the variety of their correspondence, children were preparing even at a very young age a foundation for their part in family dynamics and kinship networks that would be important for the rest of their lives. One of the most prolific letter writers in this study, Gustav Weise, wrote letters from at least age nine (and probably younger) to his father, who was often away trying to rescue a failing family business. Gustav wrote about all the familiar subjects of young children's letters: holidays, health, and quotidian aspects of life at home. Yet by the end of his father's life, the correspondence preserved in the family collection reveals such far-ranging subjects as the young man's work as a factory director in Connecticut, the political situation of the United States at the end of the American Civil War, his opinions on what his younger brother Bruno should study, and whom his sister should marry. He and his father exchanged news like any adult correspondents, but also participated in family business across an ocean. Gustav transitioned easily from writing to his father about Bruno's new teeth (at age ten) to Bruno's career path (at age twenty-six).

CONCLUSION

In 1849, one year before receiving the letter her father wrote to each of her siblings (with which this chapter began), Dora Paulsen sent a letter of her own home from school. At age fourteen, Dora had already absorbed the lessons of letter writing as a social practice, thoroughly established for child writers by the middle of the nineteenth century. She opened this particular letter with the self-deprecating trope of not having written frequently enough, and expressing her resolve to send an extra-long letter this time, though in reality, it was about the same length as her usual missives. It addressed all the necessary topics for a young person's correspondence: reports on other family members, stories from recent travel, inquiries about relatives' health, and comments on holidays and school activities. Dora's brief valediction captured the ideal style for a bourgeois child, closing with, "Adieu, dear parents. Heartfelt greetings from all and to all from your loving daughter."[79] She deployed this short letter to good purpose: for practical reasons, to communicate with her distant family, but also to secure various social ties, to make connections between her parents and other relatives, to situate herself within the family circle, and to demonstrate her mastery of genre conventions and a sentimental lexicon.

Like many other letters I have collected, the Paulsen family's correspondence illustrates how letter writing functioned for children as both pedagogic exercise and social practice in an era of newly intense attention to the education and socialization of children. The letters that bildungsbürgerlich children composed show them exploring genre conventions, learning through writing, and establishing critical social networks. As a result, correspondence aided the formation of middle-class culture early in childhood, embedding the child in modern processes of class development.

These documents include surprising moments of self-fashioning and lively, engaging voices that bring their young authors to life. They also offer frustrating mysteries: there are missing letters and absent voices in largely one-sided stacks of correspondence, the practice of corrections and multiple drafts obscure mistakes and altered language, and we have few records of the oral conversations that surrounded children's writing of letters. Yet what these sources demonstrate is the full reach of children's participation in letter writing as it facilitated the development of the modern child subject. Social ties and education were also critical to that development as young writers examined themselves in their diaries, the genre that is addressed in the next chapter.

CHAPTER FIVE

WRITING THE SELF

Growing Up with Diaries

Anyone who has experienced the regret of abandoning some design for self-improvement—say, an exercise regime, or commitment to early rising—will find this sentiment from a young writer in 1838 familiar: "Once again a long time since writing in this diary. It was a time which actually is not a time at all. One hardly knows anything about the elapsed days anymore, if one has not put it down with assiduous and active diligence, and it is a sign of a day well spent when one has also properly observed the diary writing."[1] For fifteen-year-old Wilhelm Dieckhoff, his experiences were scarcely real if he did not record his perspective on them through writing. Dieckhoff's diary tracks a repeating cycle of vowing to write more, better, more often—followed by an eventual lapse. This passage also presents a preoccupation with diligence and a desire to monitor time, periods of anxiety and self-reform, and an understanding of the diary not as a text but as a practice—elements that appear throughout the diaries gathered for this chapter.

Bourgeois European children began keeping diaries in unprecedented numbers during the Age of Revolutions. This increase in volume and in the attention paid to children's writing produced cases such as Marie Seybold and Hermann Schmidt in Württemberg. In the early 1830s, Marie kept a diary (referenced in the introduction) from at least the age of ten; in the 1850s, she ensured that her son, Hermann, did the same, and both were preserved in a family collection.[2] Diary keeping fostered a modern subjectivity for youth during this era, as bourgeois Germans came to understand it as the crucial life stage for the emergence and formation of the self. From the perspectives of pedagogues, teachers, and parents, new conceptions of children's interiority in the early nineteenth century made diary keeping a practice useful both to develop discerning, reasoning subjects and to educate the emotions. But what meaning, then, did diary keeping hold for children themselves? How did they respond to and make use of this practice?

As with letters, it would be easy to overlook these documents as simple artifacts of literacy instruction. Diaries could be dismissed as nothing more than another canvas for practicing penmanship and linguistic development, or for mechanically echoing didactic ideas about virtue and discipline. But I argue that writing instruction was only one reason—and not the most important—why these young writers kept diaries and continued writing for years. My reading of a range of examples reveals that children and youth used their diaries as rich territory for crafting and negotiating subjectivities as they grew up. Jerrold Seigel has shown "that modern conditions require individuals themselves to participate in forming their selves," in contrast to notions of the self or soul as an unchanging substance.[3] As a mechanism for both self-surveillance and self-formation, diary writing, I argue, allowed young people simultaneously

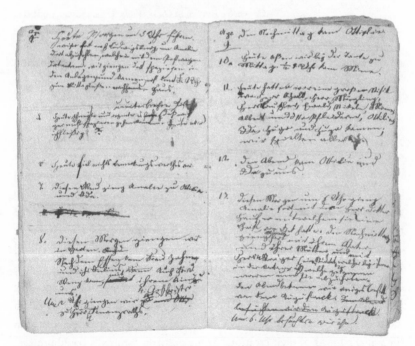

FIGURE 12. Two typical pages from Marie Seybold's diary, April 1830. Vorlage und Aufnahme: Hauptstaatsarchiv Stuttgart Q 3/48 Bü 3.

to satisfy the pedagogic imperatives that demanded continual self-evaluation through literacy, and to use their daily reflections for forging identities, asserting personal taste and opinions, and growing up. Youth diaries, perhaps more directly than any other genre, document the critical contributions of the active child writer to constructing modern European selfhood.

After taking a look at research on diary writing across historical cases, we will meet the six young German writers included in this study and review some common characteristics of the documents they created. Of particular interest are two modes of self-making: the diary as self-surveillance—through monitoring time, anticipating readers, and evaluating industry and emotions—and the diary as self-formation—through a complex process of shaping social and emotional selves.

STUDYING DIARIES

COMPARATIVE CASES
I never travel without my diary. One should always have something sensational to read on the train.

—*Gwendolyn Fairfax, in Oscar Wilde,* The Importance of Being Earnest, *1895*

As Irina Paperno writes, spending time with other people's personal papers "has long been a privilege of students of history and literature."[4] One valuable approach to reading historical diaries is to mine them for data about schooling, material culture, daily life, kinship networks, biographies, and so on.[5] My concern, however, is with how diary keeping worked as a genre and practice of self-elaboration in young people's lives. Insights into diary writing as a technology of the self from other historical contexts have shaped my analysis of German youth diaries.[6] Paperno notes the curious fact that this field insists on the marginality of diaries as a subject of inquiry, yet historians across various fields continue to reference diaries and related personal narratives as evidence. Even the landmark collection of essays on European diary writers edited by Rachael Langford and Russell West is titled *Marginal Voices, Marginal Forms.*[7] This pervasive sense that diaries remain under-theorized suggests we need to spend more time comparing how they have worked in different contexts.[8] One reason it is so difficult to locate diaries is that they are almost always catalogued by creator rather than the social context of their creation.[9] Some massive, nationally based projects do exist for identifying and collecting personal narratives and can give a sense of the range of diaries written in Europe.[10]

Exactly when diary writing began is disputed. Jürgen Schlaeger attributes the growing preoccupation with writing the self in the Renaissance to printing and the Reformation.[11] Philippe Lejeune, however, suggests that the period around 1800 was key to the evolution of the modern diary, as it emerged from bureaucratic genres and the family chronicle.[12] Lejeune also quotes Marie d'Agoult, who identified her own diary-writing impulse in 1805 as, in fact, a German custom: "In my younger years, I had felt the necessity to keep a record of my impressions, in the German manner."[13] Paperno traces a chronology of what "the self" has meant to diarists of different eras, from Puritans and Pietists monitoring "the sinful self" in the seventeenth century, to diarists in the Enlightenment pursuing moral and affective self-perfection, to Romantics "inspired by a new historicist sense," to positivists in the later nineteenth century writing for scientific self-observation, to twentieth-century writers who "absorbed the modernist impulse for deliberate self creation."[14] Karen Sánchez-Eppler wisely suggests that chronologies of diary practices cannot be drawn too starkly, because individual writers often deployed their diaries to multiple purposes simultaneously.[15] Regardless, it is clear that there was a dramatic increase in European diary writing during the early nineteenth century. Arianne Baggerman, Rudolf Dekker, and Michael Mascuch attribute this increase not only to the secularization of introspection, but to pedagogic reforms that brought a newly intense focus to children's writing.[16]

Two key observations from Peter Burke and Arianne Baggerman frame my understanding of selfhood practices in early nineteenth-century diaries of the Bildungsbürgertum. Burke identifies an active model of self-formation in European thought around 1800, in which "the self is not only the garden, but the gardener as well. The active model, including projects for self-development, illustrates what Koselleck has called the new sense of the future as constructible, but on an individual level."[17] Clearly diary writing was one such "project for self-development." Baggerman emphasizes the workings of the situated self, in which diaries indicate not "a passion to unveil one's inner self so much as the need to describe the world around one, or rather, to situate oneself in relation to that world."[18] The form of selfhood developed in the diaries I have studied was not simply that of the Romantic individual or a "true inner self," but rather a modern social subjectivity created through writing observations about family, school friends, and the world.

Turning now to what we know specifically about children and youth as diary writers, let me begin with some examples of how contemporary pedagogues encouraged the practice.[19] As early as 1772, the periodical *Leipzig Weekly for Children* (see chapter one) used a diary format to structure its moral didacticism and light entertainment. "Little Carl" was instructed by his teacher each evening to write down everything remarkable that had happened to him. The model advocated by the *Leipzig Weekly* includes a number of signature elements of Enlightenment educational practices, from the emphasis that this was Carl's "own book" to the suggestion that Carl enjoyed sharing his diary biweekly with his teacher for gentle review. The magazine made a point of the diary being kept "very secret"—except that his parents and tutor had full access, of course, and in one issue, Carl's mischievous sister Caroline took over the diary for her own observations.[20] The entries themselves did not much resemble what real children did with their diaries, being unsurprisingly longer, more literary, more polished, and more priggish. Nevertheless, the use of diary as a form in fiction demonstrates that it was an increasingly common and important practice for children to record their activities and perceptions.

Christian Felix Weiße recommended a similar writing habit for readers of his periodical *Der Kinderfreund* and also used a fictional diary by his "daughter" Charlotte to convey serial family stories. Weiße urged children to read aloud their catalogues of good and bad behavior for their teacher, siblings, and parents to hear. He also contended that diary keeping would help children organize their time and improve their writing facility.[21] *Der Kinderfreund* was translated into Dutch in 1791, and in their study *Child of the Enlightenment,* Arianne Baggerman and Rudolf Decker name it as a possible inspiration for the parents of Otto van Eck in their encouragement of his diary writing during the 1790s.[22]

Despite the fact that the most famous diary in the Western world was written by a young girl—Anne Frank—we have not yet seen many studies specifically investigating the practices of children's diaries. Baggerman and Decker's intensive reading of the diary that van Eck kept from age ten to seventeen is an exception. In many ways, his diary resembles the German examples discussed here, with the diary recording his educational progress as well as his daily activities. His writing voice was somewhat more self-critical, as seen in this entry at age ten in 1791: "Began the day crying, because, not being called early enough, I was afraid I wouldn't be able to catch up with yesterday's diary."[23] Although this anxiety about writing was not unknown to the German writers I have studied, their self-reflections were more likely to be positive than Otto's. Otto's diary also reveals persistent struggles between the writer and his parents, with Otto's writerly agency sometimes manifesting as resistance to the whole project. As Baggerman asserts elsewhere, "as a pedagogical tool, children's diaries had an entirely different impact on diary-writing than the liberating effect they were thought to have; on the contrary, such diaries led parents to exercise coercion and prompted guilt-ridden children to write very short entries."[24] As I will explore in detail, this pattern was evident in many of the diaries kept by German youth in the early nineteenth century.

Sánchez-Eppler shows that nineteenth-century middle-class children in the United States used their diary keeping as a record of reading, school work, catechism, daily habits, travel, and relationships, much like their counterparts across the Atlantic. She especially captures the contradictions of agency and pedagogy that also animate the diaries discussed in this chapter.[25] Marilyn Himmesöete's study of nineteenth-century French diarists reveals an interest in writing as agency, but specifically in what she sees as the rebellions of older children and youth. She suggests that diaries allowed their authors to "formulate the rebellion, the injustices and the dissatisfaction they felt, even if their efforts to do so were measured, limited, understated and rare."[26] Although Himmesöete may go too far in reading for these moments of rebellion (inflected, perhaps, by her choice of the anachronistic term "teenager"), this balance between self-formation and self-control was critical in the German context as well. Even for adult writers, a diary inherently marks the passage of time and self-development, which both invite introspective reflections on childhood, youth, and growing older.

Throughout the scholarly literature on diary keeping, the construction of selfhood is a recurring preoccupation. Philippe Lejeune writes about daily self-examination as an ancient practice, but one that did not result in anything like diaries *for oneself* until new religious versions appeared in the medieval era. Moving forward to the flourishing of self-surveillance through diaries in the Enlightenment, he attributes the rise of that practice to Marc-Antoine Jullien.[27] Obsessed with the efficient use of time and regular self-observation, Jullien published an 1813 booklet advising and modeling intense self-monitoring through journaling. Lejeune argues convincingly that this Enlightened mode of self-examination was aimed at "the construction of a subject who becomes autonomous only by taking responsibility for his own subjection."[28] He closes with a fascinating comment on the diary of young Stéphanie Jullien. It flouts several aspects of the practice advocated by her father, including the author addressing her diary affectionately instead of detailing of her faults and accomplishments in the "objective" third person. Young writers modeled their diaries on the guidance of adults, but also followed their own desires in crafting the self on paper.

PORTRAITS OF SIX WRITERS

Few diaries written by children and youth before the twentieth century have received extensive attention, and those that do usually belong to writers who became famous in adulthood. The sources discussed in this chapter were not preserved because their writers later became well-known, but rather simply because they belonged to families whose business and personal papers were archived at some point in time. In the course of seeking children's diaries in collections of archived family papers throughout German state archives, as well as in the Deutsches Tagebucharchiv (the German Archive for Diaries, DTA), I encountered a number of seemingly related but tangential documents. These included the travel diaries of aristocratic youth as well as daily notebooks by young people in noble families.[29] These texts share some characteristics with the diaries I read more closely in this chapter, but they were not a product of the same middle-class pedagogic impulses.

Laurel Thatcher Ulrich writes, "Opening a diary for the first time is like walking into a room full of strangers."[30] This section provides brief introductions to the diaries referred to regularly throughout the chapter, so that their authors will be more familiar.

Marie Henriette Seybold

Marie's diary makes her the youngest writer of this group at age ten. Marie was born September 12, 1819, to a Protestant family in Brackenheim, a town on the Zaber River in the wine-growing region of Heilbronn, Württemberg. Her father, Christoph Georg Jacob von Seybold (1778–1846), was the *Oberamtsrichter,* a district magistrate.[31] Her mother was Christiana Henriette Wilhelmine Nestel (1786–1864).[32] Marie was the third of four children: brother Otto and sister Amalia were five and four years older, and her sister Bertha was three years younger.

Marie began this installment of her diary on February 8, 1830, at the age of nearly ten and a half, and wrote at least one or two lines every day until the last entry on May 9, 1831 (at the age of eleven and a half). The diary filled two small notebooks of plain paper, which she divided with lines between each relatively brief entry, and dated in the margins. She was extremely diligent about her daily discipline. A lack of introductory comments or final remarks indicate that this was likely neither the first nor the last diary Marie kept, even if it was the only one to reach the archive.

On October 2, 1838, at the age of nineteen, she married twenty-six-year-old Gottlob Friedrich von Schmidt (1812–83), which is why her diary was preserved among the Schmidt family documents held at the Landesarchiv Baden-Württemberg. Gottlob Schmidt was an agricultural scientist who attended the Agricultural Academy in Hohenheim and studied beet sugar production in France before being appointed to Württemberg's Royal Building and Garden Administration. They had four children: three boys, who married and had medical and military careers, and one girl, who remained single and was active in women's organizations in Stuttgart. Marie died at age sixty-nine on November 26, 1888, in Stuttgart.[33]

Anna Krahmer

Anna Krahmer, who grew up in Prussia in the 1820s and 1830s, wrote voluminous diaries from at least as young as thirteen years old, although only portions of these have been archived.[34] Anna was born April 1, 1815, to parents Wilhelm David Friedrich (Fritz) Krahmer (1776–1844) and Wilhelmine Friederike Benecke (1786–1854). She was one of six children; her sisters Therese (eight years older) and Berta (two years younger) appeared most frequently in the pages of her diary. Anna was educated first by a tutor at home and then attended a girls' secondary school.

The document available at the DTA is an excerpted transcription of the diary Anna kept from age fifteen in 1830 to age nineteen in 1834.[35] She wrote at least a short paragraph every day, but unlike Marie Seybold, she often composed entries of four or five times that length. The primary purpose of this diary appears to have been for Anna's own benefit: to record the day's events and her memories, and to release and probe her emotions. The abridgment by Anna's descendent Rosemarie Jahnke in 1978 may have overrepresented entries in which Anna wrote about her love affair with her cousin Heinrich Honig (1809–81).[36]

At the age of twenty-three, Anna finally married Heinrich. After Heinrich's father's death, the couple managed the family estate in Egeln, Sachsen-Anhalt (near Magdeburg), and had at least six children. Anna died at seventy-five on December 24, 1890, in Berlin.[37]

Wilhelm Dieckhoff

August Wilhelm Dieckhoff was born in Göttingen on February 5, 1823. By the time he began his diary in 1838, he was attending secondary school in Clausthal in the Harz Mountains, about thirty-five miles away from his home in Adelebsen.

Wilhelm's diary has the most peculiar provenance of this group, since it was found in a flea market sometime before 2004 and accessioned into the DTA. He kept his diary from September 1, 1838, age fifteen, until June 19, 1839, age sixteen, although, like Anna Krahmer, he indicated that this was not his first attempt. Totaling about thirty-five thousand words, the diary filled half of a fine notebook with gilt edges. Wilhelm titled it *Pages from my Life*, numbered the pages, and wrote headings for himself. After opening with some religious epigraphs in German and Latin, he composed fairly long entries on his school activities and his own philosophical reflections. In Wilhelm's case, as well as for Emil Schneider (below), academic subject matter was discussed in an unpolished style quite different from the formal school essays these youths might have composed on similar subjects. Diary writing was a distinct genre with a distinct purpose.

This year of diary writing presented a young person in continual turmoil about his own development and questions of morality. Perhaps, then, it is not a surprise that Wilhelm became a Lutheran theologian of some note (with a presence in British and American religious circles). In 1847 he joined the theological faculty at Göttingen and in 1860 took a position at Rostock. He coedited a periodical for some years, conducted historical research on the Reformation, and engaged in minor doctrinal controversies. He never married, and died in Rostock on September 12, 1894.

Anna Hasenfratz

Anna Hasenfratz was born to a bourgeois Catholic family on November 4, 1823, in Donaueschingen, a town in the Black Forest. Her father was an official at the court of the Prince of Fürstenberg, a principality that was dissolved in 1806 in the Confederation of the Rhine. Anna thus grew up around, but not part of, the nobility. Her brother Fridolin, two years older, was a student at the University of Heidelberg during the years she kept this diary, and she often wrote about him and his social circle.

The diary was written between January 1, 1841, and November 24, 1843, when Anna was seventeen to twenty years old. Unlike most of the writers in this set of diaries, Anna often recorded the time of day she was writing, with several separate entries per day in some instances. Like Anna K., Anna H. wrote about her daily affairs as well as her romantic longings. Her style was influenced by her novel reading, with interrogatives and apostrophic remarks that make the diary more literary.

At age twenty-four, Anna married a man eighteen years her senior, Dr. Fidelis Würth (1805–1903). They moved for her husband's career and had two daughters. Anna died in Freiburg on June 23, 1881, at age fifty-seven.

Luise Vorwerk

Henriette Luise Vorwerk was born to a Protestant family on August 26, 1830, in Hamburg. Her mother was Christiane de Voß (1809–85). Her father, Georg Friedrich Wilhelm Vorwerk (1793–1867), was a merchant who had founded the successful (eventually transatlantic) firm Hochgreve and Vorwerk in 1823.[38] Luise was the second of ten children who lived to adulthood; her nearest siblings were a brother two years older and a sister four years younger.[39]

Written when Luise was twelve, her journal provides an example of the travel diary genre and was written in the literate but "natural" style desired of middle-class children. It chronicled a seven-week trip (April 20 to June 4, 1842) that she took with her parents and governess from Hamburg to Paris and back, traveling by coach, rail, and steamboat. The family stayed in Paris for sixteen days, visiting cultural sites on an itinerary not that different from what tourists might seek out in Paris today. The archived document may have been written up later based on Luise's original daily notes. Luise wrote fairly long entries describing each day, recording the family's activities and her own observations. This example underscores how writing was used as an essential tool of the educated traveler.

On November 12, 1850, Luise married Hamburg politician (and later mayor) Hermann Anthony Cornelius Weber (1822–86). Both her natal and marital families were active in civic life, such as when they formed a committee to establish an art museum during the 1860s.[40] The couple eventually had a mansion built outside Hamburg, near other notable Weber and Vorwerk relatives.[41] As far as I know, they did not have any children. Luise died at the age of seventy-five on February 5, 1806.

Emil Schneider

Emil Robert Schneider was born in Berlin on October 11, 1828, to a Protestant family. His father was Martin Gottlieb Schneider (1791–1858) and mother was Ida Rudorff (1804–62).[42] Emil wrote this diary while he was living at home and subject to his parents' immediate authority and instruction.[43]

Still, at age seventeen to eighteen he was on the cusp of adulthood during its composition from April 14, 1846, to August 30, 1847. Although some diaries open in medias res, Emil Schneider began his 1846 notebook with a very intentional statement of his purpose. He wrote, "Deep peace comes into my heart when I seek and find a support for my unsteadiness in the Bible, in the solace of the holy word of God. Every other feeling of earthly joy and bliss is a void compared with that of feeling like the child of a loving father, of a gentle judge of our deepest fault!"[44] By invoking the Word as part of his commitment to his diary, Emil highlighted a religious use of literacy at the outset of his writing at the same time as he interrogated his own nature. The rest of the diary proceeded as an account of his daily activities, relationships, and observations about reading. More than the other young writers in this group, Emil commented on contemporary political events.

In adulthood, Emil became a businessman, and at age thirty-six married Julie Henriette Wilhelmine de la Croix (despite her French name, she was born in Berlin to parents who were also from Brandenburg).[45] At some point, their child added a note to the front matter of this diary to record that Emil continued diligently to keep a daily journal throughout his life. However, this is the only volume that reached the archive. Emil died at age sixty-seven in 1895.

TYPICAL CHARACTERISTICS

While everyone sleeps and I know that everything is quiet, I prefer to
tend to my thoughts and memories.

–Anna Hasenfratz, January 19, 1841, 9:30 PM

While diverse in geography (hailing from cities and small towns in Baden,
Württemberg, Hamburg, Saxony, and Prussia), age (from ten to twenty years
old), gender, and schooling experiences, these six writers all came from families
embedded in the Bildungsbürgertum. The individual intellectual and moral
development of these children and youth was seen as a critical project for their
families. The diaries were written between 1830 and 1847, during an era of
Biedermeier sentimentality that emphasized interiority for middle-class youth.
This is one of the common features and themes found in this group of diaries.

Dating of the entries was also universal. Each writer did a certain amount
of self-correction and later editing, but the degree varied. Marie, for example,
occasionally crossed out entire entries, but usually not in such an aggressive
way as to obliterate what was previously written. She almost always rewrote
the offending passage, usually with fairly similar content—that is, the exci-
sion was done for reasons of handwriting mechanics rather than a reversal of
opinion or self-censorship. As with letters, there is a noticeable difference in
the sophistication of the handwriting style according to the age of the diarists.

Famous adult diarists often have become so through their commentary on
politics and world events.[46] But ordinary young writers tended to perceive a
narrower purpose for their diaries: to record daily personal events and memories,
including comments on the weather, school progress, travel, and holidays, and
to describe social relationships, especially with family and visitors at home. As
one twelve-year-old wrote in 1856, his purpose in writing a diary was to remember not only "the life and doings of this time, [but] especially *mine*" (emphasis
original). This young writer's ordinary memories were preserved because his
diary was eventually followed by works such as *Thus Spoke Zarathustra*: he was
Friedrich Nietzsche.[47] Yet his notation of quotidian experiences in these early
years is not unlike the everyday themes that the obscure diarists I have studied
address. As an inherently selective record, a diary marks some experiences as
significant and ignores others. For these writers, their diaries were mostly filled
with what Ulrich calls "the exhaustive, repetitive dailiness" of their lives.[48] A
recurring rotation of topics—walks, visitors, weather, schoolwork—facilitated
the writing of young diarists.

Indeed, it was through this "ordinariness," I argue, that children and youth
forged socially situated selves while at the same time they served the pedagogic

purpose of diary writing. Narrating everyday events was a key path to developing relational subjectivity, which stood in contrast to a more Romantic notion of the individual self that could be located in an inner spirit or psyche. Recording the day's activities, weather, and schoolwork gave ten-year-old Marie Seybold something to write about without having to rely on invention, and also allowed her to use a set of familiar phrases from entry to entry. Even so, she still sometimes resorted to comments like April 23's summary, "Today nothing happened that was remarkable."[49] When she was briefly ill and had to stay in bed, far from giving her time to write her intimate thoughts and feelings, the inactivity left her without motivation to write much at all on those days. Ubiquitous discussions of the weather remind us how much the natural world structured even these cultivated Enlightened lives. The events of the day were a starting point for each of these diarists, so that Wilhelm often commented on his studies and interactions at school and Anna K. seems to have played quite a lot of cards. For some young writers, recording what occupied their days meant writing travel narratives, as with Luise's journal. Even in this case, where young writers clearly imitated and referenced adult genres like published travel narratives or tourist guides, they understood their diaries as a space open to expressing their own tastes and feelings. For example, in the chronicle of her trip to the Jardin des Plantes in Paris, Luise noted: "I liked the giraffe the most! In fact, a beautiful animal! The figure so slender, the markings so evenly yellow with brown patches, becoming paler on the belly."[50] Although giraffes may not have populated every German child's diary in the early nineteenth century, travel did touch most writers, at least through the writing of observations about household visitors.

Diaries were also used to observe and record social relationships and to position the writers themselves within those social networks. Unsurprisingly, young people's diaries, situated as they were primarily in a domestic context, are filled with stories and observations about family and other members of the household. Friends from outside the family also appear in the pages of diaries, especially in descriptions of visitors as part of the day's events. Mina, Luise, and Julie were friends of Marie Seybold and appeared frequently as characters in her descriptions of garden walks and birthday celebrations. Diaries make it clear how middle-class children and youth in the nineteenth century had begun to rely on writing as a tool in the development of their social relationships, as when Anna H. noted in her diary that she had made a gift of a few lines and her signature as a souvenir for a friend's autograph book.[51]

Ordinary events were not the only topic addressed by young writers, however. The final most common theme across these diaries is explicit reflection on personal development. In one passage, Wilhelm Dieckhoff captured both the disciplinary element of diary writing and the diary as vessel for self-reflection and self-formation: "Although I persevered with [this diary] a whole year the first time, I still consistently let it lie fallow. This was because I recorded every little thing that I encountered with anxious exactitude, and since life at this time is a stable monotony, very uniform and with few interruptions, it soon became petty and uninteresting. . . . Therefore I have given up on my diary in order to continue it under the form: *Pages from My Life*. This way I am less tied to the everyday, and I can also concern myself more with my thoughts."[52] In addition to outlining the virtues of diary keeping, Wilhelm underscored the impermanence and irregularity of diaries through his determination to improve upon his earlier forays. This employment of diaries for self-examination and self-crafting by young writers is my primary concern in the next two sections.

DIARY AS SELF-SURVEILLANCE

Continual scrutiny of habits, relationships, and interior feelings sustained young people's self-development in their diaries. As a form, the diary presents intriguing contradictions, producing texts that are both spontaneous and quotidian and yet also crafted and edited. For these writers, diaries also constituted a disciplinary practice, one regularly performed and marked over time. Sánchez-Eppler writes of the particular inflections this takes in the hands of young writers, arguing that "the act of writing remains self-conscious for children . . . [making] the expectations and significance attached to literacy visible in ways that they would never be in more practiced hands."[53] The self-awareness of a diary became self-surveillance as writers monitored their time, considered other readers, evaluated their own industry, and examined their emotions.

TIME

Time was a key dimension for self-examination through diary keeping.[54] Weiße named this one of the virtues of diary keeping for children, that they would learn to divide their time in an orderly fashion.[55] When Wilhelm copied his school schedule into his diary, accounting for each portion of his day, he joined many other diary writers who sought to control time through writing.[56] Time especially mattered for self-surveillance in young people's diaries because writers could observe changes in themselves with the passage of weeks or years and reflect on their own development. Anna H. articulated this use of her diary on a gloomy day, writing, "I am once again alone in my room, much as I wish it, and just as I could be a few weeks ago, only I have changed quite a lot since a few days ago."[57]

The impulse to control and monitor time also reveals an awareness of potential current or future readers on the part of young writers. For example, Marie started her diary practice by providing only the month and date for each entry. A few months in, she occasionally began to include the day of the week narratively, as with her passage for May 2, which began, "This day, which is a Sunday . . .";[58] eventually, she incorporated the day of the week as regular feature in the left margin of each entry. This change marked not only a deference to form but also Marie's growing awareness of the diary as a record of her self for a future audience (or perhaps for her own re-reading), in which that kind of metadata might be useful or important.

READERS

Although none of these diaries was written for publication, that does not mean that they were written without an audience in mind. It is worth remembering Lynn Bloom's caution, "When such readers lurk at the writer's elbow, welcome or not, there is no way to rule out self-censorship."[59] Unlike diarists of a later era, these writers did not assert dialogic relationships by addressing a "dear diary."[60] That said, audience was certainly an important factor for the self-making work in each diary, ranging from the diarists themselves to adult teachers or parents to posterity. Wilhelm exhibited a sense of unknown future readers, evident in the very deliberate framing and self-editing of his journal. Although Anna K. often used her diary as a repository for intimate confessions, her writing at certain moments also indicated an awareness of a potential audience—for example, in her formal presentation of the events surrounding her confirmation at the end of March in 1831. But age generally was a dividing line: while the older diarists appear to have written primarily for themselves, the younger writers like Luise Vorwerk and Marie Seybold clearly expected an immediate audience for their diaries in the form of tutor or parent readers.[61] Luise's case illustrates a common practice in which elite children traveling with their families were expected to record their experiences and observations as a pedagogic exercise. For example, Luise wrote of Versailles, "I leave it to the writers to describe it all, it is too great a task; I will only mention the most remarkable things."[62] Her awareness of readers is evident here, as is her self-positioning within a genre. Whether performing for adults or seeking greater interiority, children and youth participated in constructing a new kind of social subject.

Marie's diary includes a great deal of evidence of adult reading and instruction. Some of her own self-editing may have been added later at the urging of her tutor. Occasional checks, question marks, and marginalia also indicate another reader. Typically, the evidence of adult instruction in Marie's diary is focused on her observations rather than her (often sloppy) handwriting.[63] Though these comments were occasionally affirming, such as a "good!" on the May 6, 1830, entry, most additions were critical, such as the demand that Marie write about more than the weather, as discussed in my introduction.

Sometimes the self-surveillance of diaries was performed explicitly for someone else's benefit. This pedagogic reality for young writers is reinforced by the audience-driven subject formation inherent to modern selfhood. As Habermas tells us, "Subjectivity, as the innermost core of the private, was always already oriented to an audience."[64] The mix of immediate self-correction, later editing, and external critiques in Marie's diary indicates how the text was used by Marie and the adults around her to externalize and scrutinize her interior development. When she wrote "Today I was diligent," anticipating that an adult would read and respond, her intentional self-presentation to that audience was part of the construction of identity that diary writing facilitated for modern bildungsbürgerlich children.

At times that external reader was the diarist's future self, since diary keeping preserved the writer's memories for later use. Anna K. wrote smugly at age sixteen, "I read my whole diary and found to my pleasure that 3 years ago I thought about certain affairs just as I do now. It is my greatest delight when I see that my feelings and opinions have not been altered, or at least not degraded, by time."[65] It is no coincidence that Anna continued seamlessly from this reflection on her past into reporting a conversation with her mother about her future (Anna's parents did not want her to marry too quickly). From the perspective of adults, diaries have often been understood to offer a record of development in an individual over time—especially in young people. However, I suspect that Anna was not alone among children and youth in holding a different view of her own growth while still in those early years, desiring consistency rather than change. Whether or not Anna's perception accurately captured the evolution she likely experienced over those years, it is striking that she used writing in her diary to fix these observations about her own sense of self.

INDUSTRY

The key category by which young writers evaluated themselves in diaries was that omnipresent goal of bildungsbürgerlich youth: diligence. Being regarded and regarding oneself as *fleißig* (industrious), rather than lazy or idle, was all-important. Diaries allowed children and youth to track their intellectual development, filial duties, schoolwork, reading, and moral or spiritual self-improvement. In Marie's short entries, her regular reports of her own industriousness often constituted an entire day's record. Interestingly, these comments usually appeared only in the positive—"Today I was diligent"—rather than reports of days when she or someone else found her work lacking.[66] One intriguing but mysterious variation came on May 26, when she observed, "Nothing else happened that deserved to be remarked upon, other than that I have been diligent."[67] In a different hand, the last line, "that I have been diligent," was later underlined and an exclamation point added at the end. Was the reader contradicting Marie's self-assessment? Or confirming and commending her hard work? Without discovering any other clues, it is still worth observing that both Marie and the adult reader of her diary understood her writing as a means to engage in this kind of self-review, and that industry and idleness were its key axis of evaluation.

Some writers surveilled their own industry through their diaries by tracking their reading. In some diaries, books made only a casual appearance, as when Marie mentioned in passing that she had returned a book she borrowed from a friend.[68] Other writers used their diaries to make more extensive commentary on their reading.[69] Literacy was part of Luise's educational tourism, as in this report: "We visited the very elaborate royal library, which in addition contains a large number of manuscripts and facsimiles. Thus I read, for example, a letter from Voltaire to Friedrich the Great."[70] For Wilhelm, books were crucial. In fact, the first thing he chose to write about in his very intentionally designed new diary was his reading, announcing, "Today I read parts of a book with the title *Spirit of Friedrich the Great's Best Writings*" (apparently a popular fellow). This was only the first of many short book reviews filling the pages of Wilhelm's journal.[71] Emil, too, frequently mentioned his reading and noted his opinions of books in his diary, writing explicitly about the development of his own taste and moral improvement through reading. For example, he observed at one point: "I am now reading: *The Rose of Tistelön* by Flygare-Carlén, a highly appealing, but dreadful novel. I am pleased with the occupation that it gives my mind." In these reviews, he made a point of not only describing his reading but also evaluating the ongoing impact on his knowledge and, most of all, his character.[72]

Observing one's industry through writing also fed the diary as a disciplinary and disciplining practice. Of these diarists, Wilhelm wrote most frequently about his anxious ambition for regular journaling. A couple of months after restarting his diary, he castigated himself, writing, "I have once again neglected to continue my diary for two days. It absolutely must change."[73] The entry then immediately launched into a review of the Goethe volume he was reading and his assessment of the characters' virtues, a performance of literary industry that seems intended to atone for forgetting the diary. Even though Wilhelm had decided intentionally at one point to eschew daily entries, it was a common pattern for him to fall away from regular practice and then admonish himself for this "laziness" in an industrious burst of new pages.

Yet Wilhelm also expressed what seems a fairly radical rejection of school-work, writing after a break, "I know that I have not been as diligent as [I was] earlier. But that does not matter! I had my reasons for it. Health comes before scholarship. The spirit demands more than intellect. I do not regret my many walks." Wilhelm continued reflecting on the list of activities outside of study that he gladly remembered from previous months. He concluded the entry:

> And so I want to and also I will be diligent next winter; but it will be a free, independent occupation that leads me ever nearer to my goals, which consists in nothing else than to cultivate myself into an outwardly and inwardly complete man and to return my spirit ever closer to the purity in which it was [given] to me from God. And everything Latin, Greek, and however it may all be called, I regard only as a means for this purpose, which each person must pursue, and as such I must and I want to chase it; and therefore I might also study the irregular verbs some time.[74]

This determination suited Wilhelm's use of his diary as a practice for which he continually reinvented great plans and then disappointed himself by failing to write as regularly or deeply as he intended. Rather than giving up on scholarship, Wilhelm actually expressed a loftier ambition for himself beyond the socially dictated purposes of schoolwork—though apparently that perfect development did require some conjugating along the way. Diaries allowed young writers to track their industry in a range of activities expected of them as dutiful, literate, middle-class youth.

EXAMINING EMOTIONS

Keeping a diary allowed writers to report and interrogate their emotions, a form of self-surveillance.[75] As much as these feelings were often recorded on paper as being *unbeschreiblich* (indescribable, literally "unwritable"), some diaries nevertheless employed a confessional mode in which emotions were indeed written, and then named, analyzed, rejected, deplored, or celebrated. In his discussion of the new interiority of diary keeping in the nineteenth century, Peter Gay writes, "The classic age for launching one, apart from the childish jottings of seven- or eight-year-olds following parents' prompting, was early adolescence . . . there was something about the awakening and turmoil of puberty most congenial to engaging in literally self-serving self-examination."[76] It is true that among the fifteen-, sixteen- and seventeen-year-old diarists, there were quite a few cases of the lovelorn. However, I contend that Gay makes too sharp a division between a true, private confession of feelings and pedagogic exercises, since this notion of the diary as vessel for emotions actually was driven in some cases by a didactic impulse.

Sometimes these feelings themselves derived from the diary practice. For example, at another time when Wilhelm felt he had neglected his diary, he wrote, "Let us harken to the causes. In the first days it was plainly laziness. These were once again odious days in which I put even my endeavors out of sight. Yes, unfortunately, this sad dreariness controls me all too often."[77] Here, after inviting explicit self-examination, he tied writing (or its absence) not only to hard work, but also to his internal turmoil or feelings of failure. In this case, writing not only recorded the evolutions of self, but actively developed it (calling back Burke's paradigm of self as both garden and gardener).

What is most interesting about the surveillance of feeling is how these young writers used their diaries to dissect their own emotional reactions and emotional logic. Anna H., the diarist who preferred to write at night when the house was quiet, also preserved some entries in her diary that were interrupted mid-stream by some distraction, indicating her other activities and preoccupations. On the afternoon of February 1, 1841, she wrote a few sentences about her low spirits, then followed a break with: "A few minutes later. In the moment as I wrote the desperate lines above, Sch. came to me with a joyful look on [her] face and announced to me that von Schweighardt was below in order to make a parting visit. Beside myself with joy, I ran down . . ."[78] Ultimately, however, this glimpse of the object of her affections only lifted her mood a little, and so she returned to her diary after the encounter to describe her feelings in writing. At another time, after a blissful evening spent dancing, Anna came back to her diary with these questions: "What presses my heart so heavily? By what is it so violently agitated? The first ball, what effects did it bring? . . . O God, if I may ask for a husband, then give me this one, because my love I bear for him is indescribable."[79] The questions are a rhetorical technique, to be sure, but she was also using this writing to find her way toward a better understanding of her own feelings. A few days later, she encountered the young man again and wrote more despondently, "But yesterday he also seemed still to think of me, because he again engaged me immediately for the first Polonaise and the first waltz, as if he already knew how happy that would make me. . . . But how do I enjoy just taking pains to write down such memories, which only make my heart bleed? Soon he will have again forgotten me and dance with another, while my heart still beats for him."[80] Her voice here rings familiar to anyone who has struggled with romantic longing and feelings of rejection or loneliness, especially as a young person. We can see from Anna's writing that she was struggling to confront and master her emotions. In the midst of this passionate expression, however, she interrupted herself to question the very purpose of diary writing.

Like Anna H., Wilhelm and Anna K. used writing as a mechanism for examining their own feelings. Wilhelm wondered why he felt compelled to minimize the joy he experienced in receiving attention on his birthday. "My heart so much wants love," he answered, but he could not leave that observation alone without also noting the "gloomy" thought of what he considered to be his inadequate academic achievement.[81] Anna K. also turned to her diary for answers to the mystery of her own emotions at the end of a long entry: "So I extinguished the light, and went to bed and did not sleep. I burst into tears and do not know why. The human heart is a strange thing, and not to be fathomed. I was dissatisfied with myself, and yet determined to remain so."[82] Her language is plaintive and touching; her use of writing reinforces the value of diary as self-examination.

These mysterious emotions about which young diarists wrote were not all feelings of despair or self-criticism, however. One morning, Anna K. tried to capture the sensation of waking up happy without knowing why: "Today upon awakening I had that beautiful feeling again, that I had a gladness in my mind I could not quite remember. Finally the thought came that the Honigs would come today, like a spark in the tinder of joy, which glows in the heart. The flame of joy blazed brightly in me, and it rose up unhindered."[83] Her joy that day, euphorically described, resulted from the anticipated arrival of her cousins (including the young man she would eventually marry). This moment is one of many illustrations of young writers using diaries to explore metaphors, literary borrowing, and other ways of writing about their own feelings. Emotional introspection was partly such a common feature of some diaries because it served the self-surveilling mode of writing. Self-examination is part of any diary keeping practice, to be sure. However, monitoring time, anticipating readers, evaluating industry, and examining emotions all contributed to the surveillance that was an especially salient contribution to self-making through diaries for young writers in the Age of Revolutions.

DIARY AS SELF-FORMATION

The distinction between "self-surveillance" and "self-formation" as descriptions of the activities in which diarists engaged may seem to exert an implicit judgment. Analyzing diaries as mechanisms of self-surveillance makes us attend to the governing aspects of writing, while looking for evidence of self-formation emphasizes the agency of children and youth. As I have argued throughout this book, however, I suggest that there is an important and inextricable link between the agency and discipline of diaries as a literacy practice for young people. Marie Seybold's diary exhibits the most explicit evidence of adult direction among this group. Her writing directly reveals little interior struggle over defining her emerging subjectivity, and yet the very fact of keeping the diary shows even Marie exerting control over time, her environment, and the way she occupied her days—*by writing about it all*. The existence and preservation of her diary is an implicit statement about the worth of recording personal experiences, even as a little girl (and even when she had "nothing to write about today").[84] Examples like this should caution us against romanticizing silent introspection as the truest form of self-making. In recording ordinary facts of daily experience, young diarists crafted selves just as they did through editing their own writing, discussing matters of taste and opinion, reporting on relationships with others, and writing about emotions.

EDITING AND VOICE

Evidence of immediate or later editing demonstrates both self-surveillance and self-formation through diaries—editing writing and editing a self. Two examples from Marie's diary demonstrate how this could mean more than the simple correction of grammatical or spelling errors. In one case, she began a sentence with "Ich habe den Nachmittag . . ." and then crossed that out to begin again with "Den Nachmittag habe ich schon . . ." She changed her initial impulse, which was not incorrect, to a slightly more sophisticated sentence structure.[85] In a second case, changes in the ink allow us to see that Marie returned to some entries at a later date to improve her writing. She made some corrections, but also embellished her plainer descriptions, inserting a word to explain that a walk was discouraged not only by wind but a *strong* wind.[86] Through this kind of editing, even in small ways, and even as part of a pedagogic project, Marie asserted individuality through the development of her voice.

Another means of experimenting with voice in diary writing was through language use. As mentioned earlier in this book, belonging to the nineteenth-century Bildungsbürgertum often entailed multilingualism. Diaries show the hard work this necessitated for young language learners. Emil frequently used his diary to practice languages. For example, while he was studying English, he wrote an entry in that language, seemingly at random. Verbatim, it read:

"Friday the 22the May. Yesterday in the afternoon the little Agnès Dagners died in the age of three months. . . . Now the question is risen to me, wether such little children, who rarely begin to live have also an immortal soul. . . . Saturday the 23the May 1846. What is the happiness of the man? wherein persists ist? in the tranquillity of his mind, in the triumph of his soul over his body."[87] Here, his own writing was likely influenced by the philosophical reading he had undertaken in his study of the English language. At other times, his linguistic shifts were concerned with more daily affairs, as in this English sequence: "As I told to mother, what Philipp yesterday had said to me from Carl, she bade me, to say nothing of it to Henriette! Why so? I can not understand it!."[88] Was he practicing the grammar of indirect speech, or is this evidence of code-switching for secret-keeping? In the following entry, he wrote in German with apparent relief, "Yesterday and the day before yesterday I copied English words," which seemed to let him off the hook for practicing English in his diary that day.[89]

The development of a personal style was also aided by code-switching or language borrowing. Although this was deployed by writers who were not equally proficient in each language, these instances of code-switching are not dissimilar to language shifts between social registers that linguists and sociologists study today.[90] These diarists moved between languages to demonstrate their bourgeois accomplishments and claim a place in transnational middle-class society. This could be at the level of a single word, as when Emil wrote: "Dr. Rupp muß morgen abreisen. Das erregt ungemein viel *indignation.*" [Dr. Rupp must depart tomorrow. This has aroused an extraordinary amount of indignation.][91] Or diary code-switching could involve more extensive interplay between the languages: Showing off his trilingualism—albeit with some creative orthography—Emil wrote a paragraph in mixed German and English that included mention of his French reading: "Ich begleitete Gustav nach Haus [I accompanied Gustav home], we entertained us in English. He speeks very well—I now am reading The mistaries of Paris by Eugèn Sue, in French language. It is very interessant."[92] At another instance, German syntax showed through the overlaid English vocabulary: "Nach Tische lasen wir etwas vor, dann schlief ich wegen Kopfschmerzen ein wenig und mother father and the two little ones went to the zoological garten, during I and Leonore, we stayed home. I was reading an interessant novelle: Sybille from A. Sternberg: Pocketbook Urania 1847, woraus ich mir auch mehreres abschrieb."[93] In this case, the code-switching also indicates how long it was comfortable for Emil to sustain his observations in a foreign language.

Other examples of code-switching are more difficult to parse. At one point, Anna H. wrote in her diary in German about attending the celebration of a princess's birthday and described the gifts everyone else brought. Then she followed in French with, "My mother did not allow me to make a gift."[94] It is possible she was worried about her mother reading the implied criticism and sought to conceal her complaint, but it is likely that Anna H.'s mother also had some command of French. Alternatively, it may be that this was simply a moment when Anna H. wanted to write with the elegance French afforded her, perhaps because of the aristocratic context. As with the use of oral code-switching in the early twenty-first century, though, this technique could genuinely be used as a code in youth diaries, particularly to conceal intimate details. At age eighteen, Emil wrote an entry in which both his expression of feeling and the names of the girls he wrote about (Jucunde and Jettchen) have been cyphered. In the middle of reporting in German on a social occasion, he began moving back and forth between languages:

Character-observations. Jucunde, very graceful an admirable very kind to me an giving more hope to my heart than ever. Bötzow gefiehl mir außerordentlich durch sein freundliches und dennoch festes und braves Benehmen . . . Oncel Eduard, den Galanten zu den jungen Damen spielend. Tante Linna. Etwas zu wenig (nach ihren Wünschen wahrscheinlich) beachtet. Fritz St. Sehr einsilbig und passiv. Jettchen a complett rebus for me. She walked ever in solitude in the garden, eated an danced almost not at all, evited the other company, was not much vivible and several times She walked alone with Mstr Meisner. I will not believe to must keep her able to be unfaithful to P. P.

Character-observations. Jucunde, very graceful an admirable very kind to me an giving more hope to my heart than ever. Bötzow pleased me exceedingly with his friendly and yet steady and well-mannered behavior . . . Uncle Eduard, playing the gallant to the young ladies. Aunt Linna. Somewhat under-attended (probably in accordance with her wishes). Fritz St. very monosyllabic and passive. Jettchen a complete riddle for me. She walked ever in solitude in the garden, eated an danced almost not at all, evited the other company, was not much vivible and several times She walked alone with Mstr Meisner. I will not believe to must keep her able to be unfaithful to P. P.[95]

Was this style chosen to conceal his inner feelings from prying family eyes— code-switching as a form of code? Or did his reading of sentimental English novels inspire this language choice when describing the young ladies he admired? Linguistic choices (both within and beyond German) and the content that written language delivered were intertwined.

Diaries allowed young people to write their way toward defined tastes and opinions, or toward seeing themselves as individuals with their own tastes, goals, and self-discipline. Recording personal opinions in a diary was another strategy for asserting the development of bourgeois selfhood. This included observations about the characters of family members and friends, activities they enjoyed, and a range of subjects from food to holiday celebrations. One of the most common arenas of taste formation commented on in the diaries was books. These diarists used notes on their reading to practice articulating critiques, to express emotional relationships with narratives and characters, and to reflect on their own personalities and values. Two entries Emil wrote on novels especially underscore this use of literacy. In the first example, his slightly pompous assessment of a French picaresque novel indicated both his intention for self-improvement through language study and his awareness that there might be morally dubious content in the book he could enjoy but critique. "My reading is now composed of the 'Histoire de Gil-Blas de Santillane par Lesage,' a book that, while it does contain a few boring parts because the sphere in which its hero moves is too low, is nonetheless written in a style that allows an attentive reader to find much morality."[96] In the second example, Emil turned to English literature (in translation), with Edward Bulwer-Lytton's popular sentimental novel *Paul Clifford* (of "it was a dark and stormy night . . ." fame). "The beginning took place in such a low sphere and revealed so many corrupted principles that I did not at all want to read further. But the more the hero of the book draws nearer to virtue and is led toward recognition of his misdeeds . . . [the more my] interest in the novel grows tremendously. The writing style of Bulwer-Lytton is of the sort that so engages everything, feeling and heart of his reader, that one can hardly wrest oneself away from the book."[97] Emil fully apprehended the purpose of sentimental literature to affect the reader's emotions. His review asserted himself as a judicious and moral audience. Here he also performed a sentimental and sympathetic self whose opinions and reactions were molded through enthusiastic reading.[98]

Novels were not the only source of taste-defining self-formation, however; Wilhelm's diary includes reports about his struggles with various philosophical and literary texts. At one point, he wrote, "I took many walks on my walking holiday, I always wanted to philosophize but could not get around to it. I read Zschokke's Alemontade and Harmonius, I did not yet quite understand them both, partly because I was not always entirely well and also occasionally not entirely pure."[99] Wilhelm's self-criticism originated in his reading, but he also expressed a hope for future understanding and self-betterment.

As with letter writing, a diary recorded the development of a young person's social self, a subjectivity embedded in and formed by the relationships fundamental to a middle-class child's life. Although some scholarship on diaries has focused on the emergence of the ego—the crafted "I" of writing—the default pronoun of Marie's diary, as one example, was plural: *we* went for a walk, *we* went to church, *we* celebrated a birthday. It was in fact this social context that allowed Marie to write her way to a sense of self by distinguishing her own personality and habits from observations about the people around her, especially her sisters. In one instance, she complained about "a truly boring hour" when her sister Bertha, three years younger, spent the evening crying miserably for their mother, who was out of the house.[100] Bertha came in for more scorn in the diary with less explanation a few months later with the entry, "Bertha is a quarrelsome child."[101] While Marie's diary gives early intonations of a self-construction project, it reflected a different practice than the more private examples from older youth. Since Marie's diary was regularly read by adult members of the household, these comments about her sister could presumably reach Bertha's ears, yet Marie still decided to record her negative feelings. These moments show Marie implicitly asserting her sense of herself as mature and pleasant in contrast to her perception of her sister.

Family and friends filled the pages of these diaries not only because they were a record of daily interactions and activities, but also because the writers' observations of this social context influenced their own ideas about growing up. Anna Krahmer's entry on the occasion of her parents' anniversary gave a hint of reflections about her own future when she wrote, "The thought that my parents have lived together for 25 years now (not entirely without sorrow, but also indeed with effusive love and joy), made me so delighted."[102] This kind of social identity formation was inspired by friends as well, as evidenced in the conversation with a family acquaintance that Anna recorded: "Madame Devrient told us her love and engagement story and blushed sweetly when she answered Mother's question of whether she really was fond of her husband—'yes, terribly!'"[103] That this exchange captured Anna's attention enough to write in her diary about it fits with her romantic preoccupations in other entries about her own desires and self-reflection.

Anna K. occasionally reported entire conversations in a scripted, imitation verbatim format in her diary. The style, and indeed the content, was novelistic, likely influenced by her own reading. The following exchange from the middle of a very long entry recorded a surprisingly direct discussion among three young people regarding the nature of individual character development in general and Anna's faults in particular:

GUSTAV: "You are not at all natural, Anna."

I: "I am natural, but my nature is contorted and refined and polished, such that it is a necessity. I am always [of] one nature, but that nature is miserably impaired, more's the pity. I am pathetic."

HE: "Yes, why are you so. You were better before, that is true."

I: "That is what you think; you liked my blunt, boisterous, open, honest character much better, when I said what I thought and did what I wanted!"

Anna made a point of observing Heinrich's silent attention to this conversation because his presence during this interrogation surely added insult to injury. She continued,

> If they had left me as I was—I thought—or only gently guided [me], like my mother; if the various relatives had let me bring myself up, I would truly be better! I have by nature a soft, clear temperament, and when one discovers his imperfections through his own experiences, then comes contrition, and thus the moment for improvement has arrived.[104]

The contrast of nature and cultivated refinement echoed Enlightenment concerns about children's education, with the older peers demonstrating the contradictions of educating someone in naturalness and the gendered tensions of that ideal. Anna also reflected on the malleability of her own character, consenting to general notions of virtue and moral improvement but still resisting the controlling judgment of these meddlesome young relatives. Most importantly, not only did she participate in this conversation about selfhood and nature in a social context, but she then returned to her diary to record it. The authority of the dialogue form elides the editing or at least imperfect remembering she surely made of these comments. She might have borrowed literary turns of phrase, made herself more persuasive, weakened their argument, or refrained from writing the cruelest of their criticisms. By composing and recording her perspective on the conversation and relationships, she inscribed the self she wanted to read in her diary.

Diaries served as a kind of nexus for the literacy work essential to the lives of middle-class children and youth. In addition to comments on the books they read, young writers' correspondence with friends and relatives received mention in diary pages as well. Letters appeared frequently among diaries' common topics, with writers recording the arrival of family news or their impatience in waiting for anticipated letters. Narrating these epistolary interactions in the pages of a diary reaffirmed the writer's place within networks of families and friends and acknowledged development in the social literacy practice of letter writing. Marie diligently recorded letters she had written to her older siblings who were away at school.[105] Anna H. wrote about correspondence with her brother Fridolin, who was studying in Heidelberg. "Out of sisterly love" and as a thank you for his repeated advice on her love affairs, she had sent Fridolin a tableau of their hometown. She was happy to hear in his letter that he enjoyed this gift, and even more glad to hear a favorable response on a particular query for his advice: "he also gave me a brief answer to my question. He wrote: 'As long as the novels do not twist your thoughts, then it is quite alright!!!' I am entirely beside myself about this message. In his view, then, I had not made the wrong choice."[106] Recording this good news in her diary, Anna H. had secured her brother's endorsement of her novel-reading—as long as it did not corrupt or change her—through these exchanged letters. This exchange further documents how bourgeois youth used literacy in the development of social selves.

INHABITING EMOTIONS

Just as emotions provided a point of self-examination in diaries, writing about sentiments and desires also contributed to the self-fashioning work of diary keeping. The diary could be a reservoir of confessions, a record of feelings about other people, a vehicle for emotional expression, or a means toward crafting an affective self. Indeed, this was feared by some early opponents of young people's diary writing, as in a 1786 pedagogical work compiled by Joachim Heinrich Campe, in which Peter Villaume wrote, "Children either feel too strongly or not at all.... they cannot handle language and writing."[107] In a way, Villaume's fear was borne out in the youth diaries I have read, as much of their self-construction was pursued through writing about emotions.

For Wilhelm, intense feeling often accompanied his ambitions for his intellectual and moral self-betterment (that is, Bildung). He wrote fervently in the final entry of his diary, after he had left school and returned to his parents' house: "I stand now more individually, freely; I want to show what I can thus accomplish. But a dull mood always remains with me. Whence does it come? I cannot conquer it. The reason is probably that I am not who I should be! [Off] fresh to Tacitus!"[108] He attributed his depression to concerns about his self-improvement. His ambitions also affected his relationships with and feelings for others. When Wilhelm rhapsodized about his affection for his parents, he framed it in terms dictated by his bourgeois education: "I really do have such good parents! Oh if only I could see your happiness for me once again! Oh, surely I will reward you one day, if I keep on living, and that shall be the best recompense for my labors."[109] His desire to demonstrate his love for his parents would be satisfied, he believed, by developing into a diligent, educated, virtuous adult self.

Parents were not always a source of delight and inspiration for self-improvement. In contrast to the unfailingly affectionate and respectful parent-child relationships written about by adults in periodicals, young writers sometimes captured family conflict in their diaries. Anna H. wrote this striking passage in her diary after an intense argument with her mother:

> I met S. on the way to church. The children's communion. Jeanette ate with us. After the meal I joked with F.—
>
> When I wrote the lines above I was very agitated, my blood in a violent boil, because I had been badly scolded by Mother about a small thing. In my heat, I took to my room and let off steam there. Only when I was completely cooled down did I repair downstairs again and repent my tempestuousness. From a distance, however, I heard that *a devilment has once again occurred. The little Anna was very naughty and headstrong, so much so that I ventured the thought of why we even have to struggle with strange children* [added italics indicate quotation]. I was on the point of my ferocity again—when I took Gerstenberg's Urgolino and removed myself.[110]

The clipped, bulletin sentences at the beginning of the entry were very different from Anna's usual style, manifesting how upset she must have been when she first sat down with the diary. The revolutions of feeling she described derived from a conflict between her self-perception and her mother's criticism. Painful as it seems the dispute must have been, writing through this incident contributed to Anna refining her sense of self through her diary.[111]

Recording romantic feelings was also part of self-formation, especially as it oriented the diarist toward growing up. Right in character, Wilhelm's primary mode of romantic writing built on his reading of philosophy. In an elaborate description of a dream, the idealized, spiritual romantic feeling he articulated was framed by his concerns about his own Bildung. He began the passage by again referencing the writer Zschokke, who described a divine, innocent love. Wilhelm vowed in his diary that "this love or none at all [is what] I want to have for a girl one day." This philosophical discussion was followed by the heading, "A DREAM," in which he visited his home on a beautiful autumn evening and reflected with wonder, "Everything was just as always! Everything! only I, I alone had changed. The lively, cheerful boy had become a youth. Where once the boy sought pleasure only in games, there sat the youth now with thoughts about God, the world . . . Where once the boy joked mischievously, the youth now mused darkly on fate and the future." Suddenly he saw standing before him, "in clear beauty, surrounded by a soft rosy radiance, a girl, a girl from the higher spheres." She told him that she was the spirit he longed for and that she would "accompany [him] through the universe back to our Father." At the end of the dream, she said to him:

Behold! I offer this pure spirit-love to you. Do not spurn it. And even if the corporeal world shall separate us for a long time, we will indeed meet some day in the eternal kingdom of the original spirit. Therefore stay true to me, do not market your love to earthly [beings]; I am your guide toward the Day of Light. Thus she spoke and still stood before me, the heavenly [being], regarding me with a radiantly joyful gaze. Then she bent to kiss my lips, I wanted to entwine my arms around her lovely figure—here I awoke.[112]

His chaste description of physical desire and intense spiritual longings here served an emerging subjectivity Wilhelm was beginning to craft and inhabit now that he perceived himself to leave childhood behind. This florid language was a form of self-fashioning. So, too, was the commitment to celibacy, which he may have kept (he certainly never married).

Anna K.'s diary betrayed perhaps the most lovesick writings of this group, filled as it was with regular reports of her feelings and hopes for a union with her cousin Heinrich. Her excited state was palpable even when writing about his absence, as in this entry: "Only Heinrich is actually not coming now, because his exam is after Easter. Good and also not good! Good?"[113] Anna was uncertain of Heinrich's changing affections, and relied on her diary as an outlet for expressions of disappointment, loneliness, embarrassment, and resentment as well as excitement and delight. Much of Anna's imagination of herself was related to her feelings about this relationship. One day, her sister Therese received a letter from their uncle and Heinrich. Therese read aloud a passage where Heinrich commented on Anna dismissively, which prompted her outburst of hurt feelings in this diary entry:

> With the most bitter, serious, unloving tone in the world he says: I certainly must have wanted to playact a novel myself, because I wanted to ascribe one to him. They must be ideas from the girls' school, which Therese would perhaps still drive out of me; little me should not yet even think of such a thing etc. Oh, how otherwise dear to me his name of "little" has always been. And now he uses it in such an unkind manner.

Here the line between reading and life was drawn directly in Anna's reference to a novel. In this case, however, the connection was used against her as an explicitly gendered criticism. She concluded that this exchange meant the end of their romance, and turned to her diary for the release or self-understanding that writing out these emotions offered. "How could I bear it, that he still interests me, when I am unremarkable or even displeasing to him. I do not even want to hate him, that would be too much interest; I want to scorn him for his inconstancy, for that he was otherwise good to me, of that I do not yet have any doubt. I feel it will be hard for me to lower myself from highest interest, from the most intimate friendship immediately down to deepest indifference.—But

I should be indifferent to him!"[114] Even while she tried to repress her feelings, Anna wrote with a passionate and insightful sense of her inner self. A final note: after reading all this anguish, perhaps it will come as relief to remember that this was not the final word on their relationship. In fact, Anna and Heinrich were married seven years after she wrote this diary entry.

CONCLUSION

In concluding her compelling analysis of early American midwife Martha Ballard's diary, Laurel Thatcher Ulrich writes, "To celebrate such a life is to acknowledge the power—and the poverty—of written records. Outside her own diary, Martha has no history."[115] What would we know about the lives of Marie Seybold, Anna Krahmer, Wilhelm Dieckhoff, Anna Hasenfratz, Luise Vorwerk, and Emil Schneider without the evidence of their diaries? Luise made a minor appearance in local history because she married a notable Hamburg politician; Marie might have shown up in the correspondence or family records of her famous male relatives. All these writers are noted as simple dates in genealogical research. The only one of our diarists who became widely known later in life is Wilhelm, and, despite making an impact on the written record through his professional career, he is also the diarist whose early life remains the most obscure out of this group. Uncovering the quotidian experiences of children and youth—documented from their own perspective—is one benefit of reading these diaries, which would inform any study of education.

As I have argued, however, diaries also reveal how the selves that young bildungsbürgerlich writers developed during their childhood and youth were continually examined and reshaped. In their diaries, young people conducted self-surveillance over time, for the purpose of moral and intellectual self-improvement. Each writer crafted a written persona, a socially embedded identity with tastes, habits, and attitudes. Though this may be seen in diaries kept by writers of any life stage, self-examination and self-fashioning played an especially important part in the developing subjectivities of diarists who were still very young.

Each of these six German diarists at some point used their diaries as instruments for separating their emerging selves from childhood. In an early entry of Emil Schneider's diary, for example, his description of the family's activities shows him intent on distinguishing himself from the little boys in his circle: "On the way I came across Jettchen, mother, and Mademoiselle Behrend, who had been out walking, and then on the boulevard Unter den Linden, [I met] Frau Majorin, Clärchen, and Adolph, who were going to the druggist. Adolph, as old and tall as I am, seemed to be of a serious nature. The boys were enjoying themselves immensely near the acrobats and gave me a lot of trouble with their wildness."[116] Emil's notion of a mature individual—his image of himself—was drawn in opposition to childish fun.

Twelve-year-old Luise observed at one point in her travels through Paris, "We were amused by the children who, under the supervision of nurses and in the shade of the trees, were playing very happily here [in the Tuileries]."[117] As a young lady on a grand journey with her parents, she now differentiated herself from the little children playing in the garden. However, even as she was writing her way toward a more grown-up identity, she was still young enough that her parents took her to a play designed for child audiences. "In the evening a delight awaited me that I had never before enjoyed,—we went to the theatre. They presented a French play—Margot, or the consequences of a good education, performed by children, which, even though I did not understand everything, still amused me endlessly."[118] Just as consuming media like this didactic play was part of the "good education" of bourgeois childhood, so, too, was the self-reflection and self-production of diary writing.

Anna Krahmer wrote explicitly about this liminality of the developing self in an 1831 entry. She reported, "I was called away from the dollhouse today to receive a visit from Herr Vogel. Just think, I lingered—and I am 16 years old!! When will the jolt come that will make me completely grown up?"[119] Even Anna, who thought she would marry young and whose diary was full of thoughts of romance, was aware that she had not yet fully left childhood behind.

When did this project of self-building finish? Certainly the cultivation and reformation of self was a lifelong process. For each of these writers, though, there came an end to diary writing and to a certain phase of self-construction. Emil decided to give up writing at age eighteen. His last entry reported the news that the young woman he loved, Luise Stachow, was engaged to be married. This disappointment had sparked a fervent plan of self-reform for Emil, aiming toward "the purest virtue" and "all attainable knowledge." He decided that this program would leave little time to continue journaling. In explaining his reasons for leaving the diary behind, however, Emil spelled out the conditions that would invite returning to it. In a rare second-person address, he wrote, "When I have become noble enough to do great deeds, when important life experiences hope to leave important memories, then I will want to seek you out again and entrust you with my secrets, because now you are too small for the great movements in me, and too big for the pettiness around me."[120] Even in leaving the diary of his youth behind him, Emil could imagine that momentous life events and internal transformations would someday require this practice again as a document of his deeds and thoughts.

The end point of each diary may be considered another way. When I sit down to read her diary again, Marie Seybold is always ten years old, fixed on its pages as the child self she recorded in 1830. But the older Marie's encouragement of her son Hermann's writing in the 1850s illustrates the popularity of diary-keeping as pedagogy in the later nineteenth century. This emphasis placed on children's literacy and self-documentation was reinforced by the subsequent preservation of both sets of papers as precious evidence of bourgeois domestic education. In the archive, then, Marie is from one view the quintessential bildungsbürgerlich parent herself—investing intensely in the literacy of the next generation. Yet from another view she is also the active child subject—challenging, satisfying, and writing a modern childhood.

FURNISHING THEIR OWN AGE

Early in Jean-Jacques Rousseau's *Émile* (1762), he conjures a compelling image: a boy between ten and twelve years old is freely following his natural curiosity and the pleasures of the open air. Then, Rousseau writes, "The hour sounds. What a change! Instantly his eyes cloud over; his gaiety is effaced. Goodbye, joy! Goodbye, frolicsome games! A severe and angry man takes him by the hand, says to him gravely, 'Let us go, sir,' and takes him away. In the room into which they go I catch a glimpse of books. Books! What sad furnishings for his age!"[1]

A century later, books had become the defining furnishings of an ideal life for middle-class children. Rousseau famously limited Émile to one story: Daniel Defoe's *Robinson Crusoe*. While the philosopher recommended free, curiosity-driven learning in nature, he believed reading supplied a dangerous unfettered autonomy. Child readers might lead themselves into moral corruption. Despite Rousseau's impact on European pedagogy, this particular proscription had little effect.[2] In fact, children's reading and writing proliferated in the Age of Revolutions. Far from limiting their charges' literacy, German pedagogues and parents in the late eighteenth century responded to Enlightenment ideas about personal development by supplying young people with even more texts designed especially for child readers. This explosion of children's literature was one of the revolutions at home illuminated in this book as part of an increasingly intense focus on education in bildungsbürgerlich families.

These children helped furnish their own age—their childhoods as well as the Age of Revolutions—by filling it with new learning practices. As young readers selected, favored, or rejected certain titles, they participated in shaping the new library of an idealized German childhood. As they wrote stories of their lives in letters and diaries, they refashioned the conventions of those genres. Against a backdrop of political and economic revolution, modern childhood emerged through further revolutions in family life, education, and fundamental conceptions of the child's nature. Through the entanglement of agency and discipline that characterized children's relationships with adults, the history of childhood thus becomes a history of politics, of the self, of the individual in society, of everyday life.

Rousseau's ideas about reading were not only contrarian but sometimes contradictory. He called for freedom while deriding children's capacity for self-control. He criticized contemporary child-rearing fashions as the corrosive result of modern civilized culture but also rejected ancient instructional tools like fables as backwards and obsolete. He wanted children to be led to a specific set of virtues and moral understanding, but to pursue this via their natural inclinations. He distrusted children's imaginations while reading, but encouraged their play. He used writing to rail against books. Rather than rendering Rousseau useless, these contradictions have made his influence on educational theory endure because they open space for diverse interpretations.[3]

The archive of childhood and youth between 1750 and 1850 documents similar contradictions, which also offered opportunities for children to participate in the socialization process in unpredictable ways. Let us return for a moment to the diary entry with which this book opened. In it, young Marie Seybold partially, reluctantly, tried to follow her teacher's instructions to write about more than the weather. Meanwhile, the adult inscription on that page paradoxically demanded that the young writer be more creative and independent. In this book, I have sought to explain such moments and also to shine light on the contradictions of children's agency. In uncovering the meaning and influence of the modern child subject, such extraordinary sources are invaluable to historians. The lively spirit revealed in these texts also makes it impossible to ignore their creators' personalities and choices.

The story of changes in German education during the years around 1800 demonstrates the continuing benefit of historicizing how children "act in and on the world."[4] Some scholars have begun to challenge the preoccupation of childhood studies with the concept of agency. Mona Gleason, for example, has identified interpretive traps that actually prevent us from seeing young people as important actors in history when we solely seek moments of resistance or presume children's contributions to be unchanging.[5] Yet the framework— examining children's agency while understanding individual choice as itself historically constituted—remains important for historians of childhood because for so long youth participation in the transformation of society was overlooked. As this book has stressed, education contains both disciplinary and emancipatory qualities. Rather than dismissing the disciplinary aspects of pedagogy, on the one hand, or overlooking the power of children to influence adults, on the other hand, my approach has emphasized the mutual constitution of agency and discipline in determining how children influenced European modernity.

Acknowledging the interplay between agency and discipline diverts an orderly narrative of progress from absolutist pedagogies based on rote memorization to emancipatory inquiry. It helps us see more nuance in earlier practices that allowed for children's creativity or imagination; furthermore, it reminds us that recent educational strategies purporting to be liberatory can also serve to discipline students. It shows the persistence of pedagogic practices that sought to govern and constrain children alongside others that celebrated independent inquiry. Juxtaposing the practices of children and the prescriptive ideology of adults deepens our understanding of developments in the history of the family, education, and the self that still influence our modern world.

Even as new educational practices worked to govern and cultivate a particular kind of middle-class subject, children still exhibited autonomy. They actively reinforced the changing ideology of childhood, as in letter writing that dutifully demonstrated literacy and affection, but also facilitated expression of the child's voice. They could make new meanings based on their own lived experience— think here of the multiplicity of possible readings offered by the sometimes ambiguous messages of fairy tales. The reader of the "Märchengroschen" story told in chapter two engaged with her reading in such an independent spirit that she chose to reject it, and yet obeyed its direction by paying the Grimms' skepticism penalty. Children also pushed back against their education through misreading or refusing to study—even altering the physical texts, as in the transgressive marginalia I found in geography textbooks.

The cultivation of a middle-class self through reading and writing wrought another revolution at home. Germans came to understand childhood as a life stage that mattered deeply in the formation of the self within a web of social relationships, and German children participated in the construction of modern bourgeois selfhood through their negotiation of relational autonomy. Youth periodicals, for example, reveal adults' presumption of children's active involvement in social life through authors' deployment of this genre to advance ideas about a gendered "selfless self" for child readers. Young writers used their diaries to write personas into being in a dialectic with observations of their friends and relations.

Reading and writing practices facilitated the construction of the modern child subject in other dimensions. Adults started to worry about entertaining and engaging children in active ways in their education. Even geography textbook authors were concerned with the amusing qualities of their work. Capturing children's attention and shaping their responses as readers became a preoccupation, as is evident in the vocative addresses from writers of youth periodicals. Sentimental attitudes and aesthetics increasingly influenced children's learning, as can be seen in the rhetoric that children practiced in their correspondence with parents. At the same time, and indeed *through* that mechanism of sentiment and affection, pedagogues and parents emphasized self-discipline. Diary writers explored this tension every day as they used writing to monitor their own feelings and relationships. When the Grimm brothers reframed their fairy tale collection explicitly for a child audience, they emphasized the moral lessons about family and class that young readers would acquire by reading fantastic stories. Personal virtues valorized by the Bildungsbürgertum were emphasized in each genre: diligence and obedience, sensibility and compassion, and intellectual development absent the threat of transgressive curiosity.

Age- and gender-appropriate reading was promoted for the moral lessons and self-discipline it could teach, but the wrong sort of reading was also regarded as a potential threat. For young writers, gender shaped many aspects of the daily lives and modes of expression that appear in their letters and diaries. However, the differences between girls and boys in their educational practices appear to have been more salient for older youth than for young children. The question of precisely when gender and age intersected to constrain children's learning experiences deserves further exploration.

Historians have neglected children's experiences and their part in the modern reimagination of selfhood partly because sources for analyzing those experiences and perspectives have been difficult to locate. In response to that methodological problem, this book has presented empirical evidence of pedagogic practices gathered across genres and archives. The question of how children learned in modern German families and how that evolved over time demands creative interpretation of the production, circulation, reading, and writing of pedagogic texts. It is also enriched by the turn toward texts composed by children. Children's literacy presents an intriguing intersection between adult aims to shape children's responses and the agency of the readers and writers themselves. Reading and writing were certainly used by teachers and parents to promote virtue, time keeping, and obedience to conventions and adult authorities. Yet children could also themselves use literacy: for humor, for resistance, in imitation, to develop a voice, for self-fashioning and self-expression, or to negotiate family relationships.

Why did middle-class German children become key actors in the development of new ideas about self-discipline, sentiment, and selfhood? Why did the Age of Revolutions witness the birth of modern childhood? For the early nineteenth-century Bildungsbürgertum, their children's education was understood as a critical component of success justified through merit rather than noble inheritance. Thus middle-class reformers promoted state schooling projects aimed at governing the working classes while focusing on cultivating self-discipline and independent thinking as a path to prosperity for their own children.[6] Anticipating the rise of "child experts" in the later nineteenth century, the genres analyzed here increasingly emphasized pedagogic authority based on knowledge of children's peculiar needs—for example, as geographic schoolbooks began to be published not by geographers but by teachers. This book has shown how education in a variety of settings within and beyond school walls—from children acting out periodical plays at home, to adults retelling fairy tales, to letter writing that connected families across distances—restructured European society, culture, and personhood. Family life and children's education were fundamental to the constitution of the German middle class.

Although these pedagogic practices developed first in this particular milieu, their development established enduring ideals for the learning experiences that would come to define a proper and happy childhood. This hegemonic notion of childhood spread far beyond Germany, albeit only ever for select children in practice. Socialist Adelheid Popp made this clear in her memoir of a working-class childhood in the 1870s:

> Most persons, if they have grown up under normal conditions, look back in times of heavy distress, with gratitude and emotion to their happy, beautiful, careless youth ... I knew nothing of what delights other children and causes them to shout for joy—dolls, playthings, fairy stories, sweetmeats, and Christmas-trees.[7]

By the turn of the twentieth century, Western childhoods began to be measured against the ideals established in bildungsbürgerlich families at the turn of the nineteenth. Furthermore, those ideals were exported and promulgated around the world. For example, think of the controversies surrounding the 1989 United Nations Convention on the Rights of the Child, which sought to impose Euroamerican values of what childhood should be like on the rest of the globe.[8]

Those values begin with the belief that youth is the key period of personal development and that the self is indelibly marked by childhood experiences. This idea was carried to an extreme by psychoanalytic thought (also born in Central Europe), but can still be seen in mainstream parenting advice that presumes the child's later behavior and personality are determined by early life. Another legacy of the developments documented in this book is evident in the intense investment in an individual child's education as the proverbial future—for example, the outrageous debt now incurred for a college degree in the United States. The modern understanding of youth ties together intellectual growth, moral virtue, and prosperity.

Transformations of educational philosophy are a lasting legacy of the innovations in childrearing surveyed here, including an emphasis on creativity and problem-solving. In the modern educational framework, children are independent thinkers capable of exerting agency in their own intellectual development. Children should be motivated to learn by affection and their emotional attachment to parents or teachers. At the same time, modern education continues to emphasize self-control and internal discipline. Think of the exhortations to sit still, pay attention, restrain impulses, and respect adults that are still part of what a "good" classroom looks like in schools around the world, even if more progressive strands have emerged for children privileged by class and race.[9]

As during the years around 1800 when formal schooling began to expand, parents and educational authorities in the early twenty-first century are concerned with the nature of children's learning at home as well as at school. The idea that children deserve their own books and learning materials, especially ones that entertain, has only intensified with the proliferation of age-graded literature. It is commonplace in the twenty-first century to hear that reading books together is the best thing a parent can do for a child's well-being. Influential genres in children's media today had their origin in the late Enlightenment, including children's magazines, primary-level social studies, fairy tales as nursery stories, and teenage diaries. Letter writing is the only genre examined in this book that was not new during the period addressed, but the participation of children in correspondence and the value placed on their early efforts increased significantly in the early nineteenth century, lasting to today. Indeed, one of the strongest connections between the story told in this book and the ideal childhood today is the value placed on children's writing.

I first encountered Marie Seybold's diary in 2012. Returning to the same archive years later, I considered a document previously overlooked: the educational record for Marie's younger sister Bertha at age four (in 1826). In entries of two or three sentences per day, Bertha's tutor logged an observation of her learning—August 25: four more letters—and conduct—August 30: industrious and well-behaved. The notebook began with an epigraph in verse that captures a moment of transition in children's education:

> This little book remains yet blank. O may your teacher
> Assign you on its pages praise instead of censure.
> This little book resembles you, young sweetheart dear:
> You still have open space for goodness, wonders here,
> Which God will give to you! And on your heart inscribe
> "Be mine you dearest child, while I with you abide."[10]

In addition to declaring a Lockean "blank slate" approach to child development, this little poem presents a number of quintessential contradictions. The language draws on ideas of the rational Enlightenment but within a Christian conceptual frame. It is written about, not by, Bertha, and prizes the adult tutor's expertise, but it also values the child's individual growth. The teacher's attitude is didactic and demanding, but also sentimental and saccharine. The book's existence reflects a new concern for girls' education, yet the approach is not especially gendered. These short lines are gripped by the power of word and page, furnishing Bertha's childhood with books. All of this reflects a society profoundly engaged with redefining socialization and subjectivity.

Middle-class German children helped construct the modern subject through their reading and writing. Yet despite the unmistakable ubiquity of children in the world, their presence is strikingly indistinct in most of the historical record. This paradox makes artifacts such as geography schoolbook marginalia or dramatic plays written for youth to perform all the more remarkable. Investigating such documents reveals the crucial contributions children made to education during the Age of Revolutions. In turn, that makes it possible to ask a host of new questions about aspects of learning, the home, class, and society that we take for granted today. Though these children may be distant in the archive, the revolutions in education, selfhood, and family life they helped set in motion continue to propel our age.

APPENDIX A
ENLIGHTENMENT YOUTH PERIODICALS

Two Examples

To illustrate the range of topics and genres included in the new Enlightenment youth periodical, I have translated here the full table of contents for each of two examples—one from the beginning of the period surveyed and one from the end.

JOHANN CHRISTOPH ADELUNG, LEIPZIGER WOCHENBLATT FÜR KINDER (LEIPZIG WEEKLY FOR CHILDREN) 1 (OCTOBER–DECEMBER 1772)

ISSUE 1
An allegory that teaches the ultimate purpose and the true use of human life in this world
An anecdote from Duke Pico della Mirandola

ISSUE 2
The Gold Piece, a Story in Letters

ISSUE 3
A list of good deeds left undone
Amru, an oriental anecdote

ISSUE 4
Travel Narrative of Three Children
Conversation, Little Carl and Little Caroline

ISSUE 5
Good Fortune and Bad, an Allegory

ISSUE 6
Dialogue about Social Deportment

ISSUE 7
Of Pearls and Pearl Fishing
Teachings of Wisdom

ISSUE 8
To Parents and Supervisors on the Purpose and Use of This Weekly

ISSUE 9
The Lost Child
Three Friends

MONAT-ROSEN: ZEITSCHRIFT FÜR BELEHRUNG UND UNTERHALTUNG
(MONTHLY ROSES: MAGAZINE FOR INSTRUCTION AND ENTERTAINMENT)
4, NO. 1 (1843)

A Story à la Kaspar Hauser
A Christmas Party in Norway (from the Revue Britannique)
The Empress and the Soldier
The Capuchin Monastery at Palermo (from Alexandre Dumas)
The Fatal Wager
Loustaunau, the French Mahratten-General
Proof of Friendship (from the youthful memories of a French officer)
A Paragon of Feminine Discretion
The Sailor, or the Cross of Mother of Pearl
A Council of the Negro
Anecdote
On Holiday in the Desert
The Sailor of Pollet

The Blackberry Bush
The Cornetkeuche (Carinthian Sage)
The Imprisonment, Arrest, Death Sentence, and Burial of General Joachim Mürat
The Battlefield of Eylau (February 9, 1807)
Battle of Friedland (June 14, 1807)
The Falkenburg
The Castle Brigitte
On the Knight-Captain's Path to Death (from Alexander Count of Württemberg)
The Journeys of Jesus Christ
The Daughter of the Governess
The Plague Ship
The Thaler
Marshal Brune and His Wife
The Three Young Women from the Lake
On the Natural History of the Elephant
Divorce, or the Human Heart Is a Wondrous Thing (from Henrietta Hohenhausen)
Public Life in Beijing (from a Russian priest)
Fanchon the Lyre Girl (the Count of E.)
One Day Prince (Farce with historical basis)
The Life Span of Some People
Prussian Folk Legends:
> 1. The Bell of Attendorn
> 2. The Cologne Cathedral

Legends from Salzburg and Its Surroundings:
> 1. King Watzmann
> 2. Of Juvavia
> 3. The Mönchsberg at Salzburg
> 4. Unterster near Salzburg

The Battle of Lutzen in 1813 (Tale from H. K.)
Scenes from the Life of a Female Dragoon
The Illness and the Last Moments of the Emperor Alexander of Taganrog
    (from an eyewitness)
The Sign Language of the Deaf
Hun Attacks and Hun Battles
The Bloody Sword at the Church of Our Lady in Halberstadt
The Profiteering Baker in Berlin
The Resurrected Woman
The Daring Girl
Jewish Crimes
Elizabeth's Roses
The Black Death
The Persecution of the Jews
St. John's Church at Altenberga
St. John's Church Will Not Stand in the Valley
The Seer of Death
The Good Idea
Windsor Castle
An Election in England
Street Clamor in London
The Card Players
The Bishop and the Cat
The Magic Ring

APPENDIX B
GEOGRAPHY SCHOOLBOOK

Typical Table of Contents

This table of contents is presented as an example of the information covered in a typical early nineteenth-century geographic schoolbook. Readers will note that Annegarn's numbering scheme is inconsistent. Although this is partly an artifact of early nineteenth-century printing technology, the shift from finer detail in the European sections to the listing of chapters on Asia and Africa hints at the asymmetrical division of the globe as discussed in chapter three.

JOSEF ANNEGARN, *HANDBUCH DER GEOGRAPHIE FÜR DIE JUGEND* (*GEOGRAPHY HANDBOOK FOR YOUTH*, 1834)

δ) Possessions of the
French

ε) Possessions of the
Danes

2. Southeast Asia

3. The East Indian Islands

   a) The Maldives

   b) Ceylon

   c) The Andaman Islands

   d) Indonesia

     α) Sumatra

     β) Java

     γ) Borneo

     δ) Celebes [Sulawesi]

     ε) The Maluku Islands

F) China

G) Japan

III. Africa

A) Egypt

B) Nubia

C) Abyssinia

D) The Berbers

   1. Barce [Marj]

   2. Tripoli

   3. Fezzan

   4. Tunisia

   5. Algeria

   6. Fez and Morocco

   7. Biledulgerid

E) The Saharan Desert

F) Senegambia

G) Guinea

H) Negroland

I) The Cape Colony

K) The Kaffirs

L) Countries on the East Coast of
Africa

   1. Sofala

   2. Mutapa

   3. Mozambique

   4. Zanzibar

   5. Ajan and Adel [Somalia]

M) The African Islands

   1. The Amirante Islands

   2. Seychelles

   3. The Comoro Islands

   4. Réunion

   5. Mauritius

   6. Madagascar

   7. St. Helena

   8. Ascension Island

   9. Guinea Islands

   10. Cape Verde Islands

   11. The Canary Islands

12. Madeira etc.

13. The Azores

IV. America

A) North America

   1. North Pole Countries

     a) Arctic Highland

     b) Greenland

     c) Svalbard

   2. British North America

   3. Russian North America

   4. The United States

   5. The Mexican Free States

   6. Federal Republic of Central
America

B) South America

   1. The Republic of Columbia

   2. The Guianas

   3. Brazil

   4. The Republic of Peru

   5. ——————Bolivia

   6. ——————Chile

   7. United Provinces of the Río
de la Plata

   8. The Republic of Paraguay

   9. ——————Cisplatina

   10. Patagonia

C) West Indies

   1. The Bahamas

   2. The Greater Antilles

   3. The Lesser Antilles

V. Australia

   1. New Holland

   2. New Zealand

   3. New Caledonia

   4. New Hebrides [Vanuatu]

   5. Queen Charlotte Islands
[Haida Gwaii]

   6. New Georgia

   7. The Louisiade Archipelago

   8. New Guinea

   9. New Britain

   10. Admiralty Islands

   11. The Caroline Islands

   12. The Mariana Islands

   13. Pescadores [The Penghu
Islands]

   14. Mulgrave [Badu] Island

   15. Samoa Islands

   16. Friendship Island

   17. The Cook Islands

   18. The Society Islands

   19. Lower Islands

   20. The Marquesas Islands

   21. Sandwich Islands

NOTES

LIST OF ARCHIVES AND RESEARCH LIBRARIES

ALEKI   Arbeitsstelle für Leseforschung und Kinder- und Jugendmedien, Cologne

BBF   Bibliothek für Bildungsgeschichtliche Forschung, Berlin

BHJ   Bibliothèque de l'Heure Joyeuse, Paris

BLHA   Brandenburgisches Landeshauptarchiv, Potsdam

BNF   Bibliothèque nationale de France, Paris

CCL   Cotsen Children's Library, Princeton

DLA   Deutsches Literaturarchiv, Marbach

DTA   Deutsches Tagebucharchiv, Emmendingen

GEI   Georg-Eckert-Institut für Schulbuchforschung, Braunschweig

GNM   Germanisches Nationalmuseum Historisches Archiv, Nuremberg

HSAH   Hauptstaatsarchiv Hannover, Niedersächsisches Landesarchiv, Hannover

HSAS   Hauptstaatsarchiv Stuttgart, Landesarchiv Baden-Württemberg, Stuttgart

IJF   Institut für Jugendbuchforschung, Frankfurt

LAB   Landesarchiv Berlin, Berlin

LAS   Landesarchiv Schleswig, Schleswig

LLB   Lippische Landesbibliothek, Detmold

SAL   Staatsarchiv Ludwigsburg, Landesarchiv Baden-Württemberg, Ludwigsburg

SBKJA   Staatsbibliothek Berlin Kinder- und Jugendbuchabteilung, Berlin

WLB   Württembergische Landesbibliothek, Stuttgart

INTRODUCTION: SENTIMENT AND SELF-CONTROL

1. See Jürgen Kocka, ed., *Bürgertum im 19. Jahrhundert* (Göttingen: Vandenhoeck & Ruprecht, 1995), especially Volumes I & II; Pia Schmid, "Deutsches Bildungsbürgertum: Bürgerliche Bildung zwischen 1750 und 1830" (PhD diss., Goethe-Universität Frankfurt am Main, 1984).

2. Marie Seybold, diary, 9–13 March 1830, Q 3/48 Bü 3, Familiennachlass Schmidt, HSAS (see above for list of archive abbreviations). Born September 12, 1819 to a Protestant family of jurists and bureaucrats in Württemberg, Marie Seybold is one of six young writers whose diaries I examine closely in Chapter Five. I have chosen to refer to children and youth by their given names in order to avoid confusion when discussing several members of the same family. Unless otherwise noted, all translations from both published texts and archival manuscripts in German or French are my own throughout.

3. Marie's father's uncle, David Christoph Seybold, was a philosopher who took a position in Strasbourg in 1792. His children had been sent ahead and made it home to Brackenheim, but Seybold was jailed on suspicion of aristocratic sentiments. Eberhard E. von Georgii-Georgenau, *Biographisch-genealogische Blätter aus und über Schwaben* (Stuttgart: Emil Müller, 1879), 915.

4. Joseph Friedrich Wilhelm von Seybold represented Heilbronn as one of the seventy elected representatives in the Second Chamber at the Württembergische Landstände (1848–1849). Frank Raberg, *Biographisches Handbuch der württembergischen Landtagsabgeordneten (1815–1933)* (Stuttgart: Kohlhammer, 2001).

5. As a field, the history of childhood has exploded in the past two decades. Despite criticisms and amendments to his bold thesis concerning "The Discovery of Childhood," Philippe Ariès continues to be cited widely in histories of childhood across comparative contexts. Philippe Ariès, *Centuries of Childhood: A Social History of Family Life*, trans. Robert Baldick (New York: Vintage Books, 1962). Developments in the literature on transformations of childhood and youth in Western European modernity can be traced through works such as Anne Digby and Peter Searby, *Children, School, and Society in Nineteenth-Century England* (London: Macmillan, 1981); John Gillis, *Youth and History: Tradition and Change in European Age Relations, 1770–Present* (New York: Academic Press, 1981); Joseph Bristow, *Empire Boys: Adventures in a Man's World* (London: Harper Collins Academic, 1991); Anna Davin, *Growing Up Poor: Home, School, and Street in London, 1870–1914* (London: River Orams, 1996); Edward Ross Dickinson, *The Politics of German Child Welfare from the Empire to the Federal Republic* (Cambridge, MA: Harvard University Press, 1996); Mary Jo Maynes, Birgitte Søland, and Christina Benninghaus, eds., *Secret Gardens, Satanic Mills: Placing Girls in European History, 1750–1960* (Bloomington: Indiana University Press, 2005); Paula S. Fass, ed., *The Routledge History of Childhood in the Western World* (London: Routledge, 2013); Colin Heywood, *Childhood in Modern Europe* (Cambridge: Cambridge University Press, 2018).

6. While undeniably Eurocentric in its formulation, the Age of Revolutions as a framework has received renewed attention in recent years from historians of the Global South. See, for example, David Armitage and Sanjay Subrahmanyam, eds., *The Age of Revolutions in Global Context, c. 1760–1840* (New York: Palgrave Macmillan, 2010); Paul E. Lovejoy, *Jihād in West Africa during the Age of Revolutions* (Athens: Ohio University Press, 2016). See also the open-access journal *Age of Revolutions* at http://ageofrevolutions.com.

7. Harvey Graff, *The Literacy Myth* (New York: Academic Press, 1979); François Furet and Jacques Ozouf, *Reading and Writing: Literacy in France from Calvin to Jules Ferry* (Cambridge: Cambridge University Press, 1982).

8. Lynn Hunt, *The Family Romance of the French Revolution* (Berkeley: University of California Press, 1992); Suzanne Desan, *The Family on Trial in Revolutionary France* (Berkeley: University of California Press, 2004); Sarah Maza, *The Myth of the French Bourgeoisie: An Essay on the Social Imaginary, 1750–1850* (Cambridge, MA: Harvard University Press, 2005).

9. Richard Gawthrop, "Literacy Drives in Preindustrial Germany," in *National Literacy Campaigns: Historical and Comparative Perspectives,* ed. Robert Arnove and Harvey Graff (New York: Plenum, 1987), 39.

10. Ibid., 42.

11. This is a broad field, but some representative works on child labor, welfare in the era of industrialization, children and consumer culture, and related topics include: Rachel Fuchs, *Abandoned Children: Foundlings and Child Welfare in Nineteenth-Century France* (Albany: State University of New York Press, 1984); Colin Heywood, *Childhood in Nineteenth-Century France: Work, Health and Education Among the "Classes Populaires"* (Cambridge: Cambridge University Press, 1988); Mary Jo Maynes, *Taking the Hard Road: Life Course in French and*

German Workers' Autobiographies in the Era of Industrialization (Chapel Hill: University of North Carolina Press, 1995); Lydia Murdoch, *Imagined Orphans: Poor Families, Child Welfare, and Contested Citizenship in London* (New Brunswick, NJ: Rutgers University Press, 2006); Peter Kirby, *Child Labour in Britain, 1750–1870* (New York: Palgrave Macmillan, 2003); David Hamlin, *Work and Play: The Production and Consumption of Toys in Germany, 1870–1914* (Ann Arbor: University of Michigan Press, 2007); Dennis Denisoff, ed., *The Nineteenth-Century Child and Consumer Culture* (Burlington, VT: Ashgate, 2008).

12. David I. Kertzer, "Living with Kin," in *History of the European Family*, vol. 2, *Family Life in the Long Nineteenth Century, 1789–1913*, ed. David I. Kertzer and Marzio Barbagli (New Haven, CT: Yale University Press, 2002), 40–72.

13. David Hamlin addresses this specifically in the context of childhood, writing in conversation with Foucault: "With the task of producing bürgerliche individuals in mind, many parents began to enforce a physical separation of their children from the world outside, creating, as the private sphere, a space 'heterogeneous to all others and closed in upon itself.'" Hamlin, *Work and Play*, 24. See also Ingeborg Weber-Kellermann, *Die deutsche Familie: Versuch einer Sozialgeschichte* (Frankfurt: Suhrkamp, 1974); Ingeborg Weber-Kellermann, *Die Kindheit: Kleidung und Wohnen, Arbeit und Spiel, eine Kulturgeschichte* (Frankfurt: Insel, 1979); Gunilla Budde, *Auf dem Weg ins Bürgerleben: Kindheit und Erziehung in Deutschen und Englischen Bürgerfamilien, 1840–1914* (Göttingen: Vandenhoeck & Ruprecht, 1994); Karin Wurst, *Fabricating Pleasure: Fashion, Entertainment, and Cultural Consumption in Germany, 1780–1830* (Detroit, MI: Wayne State University Press, 2005); Gunilla Budde, *Blütezeit des Bürgertums* (Darmstadt: Wissenschaftliche Buchgesellschaft, 2009); Jason Tebbe, "Landscapes of Remembrance: Home and Memory in the Nineteenth-Century *Bürgertum*," *Journal of Family History* 33, no. 2 (2008): 195–215.

14. See work by geographer Martin Lewis.

15. Jason Philip Coy, "Introduction: The Holy Roman Empire in History and Historiography," in *The Holy Roman Empire, Reconsidered*, ed. Jason Philip Coy, Benjamin Marschke, and David Warren Sabean (Oxford: Berghahn Books, 2010), 3.

16. Kenneth Barkin, "Social Control and the Volksschule in Vormärz Prussia," *Central European History* 16, no. 1 (1983): 50.

17. R. A. Houston, *Literacy in Early Modern Europe: Culture and Education, 1500–1800*, 2nd ed. (New York: Routledge, 2013), 194.

18. David Hamlin, "The Structures of Toy Consumption: Bourgeois Domesticity and Demand for Toys in Nineteenth-Century Germany," *Journal of Social History* 36, no. 4 (2003): 857–69; Joe Perry, *Christmas in Germany: A Cultural History* (Chapel Hill: University of North Carolina Press, 2010).

19. For the transnational influence of the Grimms, see Cay Dollerup, *Tales and Translation: The Grimm Tales from Pan-Germanic Narratives to Shared International Fairy Tales* (Amsterdam: J. Benjamins, 1999). On the impact of German children's literature in general on other traditions, see David Blamires, *Telling Tales: The Impact of Germany on English Children's Books 1780–1918* (Cambridge: OpenBook Publishers, 2009).

20. On German toys, see Hamlin, *Work and Play*; Bryan Ganaway, *Toys, Consumption, and Middle-Class Childhood in Imperial Germany, 1871–1918* (Oxford: Peter Lang, 2009).

21. On the *Kindergarten* movement inspired by Froebel, see Ann Taylor Allen, "'Let Us Live with Our Children': Kindergarten Movements in Germany and the United States, 1840–1914,"

History of Education Quarterly 28, no. 1 (1988): 23–48; Norman Brosterman, *Inventing Kindergarten* (New York: Harry N. Abrams, 1997); Roberta Wollons, ed., *Kindergartens and Cultures: The Global Diffusion of an Idea* (New Haven: Yale University Press, 2000); Anja Schoenberg Shepela, "'Meine kühnsten Wünsche und Ideen': Women, Space, Place, and Mobility in Late Eighteenth- and Nineteenth-Century Germany" (PhD diss., University of Minnesota, 2014). On Horace Mann's influential trip from the United States to report on Prussian schools, see Clarence J. Karier, *The Individual, Society, and Education: A History of American Educational Ideas,* 2nd ed. (Urbana: University of Illinois Press, 1986), 220–24.

22. Harvey Graff, *The Legacies of Literacy: Continuities and Contradictions in Western Culture and Society* (Bloomington: Indiana University Press, 1987), 14.

23. For examples of how this pattern developed in other European contexts, see Arianne Baggerman and Rudolf Dekker, *Child of the Enlightenment: Revolutionary Europe Reflected in a Boyhood Diary* (Leiden: Brill, 2009); Jennifer Popiel, *Rousseau's Daughters: Domesticity, Education, and Autonomy in Modern France* (Durham: University of New Hampshire Press, 2008); Anna Kuxhausen, *From the Womb to the Body Politic: Raising the Nation in Enlightenment Russia* (Madison: University of Wisconsin Press, 2013).

24. Louise Tilly and Miriam Cohen posed this question in a review essay published several years after the establishment of the *Journal of Family History,* reflecting on other notable developments in the field. Louise A. Tilly and Miriam Cohen, "Does the Family Have a History? A Review of Theory and Practice in Family History," *Social Science History* 6, no. 2 (1982): 131–79. Their review is organized around Michael Anderson's still-useful taxonomy of family historiography as the demographic approach, the sentiments approach, and the household economics approach. Michael Anderson, *Approaches to the History of the Western Family, 1500–1914* (Cambridge: Cambridge University Press, 1980). For an updated survey, see Mary Jo Maynes and Ann Waltner, *The Family: A World History* (Oxford: Oxford University Press, 2012).

25. He also argues that "the subjectivity of the privatized individual was related from the very start to publicity . . . [for] the familiarity (Intimität) whose vehicle was the written word, the subjectivity that had become fit to print, had in fact become the literature appealing to a wide public of readers." Jürgen Habermas, *The Structural Transformation of the Public Sphere: An Inquiry into a Category of Bourgeois Society,* trans. Thomas Burger and Frederick Lawrence (1962; Cambridge, MA: MIT Press, 1991), 50–55.

26. See, for example, Belinda Davis, "Reconsidering Habermas, Politics, and Gender: The Case of Wilhelmine Germany," in *Society, Culture, and the State in Germany, 1870–1930,* ed. Geoff Eley (Ann Arbor: University of Michigan Press, 1996), 397–426.

27. Daniel Thomas Cook, *The Moral Project of Childhood: Motherhood, Material Life, and Early Children's Consumer Culture* (New York: New York University Press, 2020).

28. For a particularly provocative analysis of selfhood in the representation of nineteenth-century children, see Stephanie O'Rourke, "Histories of the Self: Anne-Louis Girodet and the Trioson Portrait Series," *Eighteenth-Century Studies* 52, no. 2 (2019): 201–23.

29. Hamlin, *Work and Play,* 24.

30. Jerrold Seigel, *The Idea of the Self: Thought and Experience in Western Europe since the Seventeenth Century* (Cambridge: Cambridge University Press, 2005), 43.

31. David Sabean, *Power in the Blood: Popular Culture and Village Discourse in Early Modern Germany* (Cambridge: Cambridge University Press, 1984), 31.

32. The century between 1750 and 1850 rode a "virtual tidal wave of pedagogical passion." Jonathan Sheehan, *The Enlightenment Bible: Translation, Scholarship, Culture* (Princeton, NJ: Princeton University Press, 2005), 131–32.

33. Fragonard's painting was later remade as an engraving by Nicolas de Launay in 1790.

34. According to Pamela Selwyn, the bookseller Friedrich Nicolai, who published Friedrich Eberhard von Rochow's books, "saw works directed at educating both pastors and school-teachers, particularly those in the countryside, as an essential instrument in the struggle against superstition and ignorance." He reported it was "very sad to see the children of middling and common men, who are not destined for [university] studies, and yet who represent the genuine components of the nation, almost everywhere so miserably taught." Pamela Selwyn, *Everyday Life in the German Book Trade: Friedrich Nicolai as Bookseller and Publisher in the Age of Enlightenment, 1750–1810* (University Park: Pennsylvania State University Press, 2000), 52–53.

35. On the role of the state in promoting schooling during the nineteenth century and the importance of local communities in determining regional dynamics, see Mary Jo Maynes, *Schooling for the People: Comparative Local Studies of Schooling History in France and Germany, 1750–1850* (New York: Holmes & Meier, 1985).

36. Juliane Jacobi, "Girls' Secondary Education in Nineteenth- and Twentieth-Century Germany, Austria and Switzerland" (paper presented at European Conference on Educational Research, Göteborg, Sweden, September 10, 2008).

37. See Werner Gebhardt, *Die Schüler der Hohen Karlsschule: Ein biographisches Lexikon* (Stuttgart: Kohlhammer, 2011).

38. Jacobi, "Girls' Secondary Education," 10. Female illiteracy is estimated to have reached less than 10 percent by the mid-nineteenth century, if not earlier. David Vincent, *The Rise of Mass Literacy: Reading and Writing in Modern Europe* (Cambridge: Polity, 2000), 9, fig. 1.2.

39. The cast of Enlightenment pedagogues included notable philosophers and reformers such as Johann Heinrich Pestalozzi, Jean-Jacques Rousseau, John Locke, Immanuel Kant, and Joachim Heinrich Campe, but also figures lesser known today, such as Johann Bernhard Basedow, Friedrich Eberhard von Rochow, Caroline Rudolphi, Amalia Holst, and Betty Gleim. On John Locke, see Adrianne Wadewitz, "'Spare the Sympathy, Spoil the Child': Sociability, Selfhood, and the Maturing Reader, 1775–1815" (PhD diss., Indiana University, 2011); Adriana Benzaquen, "Locke's Children," *Journal of the History of Childhood and Youth* 4, no. 3 (2011): 382–402. For a print history perspective on the circulation of Basedow's reform movement, philanthropinism, see Andrea Immel, "The Shady Business of Enlightenment: John Trusler's *Progress of Man* and Johann Basedow's *Elementarwerk*," *Princeton Library Chronicle* 68, no. 3 (2007): 969–86. For an overview of Campe's position within continental Enlightenment pedagogy, see Richard B. Apgar, "Taming Travel and Disciplining Reason: Enlightenment and Pedagogy in the Work of Joachim Heinrich Campe" (PhD diss., University of North Carolina, 2008). On imitators of Campe well into the nineteenth century, see Adalbert Merget, *Geschichte der deutschen Jugendlitteratur* (Berlin: Plahn, 1882), 25–26. On women ped-agogues of the Enlightenment, see Elke Kleinau and Christine Mayer, "Caroline Rudolphi—Gemälde weiblicher Erziehung (1807); Amalia Holst—Über die Bestimmung des Weibes zur höheren Geistesbildung (1802); Betty Gleim—Erziehung und Unterricht des weiblichen Geschlechts (1810)," in *Erziehung und Bildung des weiblichen Geschlechts: Eine kommentierte*

Quellensammlung zur Bildungs- und Berufsbildungsgeschichte von Mädchen und Frauen, ed. Elke Kleinau and Christine Meyer (Weinheim, Germany: Beltz, 1996), 70–84.

40. Arianne Baggerman addresses this in the context of personal narratives: "The increasing fascination for childhood in nineteenth-century autobiographies can also be explained by the continued effect of enlightened pedagogy, in which the childhood years were seen as a separate stage of life, of vital importance to the formation of character." "Lost Time: Temporal Discipline and Historical Awareness in Nineteenth-Century Dutch Egodocuments," in *Controlling Time and Shaping the Self: Developments in Autobiographical Writing since the Sixteenth Century,* ed. Arianne Baggerman, Rudolf Dekker, and Michael Mascuch (Leiden: Brill, 2011), 529.

41. Peter Stadler, *Pestalozzi: Geschichtliche Biographie* (Zürich: Neue Zürcher Zeitung, 1988–1993).

42. On Rousseau's influence on German philosophy, see David James, *Rousseau and German Idealism: Freedom, Dependence, and Necessity* (Cambridge: Cambridge University Press, 2013). In a somewhat cranky passage of his *Confessions,* Rousseau referred to *Émile* as "the best, as well as the most important of all the works I had produced." Jean-Jacques Rousseau, *The Confessions and Correspondence, Including the Letters to Malesherbes,* ed. Christopher Kelly, Roger D. Masters, and Peter G. Stillman, trans. Christopher Kelly (Hanover, NH: University Press of New England, 1995), Book XI.

43. Paul Hensel, *Rousseau* (Leipzig: B. G. Teubner, 1912), chapter 6.

44. See Nikola Merveldt, "Multilingual Robinson: Imagining Modern Communities for Middle-Class Children," *Bookbird: A Journal of International Children's Literature* 51, no. 3 (2013): 1–11.

45. On the particular interpretation of this paradox in the bourgeois German milieu, see Budde, *Auf dem Weg ins Bürgerleben,* 78. For a fuller development of these contradictions in the case of one Dutch boy's education, see Baggerman and Dekker, *Child of the Enlightenment.*

46. For a rich engagement with Norbert Elias's classic and relevant work on *The Civilizing Process,* especially around the gendered, classed, and raced dimensions of "self-mastery," see Pavla Miller, *Transformations of Patriarchy in the West, 1500–1900* (Bloomington: Indiana University Press, 1998).

47. See Noah W. Sobe, "Concentration and Civilisation: Producing the Attentive Child in the Age of Enlightenment," *Paedagogica Historica* 46, no. 1–2 (2010): 149–60.

48. Christoph Wilhelm Hufeland, quoted in Hubert Göbels, ed., *Hundert Alte Kinderbücher aus dem 19. Jahrhundert: Eine illustrierte Bibliographie* (Dortmund: Harenberg, 1979), 2:445.

49. "The solicitude for his darling never left him, and even from a distance he guided her education according to sensible principles." Eberhard von Georgii-Georgenau, *Biographisch-genealogische Blätter aus und über Schwaben,* 924–25. This admiring description by a family chronicler in the 1870s may remind readers of similar sentiments expressed in Louisa May Alcott's novels of the same decade, a fictional treatment of her father Bronson Alcott's Romantic-era pedagogy. See especially *Little Men* (1871), *Eight Cousins* (1875), and *Rose in Bloom* (1876).

50. Jan Goldstein, *The Post-Revolutionary Self: Politics and Psyche in France, 1750–1850* (Cambridge, MA: Harvard University Press, 2005), 35 and 38.

51. Sociologist Katharina Rutschky famously coined the term "schwarze Pädagogik" ("black" or "poisonous" pedagogy) to define the corporal punishment and repressive impulses of eighteenth-century child socialization. Rutschky, ed. *Schwarze Pädagogik: Quellen zur Naturgeschichte der bürgerlichen Erziehung* (Frankfurt: Ullstein, 1977).

52. William McCarthy, "Performance, Pedagogy, and Politics: Mrs. Thrale, Mrs. Barbauld, Monsieur Itard," in *Childhood and Children's Books in Early Modern Europe, 1550–1800,* ed. Andrea Immel and Michael Witmore (New York: Routledge, 2006), 261–62.

53. Some of the scholars whose work has influenced my analysis come out of philosophy (especially Hans-Georg Gadamer) or literary criticism, including reader response theory (Wolfgang Iser, Susan Suleiman, and Inge Crosman Wimmers). As Matthew Grenby notes, it would be impossible to present a complete survey of work in the history of reading, given the prolific expansions in this field. Grenby, *The Child Reader, 1700–1840* (Cambridge: Cambridge University Press, 2011), 6. A useful review essay on key questions in literacy studies is Carl F. Kaestle, "The History of Literacy and the History of Readers," *Review of Research in Education* 12 (1985): 11–53. For the most current scholarly conversations on theories of reading and the history of the book, consider the Society for the History of Authorship, Reading and Publishing (SHARP), which fields an active listserv on these topics. See http://sharpweb.org.

54. Janice A. Radway, "Reading Is Not Eating: Mass-Produced Literature and the Theoretical, Methodological, and Political Consequences of a Metaphor," *Book Research Quarterly* 2 (1986): 7–29.

55. William St. Clair, *The Reading Nation in the Romantic Period* (Cambridge: Cambridge University Press, 2004), 5.

56. Allan Luke, "The Political Economy of Reading Instruction," in *Towards a Critical Sociology of Reading Pedagogy,* ed. Carolyn Baker and Allan Luke (Amsterdam: John Benjamins, 1991), 6.

57. Louise Rosenblatt's early transactional theory of reading has proven especially influential here across a wide range of disciplines. See, for example, *The Reader, the Text, the Poem: The Transactional Theory of the Literary Work* (Carbondale: Southern Illinois University Press, 1978). More recently, Harvey Graff has led a revitalization of the "new literacy studies," which questions the simple equation of literacy acquisition with social development. See *Literacy Myths, Legacies, and Lessons: New Studies on Literacy* (New Brunswick, NJ: Transaction, 2011) for an overview of trends and recent historical cases excavated in this field.

58. In any historical investigation of literacy, it is essential to remember the persistence of orality. Although the evidence in this book is drawn from the written word, the importance of oral communications is present as, for example, children acted out dramas they first read in youth periodicals, told and retold fairy tales, or participated in schoolroom catechism and conversation. On orality, see Walter Ong, *Orality and Literacy: The Technologizing of the Word* (New York: Meuthen, 1982); Jack Goody, *The Interface between the Written and the Oral* (Cambridge: Cambridge University Press, 1987).

59. Rolf Engelsing, *Der Bürger als Leser: Lesergeschichte in Deutschland 1500–1800* (Stuttgart: J. B. Metzler, 1974).

60. Literacy was not even absolute in one individual. As Carl Kaestle summarizes, "Some individuals learned to read but then forgot how. Some were literate but rarely read. Some perceived themselves to be literate but were perceived by others as illiterate, or vice versa. Furthermore, individuals who were unable to read participated in literate culture by listening to those who could read. The worlds of literacy and oral communication are interpenetrating." Kaestle, "The History of Literacy and the History of Readers," *Review of Research in Education* 12 (1985): 12–13.

61. Graff, *The Literacy Myth*; Vincent, *The Rise of Mass Literacy*.

62. Rolf Engelsing, *Analphabetentum und Lektüre: Zur Sozialgeschichte des Lesens in Deutschland zwischen feudaler und industrieller Gesellschaft* (Stuttgart: Metzler, 1973), 62.

63. David Vincent, "The Progress of Literacy," *Victorian Studies* 45, no. 3 (2003): figures 2 and 3.

64. Maynes, *Schooling for the People*, 104 (table).

65. On new modes of reading after 1750, see Engelsing, *Der Bürger als Leser;* Robert Darnton, *The Kiss of Lamourette: Reflections in Cultural History* (New York: W. W. Norton, 1989); Roger Chartier, *The Order of Books: Readers, Authors, and Libraries in Europe between the Fourteenth and Eighteenth Centuries* (Stanford, CA: Stanford University Press, 1994); St. Clair, *Reading Nation*; Ian Jackson, "Approaches to the History of Readers and Reading in Eighteenth-Century Britain," *The Historical Journal* 47, no. 4 (2004): 1041–54.

66. Paul Saenger, *Spaces between Words: The Origins of Silent Reading* (Stanford, CA: Stanford University Press, 1997).

67. On reference reading and the eighteenth century as the age of information, see also Ann Blair, *Too Much to Know: Managing Scholarly Information before the Modern Age* (New Haven, CT: Yale University Press, 2011); Daniel Headrick, *When Information Came of Age: Technologies of Knowledge in the Age of Reason and Revolution, 1700–1850* (Oxford: Oxford University Press, 2000).

68. Anna Hasenfratz, diary, January 1, 1841, 1491.1, DTA.

69. Johann Basedow, *Das Methodenbuch für Väter und Mütter der Familien und Völker* (Leipzig: Fritsch, 1771), 8.

70. Selwyn, *Everyday Life,* 30.

71. Engelsing, *Der Bürger als Leser,* 53.

72. Rudolf Jentzsch, *Der deutsch-lateinische Büchermarkt nach den Leipziger Ostermesskatalogen von 1740 und 1800 in seiner Gliederung und Wandlung* (Leipzig: Voigtländer, 1912), 15, 67, 146, cited in Richard Gawthrop and Gerald Strauss, "Protestantism and Literacy in Early Modern Germany," *Past & Present,* no. 104 (1984): 53.

73. The other three genres that replaced theology were political treatises, popular philosophy, and natural sciences. Helen Fronius, *Women and Literature in the Goethe Era 1770–1820: Determined Dilettantes* (Oxford: Clarendon, 2007), 140–41.

74. Selwyn, *Everyday Life,* 43.

75. On books as commodities, see Matt Erlin, *Necessary Luxuries: Books, Literature, and the Culture of Consumption in Germany, 1770–1815* (Ithaca, NY: Cornell University Press, 2014).

76. Karen Sánchez-Eppler, *Dependent States: The Child's Part in Nineteenth-Century American Culture* (Chicago: University of Chicago Press, 2005), 29.

77. Jan Fergus, *Provincial Readers in Eighteenth-Century England* (Oxford: Oxford University Press, 2007).

78. Cooper's *The Red Rover* was published originally in 1827, and translated in 1828 as *Zahlreiche Übersetzungen und Bearbeitungen für die Jugend, Der Rote Freibeuter oder Der Rote Seeräuber.* Anna Krahmer, diary, March 1, 1831, 1677/II, DTA.

79. See Budde, *Auf dem Weg ins Bürgerleben*; Miller, *Transformations of Patriarchy*; Baggerman and Dekker, *Child of the Enlightenment.*

80. Heinrich Wilhelm Weise to Friedrich Wilhelm Weise, March 8, 1813, Nachlass Hermann Weise, E Rep. 200–12 Nr. 14, LAB.

81. August Herder to Johann Gottfried Herder, 1788, in F. E. Mencken, *Dein dich zärtlich liebender Sohn: Kinderbriefe aus sechs Jahrhunderten* (Memmingen, Germany: Heimeran, 1965), 69. A surprisingly steep fine, one Saxon thaler could cover the cost of a new book

around this time according to the advertisements in M. Christian Schulz, *I. G. Stedmann's Reisen in Surinam für die Jugend bearbeitet* (Berlin: Schüppel, 1800).

82. See Mary Jo Maynes, "Age as a Category of Historical Analysis: History, Agency, and Narratives of Childhood," *Journal of the History of Childhood and Youth* 1, no. 1 (2008): 114–24; Steven Mintz, "Reflections on Age as a Category of Historical Analysis," *Journal of the History of Childhood and Youth* 1, no. 1 (2008): 91–94. John Gillis addressed the question of young people's agency as "the proposition that youth makes its own history, a history linked with and yet analytically separable from that of the family, the school, and other adult institutions." Gillis, *Youth and History,* ix.

83. Sánchez-Eppler, *Dependent States,* xv.

84. Some histories of the self that have shaped my approach include: Sabean, *Power in the Blood;* Roy Porter, ed., *Rewriting the Self: Histories from the Renaissance to the Present* (London: Routledge, 1997); Goldstein, *The Post-Revolutionary Self;* Seigel, *The Idea of the Self;* Mark G. E. Kelly, "Foucault, Subjectivity, and Technologies of the Self," in *A Companion to Foucault,* ed. Christopher Falzon, Timothy O'Leary, and Jana Sawicki (Malden, MA: Wiley-Blackwell, 2013).

85. As Andrea Immel and Michael Witmore ask, "To what degree has the 'obvious' marginality of children impeded our ability to see adults exercising a similarly middling kind of power?" "Introduction: Little Differences: Children, Their Books, and Culture in the Study of Early Modern Europe," in *Childhood and Children's Books in Early Modern Europe, 1550–1800,* ed. Andrea Immel and Michael Witmore (New York: Routledge, 2006), 14.

86. Tessie P. Liu, *The Weaver's Knot: The Contradictions of Class Struggle and Family Solidarity in Western Europe, 1750–1914* (Ithaca, NY: Cornell University Press, 1994), x.

87. Indeed, it is a consequence of the increasing importance of bourgeois children's writing that the texts I analyze were preserved in the first place. Sánchez-Eppler elegantly acknowledges the skewed nature of such an archive, writing of early American children: "Their families valued these children's writing enough to encourage this activity and to preserve the product. . . . These diaries should thus be seen as offering best instances, childhood literacy at its most personal, empowered, and liberating." Sánchez-Eppler, *Dependent States,* 19.

88. Children's imaginative or fiction writing is not a central focus of this study, but there are examples from other contexts, such as the nineteenth-century manuscript libraries examined by Sánchez-Eppler or the juvenilia of famous writers like Jane Austen, Lewis Carroll, or the Brontë sisters. Sánchez-Eppler, "Practicing for Print: The Hale Children's Manuscript Libraries," *Journal of the History of Childhood and Youth* 1, no. 2 (2008): 188–209; Liz Maynes-Aminzade, "Literary Fetishes: The Brontë Miniature Books," *Harvard Library Bulletin* 24, no. 2 (2013): 27–45; Christine Alexander and Juliet McMaster, eds., *The Child Writer from Austen to Woolf* (Cambridge: Cambridge University Press, 2010); Christine Alexander, "Playing the Author: Children's Creative Writing, Paracosms and the Construction of Family Magazines," in *Children, Childhood and Cultural Heritage,* ed. Kate Darian-Smith and Carla Pascoe, 85–103 (London: Routledge, 2013); Laurie Langbauer, *The Juvenile Tradition: Young Writers and Prolepsis, 1750–1835* (Oxford: Oxford University Press, 2016).

CHAPTER ONE: READING SERIALLY

1. On the influence of English moral weeklies on German periodicals, see Ruth-Ellen Joeres, "The German Enlightenment (1720–1790)," in *The Cambridge History of German Literature,* ed. Helen Watanabe-O'Kelly (Cambridge: Cambridge University Press, 2008), 197–98.

2. Despite the historical prevalence of these texts, Hubert Göbels's assessment that children's periodicals were neglected in German scholarship of the 1970s largely holds true today. Göbels, ed., *Das Leipziger Wochenblatt für Kinder (1772–1774): eine Studie über d. älteste deutschsprachige Kinderzeitschrift* (1772–1774; reprint of collected issues, Ratingen: Aloys Henn, 1973), 1.

3. Half of the periodicals in this set were explicitly aimed at girls and half at a general audience. Most (49) were originally published between 1770 and 1835. Publication places included traditional Central European printing strongholds such as Leipzig, Tübingen, Berlin, and Vienna, as well as smaller towns such as Altenburg and Gotha, and some French titles. Some serial publications, both annual and irregularly issued, were printed in a form more like a book than a twenty-first-century magazine, while others were collected and bound or reprinted in codex form. These volumes were more likely to have been persevered in research libraries than were individual weekly issues.

4. The surprisingly influential *Für deutsche Mädchen: Eine Wochenschrift* (1781–82) only ran for one year, for instance, while *Das Pfennig-Magazin für Kinder* (1833–55) lasted twenty-two years.

5. For example, Karl Engelhardt's homage to Weiße, the *Neuer Kinderfreund* (Leipzig, Vienna, and Prague: Barth and Franz Haas, 1796–99) was published more frequently and in a richer format in its last volume of 1799.

6. From a significant body of scholarship on women authors in the German Enlightenment (many of whom wrote for a youth audience), see Ruth-Ellen Joeres and Mary Jo Maynes, eds., *German Women in the Eighteenth and Nineteenth Centuries: A Social and Literary History* (Bloomington: Indiana University Press, 1986); Ulrike Weckel, "The Brief Flowering of Women's Journalism and Its End around 1800," in *Gender in Transition: Discourse and Practice in German-Speaking Europe, 1750–1830*, ed. Ulrike Gleixner and Marion Gray (Ann Arbor: University of Michigan Press, 2006), 175–201; Helen Fronius and Anna Richards, eds., *German Women's Writing of the Eighteenth and Nineteenth Centuries: Future Directions in Feminist Criticism* (Oxford: Legenda, 2011).

7. Christian Felix Weiße, *Der Kinderfreund: Ein Wochenblatt für Kinder* (Leipzig: Siegfried Lebrecht Crusius, 1776), I, 4.

8. Nadine Bérenguier, *Conduct Books for Girls in Enlightenment France* (Burlington, VT: Ashgate, 2011), 26.

9. *Leipziger Wochenblatt für Kinder* 1 (1773), 22.

10. Pamela Selwyn cites Reinhard Wittmann that at least one-sixth of works in German advertised between 1770 and 1810 were sold by subscription. Selwyn, *Everyday Life in the German Book Trade: Friedrich Nicolai as Bookseller and Publisher in the Age of Enlightenment, 1750–1810* (University Park: Pennsylvania State University Press, 2000), 76.

11. Jeanne-Marie Leprince de Beaumont, *Magasin des enfans, ou dialogues, entre une sage Gouvernante et plusieurs de ses Élèves de la première distinction: Dans lesquels on fait penser, parler, agir les jeunes Gens suivant la génie, le tempérament, & les inclinations d'un chacun* (1756, Leide: Luzac, 1789–90), 1.

12. Paul Nitsch, *Für deutsche Mädchen,* I (Dresde: H. W. Harpeter, 1781), 3.

13. Hubert Göbels, *Zeitschriften für die deutsche Jugend: Eine Chonographie 1772–1960* (Dortmund: Harenberg Kommunikation, 1986), 28.

14. Weckel, "The Brief Flowering," 185.

15. On the dramatic commercial success of the *Magasin des enfans,* see Barbara Kaltz, "*La Belle et la Bête:* Zur Rezeption der Werke Mme Leprince de Beaumonts im deutschsprachigen Raum," *Romanistische Zeitschrift für Literaturgeschichte* 13, no. 3–4 (1989). See also Bérenguier, *Conduct Books,* 14–15.

16. Göbels, *Zeitschriften,* 108.

17. Leprince de Beaumont, *Magasin des enfans,* v–vi.

18. Ibid., iii.

19. Johann Joachim Schwaben, introduction to *Der Frau Maria le Prince de Beaumont lehrreiches Magazin für Kinder zu richtiger Bildung ihres Verstandes und Herzens für die deutsche Jugend eingerichtet,* by Jeanne-Marie Leprince de Beaumont, trans. Johann Joachim Schwaben (Leipzig: Weidmann, 1761), viii.

20. Ibid., iv.

21. Ibid., x.

22. On Weiße's influence and his role in Enlightenment literary networks, see Katrin Löffler and Ludwig Stockinger, eds., *Christian Felix Weiße und die Leipziger Aufklärung* (Hildesheim: Georg Olm, 2006).

23. Weiße's periodical seems to have been largely unrelated to the series of schoolbooks published under the same name, spawned by Friedrich Eberhard von Rochow. Hubert Göbels, ed., *Der Kinderfreund: Ein Lesebuch zum Gebrauch in Landschulen* (Dortmund: Harenberg, 1979).

24. Adalbert Merget, *Geschichte der deutschen Jugendlitteratur* (Berlin: Plahn, 1882), 21.

25. Samuel Baur, *Charakteristik der Erziehungsschriftsteller Deutschlands: Ein Handbuch für Erzieher* (Leipzig: Johann Benjamin Georg Fleischer, 1790), 556.

26. *Allgemeine Deutsche Bibliothek* vol. 26 (1775): 248.

27. Weiße, *Der Kinderfreund* I, no. 1: 31.

28. Leprince de Beaumont, *Magasin des enfans,* ii.

29. Schwaben, introduction to *Magazin für Kinder,* vi.

30. Göbels, *Zeitschriften,* 8.

31. Kirsten Belgum, "Domesticating the Reader: Women and Die Gartenlaube," *Women in Germany Yearbook* 9 (1993): 99.

32. Weiße, *Der Kinderfreund* I, no. 1: 7.

33. See Matt Erlin, *Necessary Luxuries: Books, Literature, and the Culture of Consumption in Germany, 1770–1815* (Ithaca, NY: Cornell University Press, 2014).

34. Merget, *Geschichte der deutschen Jugendlitteratur,* 21–22.

35. Göbels, *Das Leipziger Wochenblatt für Kinder,* 7.

36. Weiße, *Der Kinderfreund* I, no. 1: 30–31.

37. Christian Carl André, *Der Mädchenfreund* (Leipzig: Crusius 1789–91).

38. "Große Geistesgegenwart einer teutschen Frau: Eine wahre Anekdote," *Flora: Deutschlands Töchtern geweiht: Ein Monatschrift von Freunden und Freundinnen des schönen Geschlechts* year 7, vol. I, no. 1 (Tübingen: Cotta, 1799), 77–79.

39. Christian Gottfried Böckh, *Kinderzeitung,* I, nos. 3 and 4 (Nuremberg: Felseker, 1780–83).

40. Two examples of such periodicals include the *Neues Wochenblatt zum Nuzzen und zur Unterhaltung für Kinder und junge Leute* (Leipzig: Sommer, 1794) and H. E. Pöschl's *Thusnelda: Zeitschrift zur Bildung und Unterhaltung der Jugend* (Vienna: A. Pichler, 1843); the latter actually made recommendations for children's books issued by other publishers.

41. Friedrich Nicolai, ed., *Allgemeine Deutsche Bibliothek* 26 (1775): 248.

42. Nitsch signed all of his essays and stories in *Für deutsche Mädchen* with the initial "N," but a portion of the pieces in this weekly were signed by "R." Göbels speculates that this unknown author may have been a woman. Göbels, *Zeitschriften*, 28.

43. *Für deutsche Mädchen* I, no. 9 (June 2, 1781): 132.

44. *Der Mädchenfreund* I, no. 1: 6.

45. On the changing nature of sociability in Europe at the end of the eighteenth century, see Gillian Russell and Clara Tuite, eds., *Romantic Sociability: Social Networks and Literary Culture in Britain, 1770–1840* (Cambridge: Cambridge University Press, 2006).

46. Weiße, *Der Kinderfreund* I, no. 1: 7–8.

47. Pamela Gay-White and Adrianne Wadewitz, "Introduction: Performing the Didactic," *The Lion and the Unicorn* 33, no. 2 (2009): v–vi.

48. Birgit Prilisauer, "Das Kinderschauspiel der Aufklärung—die Intentionen der Autoren im Kontext der Zeit" (Diplomarbeit, Universität Wien, 2009), 27.

49. *Neujahrsgeschenk für Kinder von einem Kinderfreunde* I (Frankfurt: J. J. Keßler, 1778): 12.

50. Weihnachts-Gespräch zwischen den beyden jungen Reich-Grafen Detlef und Hans, Grafen zu Ranzau und Breitenburg, 1769; Gespräche zwischen August und Konrad, 1784, Abt. 127.21 FA L 34, LAS.

51. John Randolph, *The House in the Garden: The Bakunin Family and the Romance of Russian Idealism* (Ithaca, NY: Cornell University Press, 2007), 41–45.

52. The importance of affectionate, self-sacrificing sibling relationships was paramount in these texts. The play described at the opening of this chapter, Weiße's "Sibling Love," was not even the only story published in a short period with precisely the same title. It would seem there was an epidemic of unloving brothers and sisters at the end of the eighteenth century to correct, but perhaps a more plausible explanation is that authors were deeply concerned with building lateral family bonds for children's adult lives. On sibling ties in modern Europe, see Leonore Davidoff, *Thicker than Water: Siblings and their Relations, 1780–1920* (Oxford: Oxford University Press, 2012); Christopher Johnson and David Sabean, eds., *Sibling Relations and the Transformations of European Kinship, 1300–1900* (New York: Berghahn Books, 2013).

53. J. G. Reinhardt, *Der Mädchenspiegel* (Halle: Johann Jacob Gebauer, 1794), 74.

54. Reinhardt, "Die kluge Wahl," *Der Mädchenspiegel*, 51.

55. Bérenguier, *Conduct Books,* 10.

56. Leprince de Beaumont, *Magasin des enfans,* xiii.

57. *Neujahrsgeschenk* II (1779): 37–53.

58. Ibid., 122.

59. "Wohlthätigkeit einiger jungen Mädchen," *Bildungsblätter oder Zeitung für die Jugend* (March 27, 1806): 296.

60. Weiße, *Der Kinderfreund* I, no. 1: 3–4.

61. This tension has been noted by scholars such as Andrea Kuhn and Johannes Merkel, who claim "hardly any sentimental traits may be found in the children's books of the eighteenth century," but nevertheless locate the roots of sentimental nineteenth-century children's literature in canonical Enlightenment texts. *Sentimentalität und Geschäft: Zur Sozialisation durch Kinder- und Jugendliteratur im 19. Jh.* (Berlin: Basis, 1977), 28.

62. Hina Nazar, *Enlightened Sentiments: Judgment and Autonomy in the Age of Sensibility* (New York: Fordham University Press, 2012), 1–2.

63. Weiße, *Der Kinderfreund* I, no. 1: 7.

64. Adrianne Wadewitz, "'Spare the Sympathy, Spoil the Child': Sensibility, Selfhood, and the Maturing Reader, 1775–1815" (PhD diss., Indiana University, 2011), vii.

65. Weiße, *Der Kinderfreund* I, no. 1: 9.

66. Petra Nickel, *Mädchenzeitschriften: Marketing für Medien* (Münster: Waxmann, 2000), 82.

67. Schwaben, introduction to *Magazin für Kinder,* iv.

68. Leprince de Beaumont, *Magasin des enfans,* xv.

69. Ute Dettmar, "Aufgeklärte Kindheit, Christian Felix Weiße als Autor für Kinder," in *Christian Felix Weiße und die Leipziger Aufklärung,* ed. Katrin Löffler and Ludwig Stockinger (Hildesheim: Georg Olm, 2006), 91.

70. Engelhardt, *Neuer Kinderfreund* (1797), 240.

71. L. F. Jauffret, *Programme du Courrier des enfans* (Paris: Office of the Courrier des Enfans, 1797), 3.

72. Leprince de Beaumont, *Magasin des enfans* (1756): xiii–xiv.

73. Dagmar Grenz notes the "remarkable fact" that at the very beginning of children's literature, books for girls often were the site of innovation. *Mädchenliteratur: Von den moralisch-belehrenden Schriften im 18. Jahrhundert bis zur Herausbildung der Backfischliteratur im 19. Jahrhundert* (Stuttgart: J. B. Metzler, 1981), 31.

74. Ibid., 2–3.

75. It is worth noting that the rise in girls' periodicals coincided with the rise of novels and widespread anxiety about girls' novel-reading. Samuel Richardson, author of the epistolary novels *Pamela* and *Clarissa,* was especially influential in the German book trade.

76. André, *Der Mädchenfreund* I, no. 1: 96.

77. Among this group, for example, were the girls who grew up to enjoy successful careers as authors of women's fiction themselves: Sophie von la Roche, Amalia Schoppe, and Luise Hölder.

78. One of many examples was the piece "The Consequences of Criminal Curiosity (A Story as Warning)" in Johannes Holtz's *Gemüthliche Erzählungen und Geschichten zur Veredlung des jugendlichen Herzens für gesittete Maedchen von 9–12 Jahren* (Nuremberg: C. H. Zeh, 1821), 60–75.

79. Some of the contours of this debate may be seen in Joan Landes, *Women and the Public Sphere in the Age of the French Revolution* (Ithaca, NY: Cornell University Press, 1988); Carla Hesse, *The Other Enlightenment: How French Women Became Modern* (Princeton, NJ: Princeton University Press, 2001); Dena Goodman, *Becoming a Woman in the Age of Letters* (Ithaca, NY: Cornell University Press, 2009).

80. Joan Scott, *Only Paradoxes to Offer: French Feminists and the Rights of Man* (Cambridge, MA: Harvard University Press, 1996), 2–5.

81. Grenz, *Mädchenliteratur,* 64.

82. Gunilla Budde, *Auf dem Weg ins Bürgerleben* (Göttingen: Vanderhoeck & Ruprecht, 1994), 78; David Hamlin, "The Structures of Toy Consumption: Bourgeois Domesticity and Demand for Toys in Nineteenth-Century Germany," *Journal of Social History* 36, no. 4 (2003): 859; Willemijn Ruberg, "Children's Correspondence as a Pedagogical Tool in the Netherlands (1770–1850)," *Pedagogica Historica* 41, no. 3 (2005): 297.

83. Leprince de Beaumont, *Magasin des enfans,* vi–vii.

84. See Belinda Jack, *The Woman Reader* (New Haven, CT: Yale University Press, 2012).

85. *Für Deutschlands edle Töchter, die ausser der Sorgung für den Körper die auch für den Geist können* (Leipzig: Johann Gottfried Graffe, 1801), ii–iv.

86. *Neujahrsgeschenk für Kinder von einem Kinderfreunde* II (1779): 78.

87. Leprince de Beaumont, *Magasin des enfants* (1756), 22.

88. Nancy Armstrong, *Desire and Domestic Fiction: A Political History of the Novel* (New York: Oxford University Press, 1987), 4.

89. Weiße, *Der Kinderfreund* I, no. 1: 9.

90. Ibid., 9–10.

91. Ibid., 13.

92. Ibid., 11.

93. And in fact, in Weiße's sequel publication, *Briefwechsel der Familie des Kinderfreundes* (Reutlingen: Johannes Grözinger, 1792), readers learned that in the interim Karl had left for secondary school and was living in the house of one of his teachers, while Fritz had been sent to apprentice to a tradesman in Berlin.

94. On the consequences of too much separation between bourgeois young women and men, see Edward Ross Dickinson, "'A Dark, Impenetrable Wall of Complete Incomprehension': The Impossibility of Heterosexual Love in Imperial Germany," *Central European History* 40, no. 3 (2007): 467–97.

95. "The Girl among Youths," *Für deutsche Mädchen*, June 2, 1781, 129–55.

96. Antonia Wutka, *Encyklopädie für die Weibliche Jugend* (Prague: Caspar Widtmann, 1802–16), iii.

97. Ibid., 4–9.

98. Leprince de Beaumont, *Magasin des enfans,* xiv–xv.

99. Grenz finds a similar pattern in the texts she studies, with earlier Enlightenment books providing a rational education for girls that emphasized the same virtues as for boys. Grenz, *Mädchenliteratur,* 31.

100. Ibid., 3–4.

101. Selwyn, *Everyday Life,* 38–39.

102. This formulation is borrowed from Joan Kelly, "Did Women Have a Renaissance?," in *Becoming Visible: Women in European History,* ed. Renate Bridenthal and Claudia Koonz (Boston: Houghton Mifflin, 1977), 137–64.

CHAPTER TWO: TELLING TALES

1. Wilhelm Grimm to Anna von Arnswaldt, Berlin, March 2, 1859, in *Freundesbriefe von Wilhelm und Jacob Grimm,* ed. Alexander Reifferscheid (Heilbronn: Henniger, 1878), 188–90. As Grimm noted, this story had already circulated in the German papers before he wrote to von Arnswaldt. The first recorded version of the story likely appeared sometime in 1858 in the *Kölnische Zeitung,* a major daily newspaper. It was retold in a weekly periodical edited by Gustav Kühne: "Wer's nicht glaubt, bezahlt einen Thaler!" *Europa: Chronik der gebildeten Welt* no. 4, January 22, 1859, 140. The account from Wilhelm Grimm's letter, not the newspaper version, seems to have served as source material for most later references to the Märchengroschen story, which appeared occasionally in later publications on both sides of the Atlantic, into the early twentieth century. Von Arnswaldt, née Haxthausen, had been one of the Grimms' informants for the *KHM,* contributing "The Twelve Dancing Princesses"

("Die zertanzten Schuhe," 133), among other tales. See Shawn Jarvis and Jeannine Blackwell, "Introduction to Anna von Haxthausen, 'The Rescued Princess,'" in *The Queen's Mirror: Fairy Tales by German Women, 1780–1900,* ed. Shawn Jarvis and Jeannine Blackwell (Lincoln: University of Nebraska Press, 2001), 127–31.

2. All translations in this chapter are my own. See also the currently definitive English-language translations: for the 1857 edition, Jacob and Wilhelm Grimm, *The Complete Fairy Tales of the Brothers Grimm,* trans. Jack Zipes, 3rd ed. (New York: Bantam Books, 2003); for the 1812/15 edition, Jacob and Wilhelm Grimm, *The Original Folk and Fairy Tales of the Brothers Grimm: The Complete First Edition,* trans. and ed. Jack Zipes (Princeton, NJ: Princeton University Press, 2014).

3. "She was first with Jacob, then Dortchen [Wilhelm's wife] brought her to me." Grimm to von Arnswaldt, Berlin, March 2, 1859. By comparison, the newspaper account is "a sweet anecdote which Jacob Grimm recently experienced, and whose informant is the worthy scholar himself." *Europa,* January 22, 1859, 140.

4. "The Clever Little Tailor" ("Vom klugen Schneiderlein," 114) had been part of the *KHM* since its first edition. By scholarly convention, I use tale numbers from the 1857 edition.

5. Ruth Bottigheimer mentions the Märchengroschen story in passing as an exception to the general paucity of direct evidence concerning children's reception of fairy tales. "The Publishing History of Grimms' Tales: Reception at the Cash Register," in *The Reception of Grimms' Fairy Tales,* ed. Donald Haase (Detroit: Wayne State University Press, 2004), 79. Ruth Michaelis-Jena also describes the encounter in her biography of the Grimm brothers. *The Brothers Grimm* (New York: Praeger, 1970), 156.

6. *Europa,* January 22, 1859, 140.

7. Ingeborg Weber-Kellermann, foreword to *Kinder- und Hausmärchen gesammelt durch die Brüder Grimm* (Frankfurt: Insel, 1976), 14.

8. Mary Jo Maynes, "Class Cultures and Images of Proper Family Life," in *History of the European Family,* vol. 2, *Family Life in the Long Nineteenth Century,* ed. David I. Kertzer and Marzio Barbagli (New Haven, CT: Yale University Press, 2002), 195.

9. Jacob and Wilhelm Grimm, *Kinder- und Hausmärchen: Die handschriftliche Urfassung von 1810,* ed. Heinz Rölleke (Stuttgart: Philipp Reclam, 2007). This manuscript edition is referred to hereafter as "*KHM* 1810."

10. See the discussion of these terms in Jack Zipes, "Introduction: Towards a Definition of the Literary Fairy Tale," in *The Oxford Companion to Fairy Tales,* ed. Jack Zipes (Oxford: Oxford University Press, 2000), xv–xxxii. The most useful typology of Western folklore still referenced by folklorists is the Aarne-Thompson Index (first developed by Antti Aarne in 1910), in which tale types were assigned numbers according to their common motifs and features.

11. For more on the oral versus literary origins of fairy tales, see a special issue of the *Journal of American Folklore* 123, no. 490 (2010). Also see the debate sparked by Ruth B. Bottigheimer's controversial *Fairy Tales: A New History* (Albany: State University of New York Press, 2009). For an example of a study that directly engages with folk culture and oral literature as historical evidence, see David Hopkin, *Voices of the People in Nineteenth-Century France* (Cambridge: Cambridge University Press, 2012).

12. Among others, see Linda Dégh, "What Did the Grimm Brothers Give to and Take from the Folk?," in *The Brothers Grimm and Folktale,* ed. James M. McGlathery (Urbana: University of Illinois Press, 1988), 66–90; Harvey Graff, ed., *Literacy and Social Development in the*

West: A Reader (Cambridge: Cambridge University Press, 1981); Walter Ong, *Orality and Literacy: The Technologizing of the Word* (London: Methuen, 1982).

13. Jack Zipes, "Cross-Cultural Connections and the Contamination of the Classical Fairy Tale," in *The Great Fairy Tale Tradition,* ed. Jack Zipes (New York: W. W. Norton, 2001), 845–69.

14. Straparola authored a sixteenth-century Decameron-like collection of seventy-five stories told within a frame narrative; see W. G. Waters, "Terminal Essay," *The Italian Novelists: The Facetious Nights of Straparola* (London: The Society of Bibliophiles, 1901), volume IV, 237–74. Basile's seventeenth-century collection of fifty tales, that became known as *Il Pentamerone,* was later championed by the Grimms; see Nancy L. Canepa, *From Court to Forest: Giambattista Basile's 'Lo cunto de li cunti' and the Birth of the Literary Fairy Tale* (Detroit: Wayne State University Press, 1999). D'Aulnoy, author of the first published literary fairy tale in French, was part of a group of seventeenth-century French salon and court writers of *contes de fées,* as was Charles Perrault. See Lewis Seifert, *Fairy Tales, Sexuality, and Gender in France, 1690–1715: Nostalgic Utopias* (Cambridge: Cambridge University Press, 2006); Lydie Jean, "Charles Perrault's Paradox: How Aristocratic Fairy Tales Became Synonymous with Folklore Conservation," *TRAMES: A Journal of the Humanities and Social Sciences* 11, no. 3 (2007): 276–83.

15. See Betsy Hearne, *Beauty and the Beast: Visions and Revisions of an Old Tale* (Chicago: University of Chicago Press, 1989).

16. Jeanne-Marie Leprince de Beaumont, *Magasin des enfans* (1756; Leide: Luzac, 1789–90), iv–v.

17. See Lewis Seifert, "Madame Le Prince de Beaumont and the Infantilization of the Fairy Tale," in *The Child in French and Francophone Literature,* ed. Buford Norman (Amsterdam: Rodopi, 2004), 25–40.

18. Zipes, *Oxford Companion,* xxv.

19. The German term *Märchen* is not solely limited to tales of magic and fairies, although it is most often translated as "fairy tale" in English. Etymologically, it is a diminutive derivation of the Middle German word *maere* or *māri,* meaning narration, story, or news. In the late Middle Ages, it came to mean a fictional tale. Calvert Watkins, ed., *The American Heritage Dictionary of Indo-European Roots* (New York: Houghton Mifflin Company, 2000), 51; Max Lüthi, *Märchen* (Stuttgart: J. B. Metzler, 2004), 3.

20. Christian Fürchtegott Gellert, *C. F. Gellerts sämtliche Fabeln und Erzählungen in drey Büchern* (Leipzig: Caspar Fritsch, 1795). Freiligrath's collection of children's books and school texts has been preserved at the Lippische Landesbibliothek in Detmold. In what might appear a trivial connection, it was Ferdinand Freiligrath's daughter, Käthe (Kate) Freiligrath-Kroeker, who later translated Clemens Brentano's fairy tales into English. But this was not purely coincidence. Rather, Freiligrath-Kroeker's interest in the collection reflects the cementing of an association between childhood and fairy tales from her father's generation to her own. Consider her introduction to the Brentano translation: "Familiar as these tales have been to me from my childhood, and household words as many of them have become to me, it has been with real delight that I have given them an English dress; and I am proud to be the first to introduce them to English children, trusting that they, too, may come to love the name of Brentano with those of Andersen and Grimm." *Fairy Tales from Brentano,* trans. Kate Freiligrath-Kroeker (London: T. Fisher Unwin, 1885): xxii–xxiii. Freiligrath-Kroeker likely gained her facility in English (as well as her later home and career) during the years her family lived in exile because of Ferdinand Freiligrath's political activities around the 1848 revolutions.

21. Denis Sweet, "Introduction to Beneditke Naubert, 'The Cloak,'" in *Bitter Healing: German Women Writers 1700–1830: An Anthology,* ed. Jeannine Blackwell and Susanne Zantop (Lincoln: University of Nebraska Press, 1990), 201–6.

22. Astrid Münder, "Women's Roles in Fairy Tales: A Comparison of the Portrayal of Women in 'Marienkind' of the Brothers Grimm and Benedikte Naubert's 'Ottilie'" (master's thesis, West Virginia University, 2002), 33.

23. On von Arnim, see Roswitha Burwig and Bernd Fischer, eds., *Neue Tendenzen der Arnimforschung: Edition, Biographie, Interpretation* (Bern: Peter Lang, 1990). On Brentano, see John F. Fetzer, *Clemens Brentano* (Boston: Twayne Publishers, 1981).

24. I follow Elke Frederiksen, Katherine Goodman, and others in using this version of Bettina Bretano-von Arnim's name, despite possible variations. (In chapter four, I simply use her birth name, since all references are to the writer as a child.) See Elke P. Frederiksen and Katherine R. Goodman, "'Locating' Bettina Brentano-von Arnim, a Nineteenth Century German Woman Writer," in *Bettina Brentano-von Arnim: Gender and Politics,* ed. Elke Frederiksen and Katherine Goodman (Detroit: Wayne State University Press, 1995), 32n2.

25. For more on these literary and familial circles, see Shawn Jarvis, "Trivial Pursuit? Women Deconstructing the Grimmian Model in the *Kaffeterkreis,*" in *The Reception of Grimms' Fairy Tales: Responses, Reactions, Revisions,* ed. Donald Haase (Detroit: Wayne State Press, 1993), 102–26.

26. Achim von Arnim and Clemens Brentano, *Des Knaben Wunderhorn: Alte deutsche Lieder,* ed. Heinz Rölleke (1805 and 1808; repr. Stuttgart: Philipp Reclam, 2006).

27. *KHM* 1810.

28. Wilhelm Hauff, although largely overlooked in the English-reading world, is still known and popular in Germany today, particularly for his story "Der Zwerg Nase" ("Dwarf Long Nose," 1826). In the prefatory frame to Hauff's first collection, a personified "Mährchen" disguises herself as an "Almanac" in order to gain entrance to a city after having been rejected by guards with sharp pens (allegorical censors). Even though the subtitle "for the sons and daughters of the educated classes" is misleading—Hauff intended his tales for adult eyes—it attests that by the 1820s the German market had begun to equate children and fairy tales. See Maureen Thum, "Misreading the Cross-Writer: The Case of Wilhelm Hauff's *Dwarf Long Nose,*" *Children's Literature* 25 (1997): 1–23. Ludwig Bechstein, who published his *Deutsches Märchenbuch* in 1845 and *Neues Deutsches Märchenbuch* in 1856, outsold even the Grimms for some years in the mid-nineteenth century, according to Ruth Bottigheimer's calculations. See Ruth B. Bottigheimer, "Ludwig Bechstein," in *The Teller's Tale: Lives of the Classic Fairy Tale Writers,* ed. Sophie Raynard (Albany: State University of New York Press, 2012), 153–61; Ruth Bottigheimer, "Ludwig Bechstein's Fairy Tales: Nineteenth Century Bestsellers and Bürgerlichkeit," *Internationales Archiv für Sozialgeschichte der deutschen Literatur* 15, no. 2 (1990): 55–88. Bechstein's first collection did not appear until the end of the period surveyed in this book, although Bottigheimer has suggested that the buying public were better acquainted with Bechstein than with Grimm in the 1860s. Ruth B. Bottigheimer, "The Publishing History of Grimms' Tales: Reception at the Cash Register," in *The Reception of Grimms' Fairy Tales,* ed. Donald Haase (Detroit: Wayne State University Press, 2004), 78–101.

29. Husain Haddawy, "Introduction," in *Arabian Nights,* trans. Husain Haddawy (New York: W. W. Norton, 1990), ix–xxix.

30. Galland's version of the *Arabian Nights* seems to have had more influence than did Richard Burton's "unexpurgated" edition (1885) on the popular circulation of these stories in German

markets. The first German translation, based on Galland's text, appeared in 1712. See Ernst-Peter Wieckenberg, *Johann Heinrich Voß und "Tausend und eine Nacht"* (Würzburg: Verlag Königshausen & Neumann, 2002); Otto Spies, *Orientalische Stoff in den Kinder- und Hausmärchen der Brüder Grimm* (Walldorf, Germany: H. Vorndran, 1952).

31. Maria Tatar, "Denmark's Perfect Wizard," in *The Annotated Hans Christian Andersen,* ed. Maria Tatar (New York: W. W. Norton, 2008), xv–xxxvi.

32. On the close relationship between the nineteenth-century Danish and German press (Andersen and Grimm were translated into each other's languages first), see Cay Dollerup, *Tales and Translation: The Grimm Tales from Pan-Germanic Narratives to Shared International Fairy Tales* (Amsterdam: J. Benjamins, 1999).

33. Ibid., 66–67.

34. For example, the forest holds profound metaphorical significance in the *KHM*. See Jack Zipes, *The Brothers Grimm: From Enchanted Forests to the Modern World* (New York: Palgrave Macmillan, 2002), 65–68.

35. Ibid., 9–14.

36. H. Gerstner, *Die Brüder Grimm: Ihr Leben und Werk in Selbstzeugnissen, Briefen und Aufzeichnungen* (Ebenhausen bei München: Wilhelm Langewiesche-Brandt, 1952).

37. Zipes, *The Brothers Grimm,* 2–6.

38. Ibid., 28.

39. James Sheehan writes that Jacob Grimm "believed that the aim of historical study was to discover the hidden unities at the root of contemporary complexity." *German History, 1770–1866* (New York: Oxford University Press, 1989), 449–50.

40. Dollerup, *Tales and Translation,* 5.

41. Hermann Rebel, "Why Not 'Old Marie' . . . Or Someone Very Much Like Her? A Reassessment of the Question about the Grimms' Contributors from a Social Historical Perspective," *Social History* 13, no. 1 (1988): 2.

42. The precise source for each tale in the *KHM* has been a subject of vigorous inquiry and debate for nearly two hundred years. See, among others, Wilhelm Schoof, *Zur Entstehungsgeschichte der Grimmschen Märchen* (Hamburg: Hauswedell, 1959); the polemical John M. Ellis, *One Fairy Story Too Many: The Brothers Grimm and Their Tales* (Chicago: University of Chicago Press, 1983); Heinz Rölleke, *Grimms Märchen und ihre Quellen: Die literarischen Vorlagen der Grimmschen Märchen synoptisch vorgestellt und kommentiert* (Trier: Wissenschaftlicher Verlag, 1998).

43. Jacob and Wilhelm Grimm, "Vorrede," *Kinder- und Hausmärchen* 1812/15 (Frankfurt: Fischer, 1962), 7.

44. Ibid., 12.

45. While most scholars agree that Wilhelm Grimm was primarily responsible for the editing that reshaped the *KHM* from the second full edition of 1819 onwards, I have chosen to refer to "the Grimms" as editors; the collection continued to be published under both brothers' names and Jacob did not step away entirely from the project.

46. Bottigheimer, "Reception at the Cash Register," 78–101.

47. On the Grimms' transformation of the original edition to a more stylized form intended for children, see, among others, Ellis, *One Fairy Story Too Many*; Zipes, *The Complete Fairy Tales of the Brothers Grimm,* xxiii–xxxviii; Ruth Bottigheimer, *Grimms' Bad Girls and Bold Boys* (New Haven, CT: Yale University Press, 1987); Maria Tatar, *The Hard Facts of the Grimms' Fairy Tales* (Princeton, NJ: Princeton University Press, 2003), 252.

48. "Vorrede," *KHM* 1812/15, 237.

49. "Vorrede," *Kinder- und Hausmärchen* 1819, reprinted in *Kinder- und Hausmärchen* 1857, ed. Heinz Rölleke (Stuttgart: Philipp Reclam, 1980), vol. 1: 17.

50. Hans-Jörg Uther, *The Types of International Folktales: A Classification and Bibliography, Based on the System of Antti Aarne and Stith Thompson* (Helsinki: Academia Scientiarum Fennica, 2004).

51. Psychoanlayst Bruno Bettelheim's popular book *The Uses of Enchantment: The Meaning and Importance of Fairy Tales* (New York: Knopf, 1976) provoked passionate critiques. Bettelheim's analysis was based on the 1857 edition of the Grimms' *KHM,* although he claimed universal truths could be found in these tales. By failing to reckon with the particular historical moment in which those versions were created, he neglected the social behavior and material experience reflected in fairy tales beyond their symbols of Oedipal conflict or wish fulfillment.

52. Foundational Marxist writing on fairy tales comes from Walter Benjamin and Ernst Bloch, popularized by Jack Zipes. See Andrew Teverson, "Marxism," in *The Routledge Companion to Media and Fairy Tale Cultures,* ed. Pauline Greenhill, et al. (New York: Routledge, 2018), 47–55.

53. Structuralist approaches to the fairy tale are exemplified by Vladimir Propp, *Morphology of the Folktale,* 2nd ed., trans. Laurence Scott (1928; Austin: University of Texas Press, 1968).

54. See, for example, Kay Stone, "Feminist Approaches to the Interpretations of Fairy Tales," in *Fairy Tales and Society,* ed. Ruth Bottigheimer (Philadelphia: University of Pennsylvania Press, 1986), 229–34; Donald Haase, ed., *Fairy Tales and Feminism: New Approaches* (Detroit: Wayne State University Press, 2004); Betsy Hearne and Roberta Seelinger Trites, eds., *A Narrative Compass: Stories that Guide Women's Lives* (Urbana: University of Illinois Press, 2009); Vanessa Joosen, *Critical and Creative Perspectives on Fairy Tales: An Intertextual Dialogue between Fairy-Tale Scholarship and Postmodern Retellings* (Detroit: Wayne State University Press, 2011).

55. The twenty-first century has witnessed especially meaningful exchanges between scholarly, political, and personal approaches to fairy tales in popular culture. One record of such conversations may be found at SurLaLune Fairy Tales (http://www.surlalunefairytales.com).

56. Robert Darnton, "The Meaning of Mother Goose," *New York Review of Books,* February 2, 1984; "An Exchange on Mother Goose: Jack Zipes and Irving B. Harrison, reply by Robert Darnton," *New York Review of Books,* May 10, 1984.

57. Zipes, *Oxford Companion,* xxi.

58. Exemplary sociohistorical takes on the fairy tale that inform this study include Eugen Weber, "Fairies and Hard Facts: The Reality of Folktales," *Journal of the History of Ideas* 42, no. 1 (1981): 93–113; Bottigheimer, *Grimms' Bad Girls and Bold Boys;* McGlathery, ed., *Brothers Grimm and Folktale;* Haase, ed., *Reception of Grimms' Fairy Tales;* Marina Warner, *From the Beast to the Blonde: On Fairy Tales and Their Tellers* (London: Chatto & Windus, 1994); Tatar, *Hard Facts;* Hopkin, *Voices of the People.* See also the special issue "Jack Zipes and the Sociohistorical Study of Fairy Tales," *Marvels & Tales* 16, no. 2 (2002); and Charlotte Trinquet's extensive entry on "Sociohistorical Approaches," in *The Greenwood Encyclopedia of Folktales and Fairy Tales* (Westport, CT: Greenwood Press, 2008), 887–90. For studies specifically addressing the pedagogic function of fairy tales within the German context, see Quirin Gerstl, *Die Brüder Grimm als Erzieher: Pädagogische Analyse des Märchens* (Munich: Franz Ehrenwirth, 1964); Ulrike Bastian, *Die "Kinder- und Hausmärchen" der Brüder Grimm in der literaturpädagogischen Diskussion des 19. und 20. Jahrhunderts* (Frankfurt: Haag & Herchen, 1981).

59. This includes the exhaustive work of Alan Dundes, such as his *Little Red Riding Hood: A Case Book* (Madison: University of Wisconsin Press, 1988); detailed studies of particular tale types, such as Betsy Hearne, *Beauty and the Beast: Visions and Revisions of an Old Tale* (Chicago: University of Chicago Press, 1989); and Heinz Rölleke's authoritative textual analysis and editions of the Grimms, such as *Grimms Märchen und ihre Quellen: Die literarischen Vorlagen der Grimmschen Märchen synoptisch vorgestellt und kommentiert* (Trier: Wissenschaftlicher Verlag, 1998).

60. Jacob and Wilhelm Grimm, *Kinder und Hausmärchen, dritter Band: Anmerkungen zu den einzelnen Märchen,* ed. Heinz Rölleke (1856; annotated edition, Stuttgart: Philipp Reclam, 1980), 15. However, Heinz Rölleke argues that this should really be attributed to the Wild family (Wilhelm's future in-laws), with some literary "contaminations." *KHM* 1810, 115.

61. Maria Tatar, *The Annotated Brothers Grimm* (London: W. W. Norton, 2004), 3.

62. *KHM* 1810, 46.

63. *KHM* 1812/15, 19.

64. Jacob and Wilhelm Grimm, *Kinder- und Hausmärchen* (1857; repr. Stuttgart: Reclam, 1980), vol. 1: 31–32. (This two-volume edition is referred to hereafter as "*KHM* 1857.")

65. *KHM* 1857, vol. 1: 30.

66. Particularly telling illustrations of the link between filial obedience and industry may be found in "Die zwei Brüder" ("The Two Brothers," 60), "Die Drei Spinnerinnen" ("The Three Spinners," 14), and "Rumpelstilzchen" ("Rumpelstiltskin," 55). The latter two cases present parents who are so ashamed of their children's obstinate laziness that they tell fantastic lies about those daughters' abilities. Meanwhile, girls' responses to matches arranged by their parents are especially striking in "Des Teufels rußiger Brüder" ("The Devil's Sooty Brother," 100) and "Der Bärenhäuter" ("The Bearskin," 101).

67. *KHM* 1857, vol. 1: 226.

68. Meier Teddy was possibly a pseudonym for Friedrich de la Motte Fouqué, one of many writers experimenting with fairy tale forms and material in the early nineteenth century. While the source is usually attributed to a *Frauentaschenbuch* (*Women's Pocket Book*) published in 1823, I have discovered the same poem reprinted in a digest from 1822, suggesting an earlier publication: Meier Teddy, "Klein Bäschen und Frau Trude: Ammenmährchen," *Der Sammler: Ein Unterhaltungsblatt* 14 (December 7, 1822): 586–7. See Hans-Jörg Uther, ed., *Brüder Grimm Kinder- und Hausmärchen,* vol. 4, *Nachweise und Kommentare* (Munich: Eugen Diederich, 1996), 88; Walter Scherf, *Die Herausforderung des Dämons: Form und Funktion grausiger Kindermärchen* (Munich: K. G. Saur, 1987), 135–9. For an intriguing reading of this tale, see Kay Turner, "Playing with Fire: Transgression as Truth in Grimms' 'Frau Trude,'" in *Transgressive Tales: Queering the Grimms,* ed. Turner and Pauline Greenhill (Detroit: Wayne State University Press, 2012), 245–76.

69. Teddy, "Klein Bäschen und Frau Trude," 587.

70. "Es war einmal eine alte Geis, die hatte sieben junge Geislein, und hatte sie lieb, wie eine Mutter ihre Kinder lieb hat." *KHM* 1857, vol. 1: 51. "Es war einmal eine Geis, die hatte 7 junge Geiserchen." *KHM* 1810, 18. "Eine Geis hatte sieben Junge, die sie gar lieb hatte und sorgfältig vor dem Wolf hütete." Grimm, *KHM* 1812/15, vol. 1: 17. "Eine Geis hatte sieben junge Geislein, die sie recht mütterlich liebte und sorgfältig vor dem Wolf hütete." Grimm, *KHM* 1819, vol. 1: 25.

71. *KHM* 1810, 25.

72. *KHM* 1812/15, vol. 1: 49–50.

73. *KHM* 1857, vol. 1: 100.

74. On the connection between fairy tale plots about stepmothers as villains and demographic realities, see, among others, Maryanne Kowaleski, "Singlewomen in Medieval and Early Modern Europe: The Demographic Perspective," in *Singlewomen in the European Past, 1250–1800*, ed. Judith M. Bennett and Amy M. Froide, 38–81 (Philadelphia: University of Pennsylvania Press, 1999); Harold Neeman, *Piercing the Magic Veil: Toward a Theory of the Conte* (Tübingen: Gunter Narr, 1999).

75. *KHM* 1810, 77.

76. *KHM* 1857, vol. 1: 75.

77. *KHM Anmerkungen* 1856, 52.

78. Uther, *Nachweise und Kommentare*, 50–51.

79. Johann Michael Moscherosch, *Geschichte Philanders von Sittewalt* (Straßburg: Josias Städeln, 1650), 929.

80. On the extent and meaning of companionate marriage, see Peter Borscheid, "Romantic Love or Material Interest: Choosing Partners in Nineteenth-Century Germany," *Journal of Family History* 11, no. 3 (1986): 157–68; Lynn Abrams, "Companionship and Conflict: The Negotiation of Marriage Relations in the Nineteenth Century," in *Gender Relations in German History: Power, Agency and Experience from the Sixteenth to the Twentieth Century*, ed. Lynn Abrams and Elizabeth Harvey (Durham, NC: Duke University Press, 1997), 101–21; Josef Ehmer, "Marriage," in *Family Life in the Long Nineteenth Century*, 282–321.

81. In "Die Hochzeit der Frau Füchsin" ("The Wedding of Mrs. Fox," 38), the widowed Mrs. Fox chooses a new husband who would share mice with her. The mother in "Die Brautschau" ("Choosing a Bride," 155) advises her son to watch his three prospective spouses slice into cheese and choose a wife who is not gluttonous, but thrifty, peeling off just enough rind of the cheese. Poor girls are chosen for their magical spinning ability as "dowry enough" in "The Three Spinners" and "Rumpelstiltskin."

82. *KHM* 1819, vol. 1: 206; *KHM* 1857, vol. 1: 208.

83. See, for example, "Lieb und Leid Teilen" ("Sharing Joys and Sorrows," 170) or "Die Hagere Liese" ("Lean Liese," 168).

84. *KHM* 1857, vol. 2: 360.

85. *KHM* 1857, vol. 2: 354.

86. Viviana Zelizer, *Pricing the Priceless Child: The Changing Social Value of Children* (Princeton, NJ: Princeton University Press, 1994).

87. See, for example, "Rumpelstiltskin" and "Die drei Schwestern" ("The Three Sisters," 82).

88. *KHM* 1857, vol. 1: 206. Among others, this category includes "Daumesdick" ("Thumbling," 37), "De drei Vügelkens" ("The Three Little Birds," 96), "Fundvogel" ("Foundling Bird," 51), and "Der Teufel mit dem drei goldenen Haaren" ("The Devil with the Three Gold Hairs," 29).

89. *KHM* 1812/15, vol. 1: 351.

90. *KHM* 1819, vol. 1: 272.

91. *KHM* 1812/15, vol. 1: 291–2.

92. *KHM* 1819, 434.

93. *KHM* 1812/15, vol. 2: 124.

94. *KHM* 1857, vol. 2: 108.

95. Grimm to von Arnswaldt, Berlin, March 2, 1859.

96. However, the newspaper version does report that she described the *KHM* as "beautiful fairy tales." *Europa*, January 22, 1859, 140.

97. Ibid.

98. Wolfgang Iser, *The Act of Reading: A Theory of Aesthetic Response* (Baltimore: Johns Hopkins University Press, 1978); Elizabeth Freund, *The Return of the Reader: Reader-Response Criticism* (London: New Accents, 1987).

99. Dundes, *Little Red Riding Hood*; Jack Zipes, *The Trials and Tribulations of Little Red Riding Hood* (New York: Routledge, 1993).

100. For a taste of this earlier tradition in the case of "Red Riding Hood," see Paul Delarue's synthetic tale "The Story of Grandmother," in Paul Delarue and Marie-Louise Tenèze, *Le conte populaire français: Catalogue raisonnée des versions de France* (Paris: Maisonneuve & Larose, 2002).

101. Hopkin, *Voices of the People*, 172.

102. *KHM* 1812/15, vol. 2: 93.

103. For a provocative engagement with both Zipes and Dawkins, see Gregory Schrempp, "Taking the Dawkins Challenge, or, The Dark Side of the Meme," *Journal of Folklore Research* 46, no. 1 (2009): 91–100.

104. Jack Zipes, "What Makes a Repulsive Frog so Appealing: Memetics and Fairy Tales," *Journal of Folklore Research* 45, no. 2 (2008): 110.

105. See Ong, *Orality and Literacy*, 33–36.

106. *KHM* 1857, vol. 1: 264.

107. *KHM* 1857, vol. 2: 364.

108. *KHM* 1857, vol. 2: 286.

109. Quoted in Iurii Akutin, "Aleksandr Vel'tman i ego roman 'Strannik,'" an afterword to A. F. Vel'tman, *Strannik* [The Wanderer] (Moscow: Nauka, 1978), 248–9. Thanks to Stephen Bruce for the recommendation and translation.

110. The strange position of the Virgin Mary in this tale may be a critique of Catholic piety, but it has also been read through other lenses. See, for example, G. Ronald Murphy, *The Owl, the Raven, and the Dove: The Religious Meaning of the Grimms' Magic Fairy Tales* (Oxford: Oxford University Press, 2002).

111. *KHM* 1857, vol. 1: 38.

112. *KHM* 1857, vol. 1: 41.

113. *KHM* 1857, vol. 1: 92.

114. *KHM* 1857, vol. 2: 247–8.

115. Jane Austen, *Northanger Abbey* (1817; repr., Rockville, MD: Arc Manor, 2008), 179.

116. *KHM* 1857, vol. 1: 208.

117. Rosemary Jackson, *Fantasy: The Literature of Subversion* (London: Methuen, 1981), 3–4.

118. Ibid., 10.

CHAPTER THREE: READING THE WORLD

1. In 1814, Hamburg was besieged by the French for five months during the Napoleonic Wars.

2. Luise Vorwerk, diary, April 29–30, 1842, 1682 / II, DTA.

3. On the professional development of geography, see Iris Schröder, *Das Wissen von der ganzen Welt: Globale Geographien und räumliche Ordnungen Afrikas und Europas 1790–1870*

(Paderborn: Schöningh, 2011). For connections between geographic literacy and identity formation, see Martin Brückner, *The Geographic Revolution in Early America: Maps, Literacy, and National Identity* (Chapel Hill: University of North Carolina Press, 2006).

4. This is in contrast to the medieval curriculum of the *trivium* (grammar, rhetoric, and logic) and *quadrivium* (arithmetic, geometry, astronomy, and music).

5. Georg Christian Raff, *Geographie für Kinder* (Göttingen: Johann Christian Dieterich, 1776), 2. Raff's book, covering the geography of Europe and Russia in two parts with a foreword by Johann Georg Heinrich Feder, went through multiple editions from 1776 to 1792 in Göttingen, including a posthumous publication by the well-known pedagogue Christian Carl André.

6. Ibid., vi–vii.

7. Thomas Nipperdey summed up the fundamental importance of Napoleon to this period of German history best with the pithy opening sentence of his more than eight-hundred-page survey: "In the beginning was Napoleon." *Deutsche Geschichte 1800–1866: Bürgerwelt und starker Staat* (Munich: Beck, 1983), 11. On the German colonial imagination in the eighteenth century, see Susanne Zantop, *Colonial Fantasies: Conquest, Family, and Nation in Precolonial Germany, 1770–1870* (Durham, NC: Duke University Press, 1997). On the eighteenth-century revolution in technologies of knowledge, see Daniel Headrick, *When Information Came of Age: Technologies of Knowledge in the Age of Reason and Revolution, 1700–1850* (Oxford: Oxford University Press, 2000).

8. Charles W. J. Withers and David N. Livingstone, *Geography and Enlightenment* (Chicago: University of Chicago Press, 1999), 19.

9. Chenxi Tang, *The Geographic Imagination of Modernity: Geography, Literature, and Philosophy in German Romanticism* (Stanford, CA: Stanford University Press, 2008), 36.

10. Johann W. M. Henning, *Leitfaden beim methodischen Unterricht in der Geographie* (Iferten [Yverdon-les-Bains]: Literarische Büreau, 1812), 13.

11. Luise Hölder, *Kleine Weltgeschichte: von den ältesten bis auf die neuesten Zeiten in anziehenden, regelmässig fortlaufenden Erzählungen für Kinder von 6 bis 12 Jahren* (Nuremberg & Leipzig: C. H. Zeh, 1823).

12. Raff, *Geographie für Kinder*, 2–3.

13. Johann Günther Friedrich Cannabich, *Kleine Schulgeographie, oder erster Unterricht in der Erdbeschreibung für die unteren und mittleren Schulklassen* (Sondershausen & Weimar: Bernhard Friedrich Voigt, 1818; 1838; 1851), based on his *Lehrbuch der Geographie* (1816).

14. Johann Matthias Schröckh, *Lehrbuch der allgemeine Weltgeschichte: Einleitung zur Universalhistorie: zum Gebrauche bey dem ersten Unterrichte der Jugend* (Berlin & Stettin: Friedrich Nicolai, 1774), viii.

15. Friedrich Nösselt, *Lehrbuch der Weltgeschichte für Töchterschulen und zum Privatunterricht heranwachsender Mädchen*, 2nd ed. (Breslau: Josef Mar, 1827), I:vii.

16. Ibid., I:v.

17. Heinrich Rockstroh, *Erzählungen aus der älteren und mittleren Geschichte: zum ersten gründlichen Unterricht in der Weltgeschichte* (Leipzig: Carl Cnoblauch, 1829), vi; Karl Stein, *Allgemeine Weltgeschichte für die Jugend, zunächst zum Gebrauche für Söhne und Töchter aus den gebildeten Ständen und für Schulen* (Berlin: G. Hayn, 1810).

18. Carl and Adolph von Lüneburg, Schulhefte, 1816–21, Dep. 122 Nr. 92, HSAH.

19. *Vermehrtes Geographisches Handbüchlein für die zarte Jugend* (Mühlhausen: Leopold Andreas Beck, 1770).

20. Friedrich Christian Franz, *Lehrbuch der Länder- und Völkerkunde: Asien, Afrika, Amerika und die neu entdekten Länder* (Stuttgart: Erhard & Löslund, 1790).

21. See Ann Blair, *Too Much to Know: Managing Scholarly Information before the Modern Age* (New Haven, CT: Yale University Press, 2011).

22. Rockstroh, *Erzählungen*, vi.

23. Henning, *Geographie*, 15.

24. August Lüben, *Leitfaden zu einem methodischen Unterricht in der Geographie für Bürgerschulen: mit vielen Aufgaben und Fragen zu mündlicher und schriftlicher Lösung* (Helmstedt: E. G. Fleckeisen, 1850), iii.

25. Schröckh, *Lehrbuch*, iv–v. The *Lehrbuch* was published in at least six editions between 1774 and 1816; the longer, multi-volume *Allgemeine Weltgeschichte für Kinder* was published in at least four editions between 1779 and 1784 in Leipzig.

26. Lüben, *Geographie für Bürgerschulen*, iii–iv.

27. Tang, *Geographic Imagination*, 10.

28. Schröckh, *Lehrbuch*, xi.

29. Cannabich, *Kleine Schulgeographie* (1851).

30. Henning, *Geographie*, 490.

31. Ibid., 31–32.

32. Mark Monmonier, *How to Lie with Maps* (Chicago: University of Chicago Press, 1991), 1.

33. Adam Christian Gaspari, *Lehrbuch der Erdbeschreibung: zur Erläuterung des neuen methodischen Schulatlasses* (Weimar: Geographischen Institut, 1806), 7–8.

34. M. Christian Schulz, *Mungo Park's Reise in Afrika für die Jugend bearbeitet* (Berlin: Schüppel, 1805), 8.

35. Historical atlases were especially popular after the French Revolution. See Jeremy Black, *Maps and History: Constructing Images of the Past* (New Haven, CT: Yale University Press, 1997), 26.

36. For a discussion of the major Justus Perthes publishing house that printed revisions of Stieler's atlases for more than a century, see Max Linke, M. Hoffman, and J. A. Hellen, "Two Hundred Years of the Geographical-Cartographical Institute in Gotha," *The Geographical Journal* 152, no. 1 (1986): 75–80.

37. Karl Ferdinand Weiland, *Compendiöser allgemeiner Atlas der ganzen Erde* (Weimar: Geographischen Institut, 1833).

38. Johann Heckel, *Atlas für die Jugend: und alle Liebhaber der Geographie* (Augsburg: Conrad Heinrich Stage, 1791).

39. Luise Hölder, *Neue Gesellschaftspiele und Unterhaltungen: zum Vergnügen und zur Uebung des Scarfsinns für die Jugend* (Ulm: J. Ebner, 1824), 14.

40. Johann Peter Voit, *Schule des Vergnügens für kleine Kinder* (Nuremberg: Schneider and Weigel, 1803).

41. Nösselt, *Lehrbuch der Weltgeschichte für Töchterschulen*, I:iv.

42. Cannabich, *Kleine Schulgeographie* (1818), I:iv.

43. Feder, foreword to *Geographie für Kinder*, by Raff, ix.

44. Ibid., iv.

45. Schröckh, *Lehrbuch*, iv–v.

46. Just as these developments did not entail utter freedom for children, the previous memorization-driven pedagogy was not always repressive. For example, composer Georg Philipp Telemann created a *Singing Geography* in 1708 with thirty-six songs for voice and continuo based on the geography textbook of Johann Christoph Losius as an entertaining way to aid memorization.

47. Gaspari, *Lehrbuch der Erdbeschreibung*, 12.

48. Carl Grumbach, *Die Reisemappe: enthaltend Auszüge aus Reisebeschreibungen Städteräthsel und Sinngedichte, zur angenehmen und nützlichen Unterhaltung für die mittlere Jugend* (Meißen: C. E. Klinkicht & Sohn, 1828), iii.

49. Henning, *Geographie*, 19.

50. *Die Reise von Prag nach Wien: Ein geographisches Spiel für die Jugend*, c. 1800, Cotsen Children's Library, Princeton University Library, Princeton, NJ. For further discussion of this particular game, see Emily Bruce and Elise Klarenbeek, "Playing on the Map: An Educational Game from the Age of Revolutions," *Journal of the History of Childhood and Youth* 13, no. 1 (Winter 2020): 9–17. Board games have been played for thousands of years around the world, and began to be marketed for European children's use in the late eighteenth century. See David Sidney Parlett, *The Oxford History of Board Games* (Oxford: Oxford University Press, 1999); Caroline G. Goodfellow, "The Development of the English Board Game, 1770–1850," *Board Game Studies*, no. 1 (1998): 70–80; Jill Shefrin, *The Dartons: Publishers of Educational Aids, Pastimes & Juvenile Ephemera, 1787–1876* (Los Angeles: Cotsen Occasional Press, 2009).

51. Bryan Ganaway, *Toys, Consumption, and Middle-class Childhood in Imperial Germany, 1871–1918* (Bern: Peter Lang, 2009); David Hamlin, *Work and Play: The Production and Consumption of Toys in Germany, 1870–1914* (Ann Arbor: University of Michigan Press, 2007).

52. Gotthold Emmanuel Friedrich Seidel, *Jugendkalender für das Jahr 1805* (Nuremberg: J. E. Seidel, 1805). The author was a theologian and occasional writer of works for young readers. Ernst Mummenhoff, "Seidel, Gotthold Emanuel Friedrich," in *Allgemeine Deutsche Biographie* 33 (1891), 619–20. Either the mounted game held at the Cotsen or the periodical version might have been the original—or both could have been copied from an unknown source.

53. Goodfellow, "English Board Game," 74–75. *The Journey from Prague to Vienna* may have been inspired by an earlier English race game made by John Jefferys, *A Journey through Europe, or the Play of Geography* (1759), although they differed significantly in form. Notably, *The Journey from Prague to Vienna* reorients the center of the world from London to the cities of Central Europe. See F. R. B. Whitehouse, *Table Games of Georgian and Victorian Days* (London: Peter Garnett, 1951); Margaret Drabble, *The Pattern in the Carpet: A Personal History with Jigsaws* (New York: Houghton Mifflin, 2009), 106–10.

54. Mary Flanagan, *Critical Play: Radical Game Design* (Cambridge, MA: MIT Press, 2009), 11.

55. Elizabeth Segel, "'As the Twig is Bent . . .': Gender and Childhood Reading," in *Gender and Reading: Essays on Readers, Texts, and Contexts*, ed. Elizabeth Flynn and Patrocinio Schweickart (Baltimore: Johns Hopkins University Press, 1986), 165.

56. Wilhelm Fornet, *Allgemeine Weltgeschichte für Töchter gebildeter Stände: Ein Leitfaden zum Gebrauche in Schulen und zum Selbst-Unterrichte* (Berlin: Rubach, 1840); Christian Oeser, *Weltgeschichte für Töchterschulen und zum Privatunterricht: Mit besonderer Beziehung auf das weibliche Geschlecht* (Leipzig: Einhorn, 1843); Christian Gotthold Neudecker, *Weltgeschichte für Töchterschulen und zum Privatunterrichte für das weibliche Geschlecht von Chr. Oeser*, 3rd ed./1st ed. under Neudecker (Leipzig: Brandstetter, 1848).

57. The *Damen Conversations Lexikon,* a nineteenth-century encyclopedia of topics relating to the instruction of middle-class young ladies, commented on the breadth of Nösselt's publishing for girls, ranging from a geography textbook to a world history reader to a collection of Greek and Roman mythology. Carl Herloßsohn, ed., *Damen Conversations Lexikon,* vol. 7 (Leipzig: Friedrich Volkmar, 1836), 452. In addition to the *Short* and *Long Geography,* Nösselt wrote a *World History Reader for Girls' Schools and the Private Instruction of Young Women* that was published in at least ten editions during his lifetime (*Lehrbuch der Weltgeschichte für Töchterschulen und zum Privatunterricht heranwachsender Mädchen;* my analysis deals with the editions from 1827, 1830, 1835, 1838, and 1842).

58. See Susanne Barth, "Das Goldtöchterchen: Zur geschlechtsspezifischen Erziehung von kleinen Mädchen im Kinderbuch um nach 1800," *Der Deutschunterricht: Beiträge zu Seiner Praxis und Wissenschaftlichen Grundlegung* 42, no. 3 (1990): 61–75; Jennifer Popiel, *Rousseau's Daughters: Domesticity, Education, and Autonomy in Modern France* (Durham: University of New Hampshire Press, 2008).

59. Nösselt, *Lehrbuch der Weltgeschichte für Töchterschulen,* I:iv.

60. Ibid.

61. Ibid., iii–iv.

62. Nösselt also published a book of mythology that apparently influenced a young Thomas Mann. Lewis Lawson, *A Gorgon's Mask: The Mother in Thomas Mann's Fiction* (Amsterdam: Editions Rodopi, 2005), 37.

63. Nösselt, *Lehrbuch der Weltgeschichte für Töchterschulen,* I:iv.

64. Ibid., v–vi.

65. Christian Gotthold Neudecker, *Weltgeschichte für Töchterschulen, und zum Privatunterrichte für das weiblich Geschlecht von Chr. Oeser* (Leipzig: Brandstetter, 1848), I:v.

66. Among others, see Joan Scott, *Only Paradoxes to Offer: French Feminists and the Rights of Man* (Cambridge, MA: Harvard University Press, 1996).

67. Raff, *Geographie für Kinder,* 2–3.

68. Nösselt, *Lehrbuch der Weltgeschichte für Töchterschulen,* I:v.

69. Ibid., viii.

70. Schröckh, *Lehrbuch,* ix.

71. Gaspari, *Lehrbuch der Erdbeschreibung,* 4–5.

72. Henning, *Geographie,* 22–23.

73. Ibid., 52–53, 65.

74. Ibid., 564.

75. Ibid., 483.

76. Schröckh, *Lehrbuch,* ix.

77. Gaspari, *Lehrbuch der Erdbeschreibung,* 6.

78. Rockstroh, *Erzählungen,* I:ix–x.

79. See Roger Stoddard, "Looking at Marks in Books," *Gazette of the Grolier Club,* n.s., 51 (2000); H. J. Jackson, *Marginalia: Readers Writing in Books* (New Haven, CT: Yale University Press, 2001); William H. Sherman, *Used Books: Marking Readers in Renaissance England* (Philadelphia: University of Pennsylvania Press, 2008).

80. Jackson, *Marginalia,* 19.

81. Sherman, *Used Books,* 164.

82. Stephen Orgel, "Margins of Truth," in *The Renaissance Text: Theory, Editing, Textuality*, ed. Andrew Murphy (Manchester: Manchester University Press, 2000), 92.

83. Friedrich Nösselt, *Kleine Geographie für Töchterschulen und die Gebildeten des weiblichen Geschlechts* (Königsberg: Gebrüder Bornträger, 1857). Copy held at location GDG-I 2 (8, 1857) at the Georg-Eckert-Institut für Schulbuchforschung, Braunschweig.

84. Paul Friedrich Achat Nitsch, *Kurzer Entwurf der alten Geographie* (Leipzig: Heinsius, 1792). Copy held at location GEG-I 26 (2, 1792) at the Georg-Eckert-Institut für Schulbuchforschung.

85. Ibid., 292 and 75.

86. Schröckh, *Lehrbuch*. This copy held at location HDG-I 23 (1, 1774) at the Georg-Eckert-Institut für Schulbuchforschung.

87. Schröckh, *Lehrbuch*, 83.

88. *Nouveau dictionnaire de poche français-allemand et allemand-français*, 3rd ed. (Leipzig: Chrétien Théophile Rabenhorst, 1802), vii. This preface is presented bilingually, side-by-side.

89. Johann Günther Friedrich Cannabich, *Lehrbuch der Geographie nach den neuesten Friedensbestimmungen*, 7th ed. (1816; Sondershausen: Bernhard Friedrich Voigt, 1820).

90. Cannabich, *Kleine Schulgeographie* (1851), vi.

91. Tang, *Geographic Imagination*, 42.

92. Henning, *Geographie*, 45–46.

93. According to Iris Schröder, Mungo Park's narrative was a key text in the transnational development of professional and public geography. *Das Wissen von der ganzen Welt*, 9. The legacy of Mungo Park for young readers has stretched far and wide. Kate Ferguson Marsters notes that throughout the nineteenth century, copies of Park's *Travels* were given as school prizes to boys in the United States and Britain. "Introduction," in *Travels in the Interior Districts of Africa, by Mungo Park* (Durham, NC: Duke University Press, 2000), 1–2. In 1997, a journalist for *Natural History* interviewed a Cameroonian who explained his motivation to pursue the so-called bushmeat trade this way: "In school I read the diaries of Mungo Park and *The Adventures of Huckleberry Finn*. I thought if these men can have their adventures, I can have mine too." Michael McRae, "Road Kill in Cameroon," *Natural History*, February 1997, 36–50.

94. Marsters, "Introduction," 2.

95. Schulz, *Mungo Park*, 2.

96. Ibid., 4–5.

97. Ibid., 12–13.

98. On the long history of sexual and spatial metaphors that framed European imaginings of the African continent as an empty, penetrable body, see Jan Nederveen Pieterse, *White on Black: Images of Africa and Blacks in Western Popular Culture* (New Haven, CT: Yale University Press, 1992); Johannes Fabian, *Out of Our Minds: Reason and Madness in the Exploration of Central Africa* (Berkeley: University of California Press, 2000); Jean Comaroff and John Comaroff, "Africa Observed: Discourses of the Imperial Imagination," in *Perspectives on Africa: A Reader in Culture, History, and Representation*, ed. Rory Richard Grinker, Stephen C. Lubkemann, and Christopher B. Steiner (Oxford: Wiley-Blackwell, 2010), 31–43.

99. Schulz, *Mungo Park*, 4.

100. Ibid., 8.

101. Ibid., 6.

102. Ibid., 5.

103. Tim Fulford and Debbie Lee, "Mental Travelers: Joseph Banks, Mungo Park, and the Romantic Imagination," *Nineteenth-Century Contexts* 24, no. 2 (2002): 118.

104. Joachim Heinrich Campe, *Robinson der Jüngere: zur angenehmen und nützlichen Unterhaltung für Kinder* (1780; repr. Stuttgart: Reclam, 2014). See Richard Apgar, "Taming Travel and Disciplining Reason: Enlightenment and Pedagogy in the Work of Joachim Heinrich Campe" (PhD diss., University of North Carolina Press, 2008).

105. Raff, *Geographie für Kinder*, 3.

106. Grumbach, *Die Reisemappe*, iv.

107. Tang, *Geographic Imagination*, 45.

108. Feder in Raff, *Geographie für Kinder*, v–vi.

109. Henning, *Geographie*, 11–12.

110. Tang, *Geographic Imagination*, 249.

111. Josef Annnegarn, *Handbuch der Geographie für die Jugend: mit vielen eingestreuten ausführlichen Nachrichten über die Sitten, Religionen, Lebensweisen fremder Völker, nebst andern nützlichen Notizen* (Münster: Deiter, 1834).

112. J. F. Robert Schneider, *Deutsche Vaterlandskunde, oder das Land der Deutschen mit seinen Gebirgen, Gewässern, Gesteinen, Pflanzen, Thieren und Menschen: Ein Lehr- und Lesebuch für Schule und Haus* (Erlangen: Carl Heyder, 1840), iii–iv.

113. *Vermehrtes Geographisches Handbüchlein*, 15–33.

114. Schneider, *Deutsche Vaterlandskunde*, 2.

115. Ibid., 58.

116. Ibid., 59.

117. For two landmark examinations of *Heimat*, see Celia Applegate, *A Nation of Provincials: The German Idea of Heimat* (Berkeley: University of California Press, 1990); Alon Confino, *The Nation as a Local Metaphor: Württemberg, Imperial Germany, and National Memory, 1871–1918* (Chapel Hill: University of North Carolina Press, 2000).

118. Cannabich, *Kleine Schulgeographie* (1818), I:iii.

119. Johann Joachim Schwaben, "Vorrede des deutschen Herausgebers," *Leprince de Beaumonts Magazin für Kinder* (Leipzig: Weidmann, 1761), xiii.

120. Henning, *Geographie*, 76.

121. For a historical overview of European and American spatial systems for subdividing the globe, see Martin W. Lewis and Kären E. Wigen, *The Myth of Continents: A Critique of Metageography* (Berkeley: University of California Press, 1997).

122. Henning, *Geographie*, 554.

123. On the epistemic violence of defining "civilization" and "progress" by cities, see Thomas C. Patterson, *Inventing Western Civilization* (New York: New York University Press, 1997); Dipesh Chakrabarty, *Provincializing Europe: Postcolonial Thought and Historical Difference* (Princeton: Princeton University Press, 2000); Martin Hall and Patrick Thaddeus Jackson, *Civilizational Identity: The Production and Reproduction of "Civilizations" in International Relations* (New York: Palgrave Macmillan, 2007).

124. Grumbach, *Die Reisemappe*, 218.

125. The orientalist misconception of the harem system has received significant attention by scholars of the Middle East. See, for example, Reina Lewis, *Rethinking Orientalism: Women, Travel and the Ottoman Harem* (London: I.B. Tauris, 2004).

126. Grumbach, *Die Reisemappe*, 63–65.

127. Nösselt, *Lehrbuch der Weltgeschichte für Töchterschulen*, II:11.

128. Zantop, *Colonial Fantasies*, 11.

129. Nösselt, *Lehrbuch der Weltgeschichte für Töchterschulen*, II:13.

130. On the history of racial thought in Europe, see, among others, Michael Banton, *Racial Theories* (Cambridge: Cambridge University Press, 1987).

131. John P. Jackson Jr. and Nadine M. Weidman, *Race, Racism, and Science: Social Impact and Interaction* (New Brunswick, NJ: Rutgers University Press, 2006), 13–24.

132. Friedrich Christian Franz, *Lehrbuch der Länder- und Völkerkunde* (Stuttgart: Erhard & Löslund, 1790), II:142.

133. Karl May, *Mein Leben und Streben: Selbstbiographie* (Freiburg: Friedrich Ernst Fehsenfeld, 1910), 22.

134. Marlies Bugmann, *Savage to Saint: The Karl May Story* (self-pub., 2008), 2.

135. May's autobiography began with a "retelling" of the Fable of Sitara (an Orientalist story mostly of May's invention). The tale is set in an imaginary world whose landmasses form a Pangaea-type continent. The physical connection of these diverse places worked as a geographic fantasy for a travel writer who famously never traveled until the end of his life.

136. Raff, *Geographie für Kinder*, 4.

137. Lucy Sprague Mitchell, *Young Geographers: How They Explore the World and How They Map the World* (New York: Basic Books, 1934), 33.

138. Ibid., 34.

139. Ibid., 35.

CHAPTER FOUR: WRITING HOME

1. Peter Paulsen to his wife and children, October 14, 1850, Nachlass Peter Paulsen, Abt. 399.1113 Nr. 5, LAS.

2. Paulsen eventually became the director of the school for the deaf in Schleswig.

3. An earlier version of this chapter appeared as Emily C. Bruce, "'Each Word Shows How You Love Me': The Social Literacy Practice of Children's Letter Writing (1780–1860)," *Paedagogica Historica* 50, no. 3 (2014): 247–64.

4. Exceptions include some essays in David Barton and Nigel Hall, eds., *Letter Writing as a Social Practice* (Amsterdam: John Benjamins Publishing Company, 2000); Willemijn Ruberg, "Children's Correspondence as a Pedagogical Tool in the Netherlands (1770–1850)," *Pedagogica Historica* 41, no. 3 (2005): 295–312; Kaisa Vehkalahti, "The Urge to See Inside and Cure: Letter-writing as an Educational Tool in Finnish Reform School Education, 1915–1928," *Paedagogica Historica* 44 (2008): 193–205; Amy Harris, "'This I Beg my Aunt May Not Know': Young Letter-Writers in Eighteenth-Century England, Peer Correspondence in a Hierarchical World," *Journal of the History of Childhood and Youth* 2, no. 3 (2009): 333–60; Christopher J. Lee, "Children in the Archives: Epistolary Evidence, Youth Agency, and the Social Meanings of 'Coming of Age' in Interwar Nyasaland," *Journal of Family History* 35, no. 1 (2010): 25–47; Adriana Benzaquén, "'Pray Let None See this Impertinent Epistle': Children's Letters and Children in Letters at the Turn of the Eighteenth Century," *Literary Cultures and Eighteenth-Century Childhoods*, ed. Andrew O'Malley (New York: Palgrave Macmillan, 2018), 75–96; several essays in Kristine Moruzi, Nell Musgrove, and Carla Pascoe Leahy, eds., *Children's Voices from the Past: New Historical and Interdisciplinary*

Perspectives (Basingstoke, UK: Palgrave Macmillan, 2019); Danni Cai, "Power, Politeness, and Print: Children's Letter Writing in Republican China," *Journal of the History of Childhood and Youth* 13, no. 1 (2020): 38–62. From education research, see Criss Jones Díaz, "Literacy as Social Practice," in *Literacies in Childhood: Changing Views, Challenging Practice,* ed. Laurie Makin, Criss Jones Díaz, and Claire McLachlan (Sydney: MacLennan Petty, 2007), 31–42.

5. For valuable studies that examine letters as a genre across historical cases, but do not consider the particular characteristics of children's correspondence, see Alexandru Duțu, Edgar Hösch, and Norbert Oellers, eds., *Brief und Briefwechsel in Mittel- und Osteuropa im 18. und 19. Jahrhundert* (Essen, Germany: Reimar Hobbing, 1989); Roger Chartier, ed., *La Correspondance: Les Usages de la Lettre au XIXe Siècle* (Paris: Arthème Fayard, 1991); Rainer Baasner, ed., *Briefkultur im 19. Jahrhundert* (Tübingen: Max Niemeyer Verlag, 1999); Rebecca Earle, ed., *Epistolary Selves: Letters and Letter-Writers, 1600–1945* (Farnham, UK: Ashgate, 1999); Liz Stanley, "The Epistolarium: On Theorizing Letters and Correspondences," *Auto/Biography* 12 (2004): 201–35.

6. In this attention to the dual nature of letters as sources, I am following recent scholarship that turns to letters not only for historical evidence, but letters *as* evidence. See Mary Jo Maynes, Jennifer Pierce, and Barbara Laslett, *Telling Stories: The Use of Personal Narratives in the Social Sciences and History* (Ithaca, NY: Cornell University Press, 2008), 82–90.

7. Jürgen Habermas, *The Structural Transformation of the Public Sphere: An Inquiry into a Category of Bourgeois Society,* trans. Thomas Burger and Frederick Lawrence (1962; Cambridge, MA: MIT Press, 1991), 48. On the eighteenth century as the "pedagogical century," see, among others, Marion Gray, *Productive Men, Reproductive Women: The Agrarian Household and the Emergence of Separate Spheres during the German Enlightenment* (New York: Berghahn Books, 2000), 135–39.

8. See Liz Stanley, "The Epistolary Gift, the Editorial Third-Party, Counter-Epistolaria: Rethinking the Epistolarium," *Life Writing* 8 (2011): 135–52; Emma Moreton, "Profiling the Female Emigrant: A Method of Linguistic Inquiry for Examining Correspondence Collections," *Gender and History* 24, no. 3 (2012): 617–46.

9. Here and in chapter 5, I have chosen to refer to young writers by their given names to avoid confusion when I am discussing several children from the same family.

10. On the postal system, see Elemér Hantos, *Mitteleuropäischer postverein* (Vienna: W. Braumüller, 1929); Gerhard Brandtner, *Die Post in Ostpreussen: ihre Geschichte von den Anfängen bis ins 20. Jahrhundert* (Lüneburg, Germany: Nordostdeutsches Kulturwerk, 2000); Daniel Headrick, *When Information Came of Age: Technologies of Knowledge in the Age of Reason and Revolution, 1700–1850* (Oxford: Oxford University Press, 2000); Siegfried Grillmeyer, *Habsburgs Diener in Post und Politik: das "Haus" Turn und Taxis zwischen 1745 und 1867* (Mainz: Von Zabern, 2005).

11. Briefe von Charlotte Marie Agnes von Neurath geb. von Erath, Familienarchiv Freiherren von Neurath, Q 3/11 Bü 41, HSAS.

12. A notable example from the French context is Dena Goodman, *Becoming a Woman in the Age of Letters* (Ithaca, NY: Cornell University Press, 2009).

13. Ruth-Ellen Boetcher Joeres, "The German Enlightenment (1720–1790)," in *The Cambridge History of German Literature,* ed. Helen Watanabe-O'Kelly (Cambridge: Cambridge University Press, 2008), 161.

14. Ibid., 162.

15. Brief von Eugen von Seeger, 1801, Familienarchiv von Seeger, Q 3/28 Bü 104–112, HSAS; Briefwechsel zwischen dem Legationsrat Schiffmann und den Prinzen, 1779–82, Herzöge von Schleswig-Holstein-Sonderburg-Augustenburg, Abt. 22 Nr. 95, LAS.

16. Konstantin Dierks, "The Familiar Letter and Social Refinement in America, 1750–1800," in *Letter Writing as a Social Practice*, ed. David Barton and Nigel Hall (Amsterdam: John Benjamins, 2000), 31.

17. "lieber Vater! Kommen Sie bald, u haben Sie mich lieb, und erzehlen mir von den Gemslis [gemsen] u. da will ich wieder an ihnen hinaufe klettern. u. ich will sie auh lieb haben, u wenn sie kommn, bringen Sie Von die schönen Abrilicosen [aprikosen] mit. Dein getreuer Bruder Emil." Emil Herder to Johann Gottfried Herder, September 1788, in *Dein dich zärtlich liebender Sohn: Kinderbriefe aus sechs Jahrhunderten*, ed. F. E. Mencken (Munich: Heimeran, 1965), 76. The late eighteenth and early nineteenth century was a transitional period in German children's use of formal or informal pronouns to address their parents (the "T-V distinction"). Some continued to "siezen" their parents with the formal second person, as in this example. In other cases, children had already begun to use more intimate grammatical structures with their adult relatives. Both forms of address are evident across the letters cited in this study.

18. Nigel Hall, Anne Robinson, and Leslie Crawford, "Young Children's Explorations of Letter Writing," in *Letter Writing as a Social Practice*, 144.

19. Heinrich Lehmann to Caroline Amalie Jessen Lehmann, August 12, 1859, Nachlass Theodor Lehmann, Abt. 399.1094 Nr. 1–2, LAS.

20. Caroline Amalie to Herzog Friedrich Christian II, January 1, 1806, Herzöge von Schleswig-Holstein-Sonderburg-Augustenburg, Abt. 22 Nr. 135, LAS.

21. "grüße ale filmals und blaibe so gesund wi wir dic ferlasen haben ich bin dein dich libender Sohn." Otto von Bismarck to Wilhelmine Luise Mencken, April 27, 1822, in Mencken, *Dein dich zärtlich liebender Sohn*, 180.

22. August Graf von Platen to Friederike Luise Eichler von Platen (née von Auritz), December 19, 1806, in Mencken, *Dein dich zärtlich liebender Sohn*, 124.

23. On the costs associated with the postal system, see Headrick, *When Information Came of Age*, 192.

24. Carl Heinrich Pathe to Johann Peter Pathe and Caroline Dorothea Sophie Pathe (née Bastian), January 1, 1832, Nachlass Carl Heinrich Pathe, E Rep. 200–09, LAB.

25. Wilhelm Herder to Johann Gottfried Herder, February 13, 1789, in Mencken, *Dein dich zärtlich liebender Sohn*, 71.

26. Carl Christian von Seeger to Christoph Dionysius von Seeger, October 30, 1783, Familienarchiv von Seeger, Q 3/28 Bü 7, HSAS.

27. Gabriele von Humboldt to Wilhelm von Humboldt, November 19, 1808, in Mencken, *Dein dich zärtlich liebender Sohn*, 156.

28. Dorothea von Schlözer to August Ludwig von Schlözer, January 29, 1782, in Mencken, *Dein dich zärtlich liebender Sohn*, 53.

29. Gustav Weise to Hermann Weise, 1849, Nachlass Hermann Weise, E Rep. 200–12 Nr. 96, LAB; Luise Herder to Johann Gottfried Herder, October 24, 1788, in Mencken, *Dein dich zärtlich liebender Sohn*, 76.

30. Conrad Meyer to Ferdinand Meyer, August 2, 1831, in Mencken, *Dein dich zärtlich liebender Sohn*, 193.

31. Gustav Weise to Hermann Weise, May 30, 1854, Nachlass Hermann Weise, E Rep. 200–12 Nr. 169, LAB.

32. Similarly, Goodman writes that instruction in letter writing was necessary for French girls because "it was part of the equipment of a modern woman and a primary means of social mobility." *Becoming a Woman,* 2.

33. Examples include G. C. Claudius, *Allgemeiner Briefsteller, nebst einer kurzen Anweisung zu verschiedenen schriftlichen Aufsätzen für das gemeine bürgerliche Geschäftsleben* (Leipzig: Heinrich Gräff, 1804); *Briefe für Kinder, nebst einer kurzen Anleitung zum Briefschreiben* (Passau: Pustet, 1821); C. F. Mayer, *Kinderbriefe zum Gebrauch für Schule und Haus* (1830); August Edmund Engelbrecht, *Neunzig drei Briefe für Kinder, nebst Aufsätzen für's bürgerliche Leben* (Augsburg: K. Kollmann, 1844); Margarete Wulff, *Funfzig Kinderbriefe für kleine Kinder* (Berlin: Winckelmann, 1845). On letter manuals in general, see Cécile Dauphin, "Letter-Writing Manuals in the Nineteenth Century," in *Correspondence,* ed. Roger Chartier, Alain Boureau, and Cécile Dauphin, trans. Christopher Woodall (Princeton, NJ: Princeton University Press, 1997), 112–57; Carol Poster and Linda C. Mitchell, *Letter-Writing Manuals and Instruction from Antiquity to the Present* (Columbia: University of South Carolina Press, 2007); Willemijn Ruberg, *Conventional Correspondence: Epistolary Culture of the Dutch Elite, 1770–1850* (Leiden: Brill, 2011), especially 18–22 and 125–27.

34. Poster and Mitchell, *Letter-Writing Manuals,* 196.

35. Mayer, *Kinderbriefe,* 8.

36. On the use of letters in periodicals, see Hubert Göbels, *Das Leipziger Wochenblatt für Kinder (1772–1774): eine Studie über den älteste deutschsprachige Kinderzeitschrift* (Ratingen: Aloys Henn, 1973), 85.

37. Janet Gurkin Altman, *Epistolarity: Approaches to a Form* (Columbus: Ohio State University Press, 1982); Amanda Gilroy and W. M. Verhoeven, ed., *Epistolary Histories: Letters, Fiction, Culture* (Charlottesville: University of Virginia Press, 2000).

38. Thomas O. Beebee, *Epistolary Fiction in Europe 1500–1850* (Cambridge: Cambridge University Press, 1999), 6.

39. Erziehung der Prinzen Christian August und Friedrich Emil August, 1800–1813, Herzöge von Schleswig-Holstein-Sonderburg-Augustenburg, Abt. 22 Nr. 120, LAS.

40. Else von Arnim to Heinrich-Alexander von Arnim-Suckow, 1843, in Mencken, *Dein dich zärtlich liebender Sohn,* 224.

41. Conrad Meyer to Ferdinand Meyer, August 17, 1835, in Mencken, *Dein dich zärtlich liebender Sohn,* 193.

42. Adelheid von Alvensleben to Johann August Ernst von Alvensleben, August 7, 1801, Familie von Alvensleben, Dep. 83 B Nr. 238, HSAH.

43. Gustav Weise to Hermann Weise, March 24, 1850, Nachlass Hermann Weise, E Rep. 200–12 Nr. 106, LAB.

44. Dorothea Schlözer to Luise Michaelis, June 19, 1785, in Mencken, *Dein dich zärtlich liebender Sohn,* 57.

45. Heinrich Lehmann to Theodor Lehmann, January 21, 1861, Nachlass Theodor Lehmann, Abt. 399.1094 Nr. 1–2, LAS.

46. Bettina Brentano to Kunigunde Brentano, September 7, 1796, in Mencken, *Dein dich zärtlich liebender Sohn,* 101.

47. Caroline Amalie to Herzog Friedrich Christian II, January 1, 1806, Herzöge von Schleswig-Holstein-Sonderburg-Augustenburg, Abt. 22 Nr. 135, LAS.

48. Adelbert Herder to Johann Gottfried Herder, September 22, 1788, in Mencken, *Dein dich zärtlich liebender Sohn*, 73.

49. Carl Seeger to Christoph Dionysius Seeger, October 30, 1783, Familienarchiv von Seeger, Q 3/28 Bü 7, HSAS.

50. August von Tschirschnitz to Wilhelm von Tschirschnitz and Zeugnis, May 16, 1841, Wilhelm von Tschirschnitz, Hann. 91 Acc. 183/95 Nr. 112, HSAH.

51. Heinrich Wilhelm Weise to Friedrich Wilhelm Weise, March 8, 1813, Nachlass Hermann Weise, E Rep. 200–12 Nr. 14, LAB.

52. Familie von Alvensleben, Dep. 83 B Nr. 238, HSAH.

53. See Ruberg, "Children's Correspondence."

54. Jacob Burckhardt and Susanna Maria Burckhardt (née Schorndorff), October 4, 1823, in Mencken, *Dein dich zärtlich liebender Sohn*, 186. The original German here (specifically, "Wüste") is archaic or only in regional use today to mean something like "jumbled, disordered." Burckhardt scholars who looked at his juvenilia have interpreted the sentence in a similar fashion. See Fritz Kaphahn, ed., *Jacob Burckhardt Briefe, mit einer biographischen Einleitung* (Leipzig: A. Kröner, 1935), xxii–xxiii; Otto Markwart, *Jacob Burckhardt: Persönlichkeit und Jugendjahre* (Basel: Schwabe, 1920), 180.

55. John Hinde, *Jacob Burckhardt and the Crisis of Modernity* (Montreal: McGill-Queen's University Press, 2000).

56. Ruberg, *Conventional Correspondence*, 139.

57. Fritz Claudius to Matthias Claudius, Anna Rebbekka Behn, and Hans Claudius, August 18, 1795, in Mencken, *Dein dich zärtlich liebender Sohn*, 106–7.

58. Andreas Heusler to Andreas Heusler-Ryhiner, 1840, in Mencken, *Dein dich zärtlich liebender Sohn*, 221.

59. Adelbert Herder to Johann Gottfried Herder, August 8, 1788, in Mencken, *Dein dich zärtlich liebender Sohn*, 72.

60. Habermas, *Structural Transformation*, 48–49.

61. Annette von Droste-Hülshoff to her grandmother, December 31, 1805, in Mencken, *Dein dich zärtlich liebender Sohn*, 143. In addition to her own poetry and novels, von Droste-Hülshoff contributed several fairy tales to the Grimms' *Kinder- und Hausmärchen* in her youth (see chapter 2).

62. Ferdinand Freiligrath to his aunt, March 31, 1824, Fr. S 320, LLB.

63. Anna Krahmer, diary, February 11, 1831, 1677/II, DTA.

64. Ibid., April 28, 1831.

65. Emil Schneider, diary, June 22, 1847, 1754 / I.2, DTA.

66. Ibid., August 30, 1847.

67. Henriette and Lisette Pathe to Johann Peter Pathe, April 25, 1819, Nachlass Carl Heinrich Pathe, E Rep. 200–09, LAB.

68. Gottfried Herder to Werner, November 14, 1788, in Mencken, *Dein dich zärtlich liebender Sohn*, 65–66. According to Johann Gottfried Herder, when Werner saw beautiful Venetian fishing boats during their trip to Italy, he cried out, "'Oh, if only the children were here!' and mentioned what each of them would have said." Johann Gottfried Herder to Caroline

Herder, September 11, 1788, in *Herders Reise nach Italien: Herders Briefwechsel mit seiner Gattin,* ed. Heinrich Düntzer and Ferdinand Gottfried von Herder (Gießen, Germany: Ricker, 1859), 67.

69. Fritz Schnizlein to Friederike Luise Eichler von Platen (née von Auritz), October 6, 1808, in Mencken, *Dein dich zärtlich liebender Sohn,* 139.

70. Bettina Brentano to Sophie Brentano, February 27, 1797, in Mencken, *Dein dich zärtlich liebender Sohn,* 101.

71. Eduard Mörike to Karl Mörike, July 20, 1812, in Mencken, *Dein dich zärtlich liebender Sohn,* 161.

72. Roller children to Auguste Roller, February 23, 1808, Nachlass Theodor Roller, Q 2/9 Bü 145, HSAS.

73. Sophie and Felix von Brüsselle to Felix von Brüsselle, c. 1860, Nachlass Familie von Brüsselle, PL 13 Bü 791, SAL.

74. For Foucault's writings on "technologies of the self," see Luther H. Martin, Huck Gutman, and Patrick H. Hutton, eds., *Technologies of the Self: A Seminar with Michel Foucault* (Amherst: University of Massachusetts Press, 1988). On selfhood in modern Europe, see literature cited in the introduction and chapter five.

75. Goodman, *Becoming a Woman,* 3.

76. Caroline Dorothea Pathe to Johann Peter Pathe and Caroline Dorothea Sophie Pathe (née Bastian), January 1, 1831, Nachlass Carl Heinrich Pathe, E Rep. 200–09, LAB.

77. Philippe Lejeune, *On Diary,* ed. Jeremy D. Popkin and Julie Rak, trans. Katherine Durnin (Mānoa: University of Hawai'i Press, 2009), 109.

78. Caroline Amalie to Herzog Friedrich Christian II, January 1, 1806, Herzöge von Schleswig-Holstein-Sonderburg-Augustenburg, Abt. 22 Nr. 135, LAS.

79. Dora Paulsen to Peter Paulsen and Maria Paulsen, September 22, 1849, Nachlass Peter Paulsen, Abt. 399.1113 Nr. 5, LAS.

CHAPTER FIVE: WRITING THE SELF

1. Wilhelm Dieckhoff, diary, December 14, 1838, 644, DTA.

2. The earliest document labeled in the archive as Hermann's diary was in fact written by Marie and her husband, Gottlob Friedrich Schmidt; Hermann was fifteen years old at the beginning of the preserved diary he authored.

3. Jerrold Seigel, *The Idea of the Self: Thought and Experience in Western Europe since the Seventeenth Century* (Cambridge: Cambridge University Press, 2005), 43.

4. Irina Paperno, "What Can Be Done with Diaries?," *Russian Review* 63, no. 4 (2004): 561.

5. One example of this approach is a study by economic historian Jane Humphries, in which she scoured more than six hundred autobiographies by working-class British men in the eighteenth and nineteenth centuries for data about child labor and industrialization. Jane Humphries, *Childhood and Child Labour in the British Industrial Revolution* (Cambridge: Cambridge University Press, 2010).

6. Mary Jo Maynes, Jennifer Pierce, and Barbara Laslett make a case for scrutinizing both the social context and life cycles of diaries when using them for historical evidence. *Telling Stories: The Use of Personal Narratives in the Social Sciences and History* (Ithaca, NY: Cornell University Press, 2008), 92. One celebrated work that does this is Laurel Thatcher Ulrich's excavation of a diary kept by eighteenth-century American midwife Martha Ballard. I suggest

that examining the diaries kept by children and youth similarly "restore[s] a lost substructure" by revealing not only what pedagogues wrote that young people should be doing and thinking, but also what these diarists recorded of their own experiences. *A Midwife's Tale* (New York: Vintage Books, 1991), 27.

7. Rachel Langford and Russell West, eds., *Marginal Voices, Marginal Forms: Diaries in European Literature and History* (Amsterdam: Rodopi, 1999), 6.

8. See Suzanne L. Bunkers and Cynthia Huff, eds., *Inscribing the Daily: Critical Essays on Women's Diaries* (Amherst: University of Massachusetts Press, 1996); Marlene Kadar, *Reading Life Writing: An Anthology* (Oxford: Oxford University Press, 1993); Jeroen Blaak, *Literacy in Everyday Life: Reading and Writing in Early Modern Dutch Diaries* (Leiden: Brill, 2009); Rüdiger Görner, *Das Tagebuch: Eine Einführung* (Munich: Artemis, 1986); Manfred Jurgensen, *Das fiktionale Ich: Untersuchungen zum Tagebuch* (Bern, Switzerland: Francke, 1979); Helmut Ottenjann and Günter Wiegelmann, eds., *Alte Tagebücher und Anschreibebücher: Quellen zum Alltag der ländlichen Bevölkerung in Nordwesteuropa* (Münster: F. Coppenrath, 1982).

9. Heather Beattie, "Where Narratives Meet: Archival Description, Provenance, and Women's Diaries," *Libraries and the Cultural Record* 44, no. 1 (2009): 82–100.

10. These include the Deutsches Tagebucharchiv (German Archive for Diaries), the Onderzoeksinstituut Egodocument en Geschiedenis (Center for the Study of Egodocuments and History), and the Association pour l'autobiographie et le Patrimoine Autobiographique (Association for Autobiography and Autobiographical Heritage).

11. Jürgen Schlaeger, "Self-Exploration in Early Modern Diaries," in *Marginal Voices, Marginal Forms*, 23.

12. Philippe Lejeune, *On Diary*, ed. Jeremy D. Popkin and Julie Rak, trans. Katherine Durnin (Mānoa: University of Hawai'i Press, 2009), 51. See also Jeremy D. Popkin, "Philippe Lejeune, Explorer of the Diary," in *On Diary*, 7.

13. Lejeune, *On Diary*, 135.

14. Paperno, "What Can Be Done," 563.

15. Karen Sánchez-Eppler, *Dependent States: The Child's Part in Nineteenth-Century American Culture* (Chicago: University of Chicago Press, 2005), 19.

16. Arianne Baggerman, Rudolf Dekker, and Michael Mascuch, eds., *Controlling Time and Shaping the Self: Developments in Autobiographical Writing since the Sixteenth Century* (Leiden: Brill, 2011), 3–4.

17. Peter Burke, "Historicizing the Self, 1770–1830," in *Controlling Time*, ed. Baggerman, Dekker, and Mascuch, 19.

18. Arianne Baggerman, "Lost Time: Temporal Discipline and Historical Awareness in Nineteenth-Century Dutch Egodocuments," in *Controlling Time*, ed. Baggerman, Dekker, and Mascuch, 466.

19. For a discussion of advice books in French, German, and Dutch that began advocating diaries for children at the end of the eighteenth century, see Baggerman, "Lost Time," 474.

20. *Leipziger Wochenblatt für Kinder*, November 2, 1772 (repr., Ratingen: Aloys Henn, 1973).

21. Christian Felix Weiße, *Der Kinderfreund* I, no. 1 (1776; repr., Leipzig: Crusius, 1778), 33.

22. Arianne Baggerman and Rudolf Dekker, *Child of the Enlightenment: Revolutionary Europe Reflected in a Boyhood Diary* (Leiden: Brill, 2009), 108–10.

23. Ibid., 43.

24. Baggerman, "Lost Time," 470–71.

25. Sánchez-Eppler, *Dependent States*.

26. Marilyn Himmesoëte, "Writing and Measuring Time: Nineteenth-Century French Teenagers' Diaries," in *Controlling Time*, ed. Baggerman, Dekker, and Mascuch, 165. See also Philippe Lejeune, *Le moi des demoiselles: Enquête sur le journal de jeune fille* (Paris: Éditions de Seuil, 1993).

27. Lejeune, *On Diary*, 102.

28. Lejeune, *On Diary*, 109.

29. The travel journals of young aristocrats I located include the 1748 journal kept by Friedrich Eugen, the sixteen-year-old future Duke of Württemberg (HSAS G 236 Bü 6), or the 1837 account of Maximilian zu Lynar's trip to Bad Kösen at age twelve (BLHA Rep. 37 Nr. 5761/5). Prince Christian August of Schleswig-Holstein-Sonderburg-Augustenburg recorded from age thirteen to seventeen his "Thoughts, Ambitions, Words, and Deeds" (LAS Abt. 22 Nr. 96). Mathilde Countess von Voß, later zu Lynar, began a diary at age fifteen with the expectation, "I think it will give me much pleasure." Mathilde de Voß, May 23, 1818, Rep. 37 Lübbenau Nr. 5234, BLHA.

30. Ulrich, *Midwife's Tale*, 35.

31. Although some members of Marie's family had been ennobled, this particle "von" did not indicate a high inherited nobility (Marie's grandfather was called simply Joseph Johann Friedrich Seybold and her brother Otto did not inherit the "von"). The Landesarchiv Baden-Württemberg archival finding aid refers to the Seybold and Schmidt family collection as documenting the social history of the "württembergischen Bürgertum."

32. Through the Seybolds and Nestels, Marie was related to a few well-known literati, including her great-uncle David Christoph Seybold (1747–1804), editor of a moral weekly and professor of classical philology at Jena and Tübingen. Theodor Schön, "Seybold, David Christoph," *Allgemeinen deutschen Biographie* 34 (1892): 79–80. https://www.deutsche-biographie.de/pnd117475165.html#adbcontent. (ADB).

33. Seybold biographical information comes primarily from "Zur Geschichte der Familie (von) Schmid(t)," Bestand Q 3/48, *Landesarchiv Baden-Württemberg*, accessed December 21, 2020, https://www2.landesarchiv-bw.de/ofs21/olf/einfueh.php?bestand=6848.

34. Wherever the context is unclear throughout the rest of the chapter, I refer to Anna Krahmer as Anna K. and Anna Hasenfratz as Anna H.

35. Although it is a challenge not to have access to the complete source, the presentation of Anna Krahmer's diary is an intriguing example of how personal narratives have been preserved, passed down, and understood within the context of a family.

36. Their mothers were sisters.

37. Most biographical details on Anna Krahmer are drawn from the record at the DTA.

38. Renate Hauschild-Thiessen, *Zwischen Hamburg und Chile: Hochgreve & Vorwerk, Hamburg; Vorwerk & Co., Chile; Vorwerk Gebr. & Co.; Hamburg Vorwerk y Cia. S.A., Chile* (Hamburg: Vorwerk y Cía S. A., 1995).

39. Some biographical details come from the DTA. See also Hans Joachim Schröder, *Die Brüder Augustus Friedrich und Gustav Adolph Vorwerk: Zwei Hamburger Kaufleute* (Hamburg: Hamburgische Wissenschaftliche Stiftung, 2007).

40. Hauschild-Thiessen, *Zwischen Hamburg und Chile*, 50.

41. Paul Hoffmann, *Die Elbchaussee, ihre Landsitze, Menschen, und Schicksale* (Hamburg: Broschek, 1937), 85.

42. Emil Robert Schneider, "Deutschland Geburten und Taufen, 1558–1898," FamilySearch, accessed May 26, 2015, https://familysearch.org/ark:/61903/1:1:NP2Q-K2N.

43. The DTA transcription of his diary includes indications of Emil's additions and self-corrections.

44. Emil Schneider, diary, April 14, 1846, 1754 / I.2, DTA.

45. "Deutschland, ausgewählte evangelische Kirchenbücher 1500–1971," vol. A79 (Berlin Brandenburg, St. Marien, 1855–66), Ancestry.com, accessed in 2016, https://www.ancestry.com/search/collections/61229.

46. Think here, for example, of Samuel Pepys. And indeed, some of the diaries I have examined also include elements of this kind of commentary, as with Emil's comments in 1847 on planning for the Prussian Landtag. Schneider, diary, April 11, 1847. But these moments were exceptions rather than typical of young diarists' preoccupations.

47. Friedrich Nietzsche, diary, December 26, 1856, quoted in Rüdiger Görner, *Das Tagebuch*, 5.

48. Ulrich, *Midwife's Tale*, 9.

49. Marie Seybold, diary, April 23, 1830, Q 3/48 Bü 3, Familiennachlass Schmidt, HSAS.

50. Luise Vorwerk, diary, May 11, 1842, 1682 / II, DTA.

51. Anna Hasenfratz, diary, June 13, 1841, 1491.1, DTA.

52. Dieckhoff, diary, September 1838.

53. Sánchez-Eppler, *Dependent States,* 21.

54. Baggerman, Dekker, and Mascuch, *Controlling Time,* 5. My observations are also shaped by E. P. Thompson's classic "Time, Work-Discipline and Industrial Capitalism," *Past & Present* 38, no. 1 (1967): 56–97.

55. Weiße, *Der Kinderfreund* I, no. 1 (1776; repr., Leipzig: Crusius, 1778), 33.

56. Dieckhoff, diary, December 1838.

57. Hasenfratz, diary, January 24, 1841.

58. Seybold, diary, May 2, 1830.

59. Lynn Bloom, "'I Write for Myself and Strangers': Private Diaries as Public Documents," in Bunkers and Huff, ed., *Inscribing the Daily,* 24.

60. On the vocative address to a diary, see Lejeune, *On Diary,* 100.

61. This runs contrary to the model expected from other examples, such as Otto van Eck's heavily supervised diary; see Baggerman and Dekker, *Child of the Enlightenment.*

62. Vorwerk, diary, May 16, 1842.

63. Meredith McGill observes that moving from the late eighteenth to the early nineteenth centuries, letter manual pedagogues "worry less about a child's ability to control his hand, and more about the fact that he might exercise faulty judgment or become the victim of a false impression." "The Duplicity of the Pen," in *Language Machines: Technologies of Literary and Cultural Production,* ed. Jeffrey Masten, Peter Stallybrass, and Nancy Vickers (New York: Routledge, 1997), 47.

64. Jürgen Habermas, *The Structural Transformation of the Public Sphere: An Inquiry into a Category of Bourgeois Society,* trans. Thomas Burger and Frederick Lawrence (1962; Cambridge, MA: MIT Press, 1991), 49.

65. Krahmer, diary, October 3, 1831.

66. Note the contrast to Otto van Eck's self-castigation. In *Child of the Enlightenment,* Baggerman and Dekker read that as performed self-criticism for the benefit of his parents. While Marie also evaluated herself for adult readers, she generally gave herself high marks.

67. Seybold, diary, May 26, 1830.

68. Seybold, diary, July 6, 1830.

69. We should not over-extrapolate from this small corpus, but it does feature a gendered pattern of reading: Emil and Wilhelm used their diaries to comment on a wide range of books, including religion and philosophy, while their peers Anna K. and Anna H. only mentioned novels.

70. Vorwerk, diary, May 17, 1842.

71. Dieckhoff, diary, September 1, 1838.

72. Schneider, diary, December 18, 1846. Emilie Flygare-Carlén was a Swedish novelist who wrote on nautical and domestic themes. Her 1842 work *Rosen på Tistelön* was translated into German as *Die Rose von Tistelön: Erzählung aus den Scheeren* in 1843.

73. Dieckhoff, diary, November 27, 1838.

74. Dieckhoff, diary, September 28, 1838.

75. For a list of references in the rapidly expanding history of youth emotions, see Emily Bruce, "Encountering Emotions in the Archive of Childhood and Youth," in *Children and Youth as Subjects, Objects, Agents: Innovative Approaches to Research across Space and Time,* ed. Deborah Levinson, Mary Jo Maynes, and Frances Vavrus (New York: Palgrave Macmillan, forthcoming).

76. Peter Gay, *The Naked Heart: The Bourgeois Experience, Victoria to Freud* (New York: W. W. Norton, 1995), 331.

77. Dieckhoff, diary, November 7, 1838.

78. Hasenfratz, diary, February 1, 1841.

79. Hasenfratz, diary, January 29, 1841.

80. Hasenfratz, diary, February 1, 1841.

81. Dieckhoff, diary, February 5, 1839.

82. Krahmer, diary, September 25, 1831.

83. Krahmer, diary, December 28, 1830.

84. Seybold, diary, March 10, 1830.

85. Seybold, diary, February 26, 1830.

86. "Diesen Nachmittag war es so schön, Mutter und–––deßwegen giengen wir spazieren gehen wir, wo wir bald wieder heimkehrt weil so ein starker Wind wehte." Seybold, diary, March 3, 1830.

87. Schneider, diary, May 22 and 23, 1846.

88. Schneider, diary, June 15, 1846.

89. Schneider, diary, June 18, 1846.

90. On code-switching, see Ludmila Isurin, Donald Winford, Kees de Bot, eds., *Multidisciplinary Approaches to Code Switching* (Amsterdam: John Benjamins, 2009); Penelope Gardner-Chloros, *Code-Switching* (Cambridge: Cambridge University Press, 2009).

91. Schneider, diary, September 7, 1846.

92. Schneider, diary, June 18, 1847.

93. "After dinner we read something aloud, then I slept a little because I had a headache and mother father and the two little ones went to the zoological garten, during I and Leonore, we stayed home. I was reading an interesting novel: Sybille from A. Sternberg: Pocketbook Urania 1847, from which I also copied several things." Schneider, diary, July 4, 1847.

94. Hasenfratz, diary, June 11, 1841.

95. Schneider, diary, August 3, 1847.

96. Schneider, diary, May 7, 1846. *L'Histoire de Gil Blas de Santillane* is a picaresque novel written by Alain-René Lesage between 1715 and 1731.

97. Schneider, diary, May 13, 1846. Published originally in 1830, *Paul Clifford* was translated into German in 1834.

98. On this notion of selfhood, see Adrianne Wadewitz, "'Spare the Sympathy, Spoil the Child': Sensibility, Selfhood, and the Maturing Reader, 1775–1815" (PhD diss., Indiana University, 2011).

99. Dieckhoff, diary, October 16, 1838. The Swiss writer Johann Heinrich Daniel Zschokke published his moralistic novellas *Harmonius* circa 1801 and *Alamontade der Galeerensklave* (*Alamontade the Galley-Slave*) in 1802.

100. Seybold, diary, April 14, 1830.

101. Seybold, diary, July 2, 1830.

102. Krahmer, diary, March 3, 1831.

103. Krahmer, diary, May 16, 1831.

104. Krahmer, diary, September 25, 1831.

105. Seybold, diary, February 27, 1830.

106. Hasenfratz, diary, January 1, 1841.

107. Quoted in Baggerman and Dekker, *Child of the Enlightenment,* 95.

108. Dieckhoff, diary, June 19, 1839.

109. Dieckhoff, diary, November 27, 1838.

110. Hasenfratz, diary, April 18, 1841.

111. It is fitting that her report of her self-controlled restraint in the end was facilitated through retreating to a *Sturm und Drang* play such as Heinrich Wilhelm von Gerstenberg's *Ugolino.*

112. Dieckhoff, diary, December 17, 1838.

113. Krahmer, diary, April 2, 1831.

114. Krahmer, diary, February 11, 1831.

115. Ulrich, *Midwife's Tale,* 343.

116. Schneider, diary, April 22, 1846.

117. Vorwerk, diary, May 17, 1842.

118. Vorwerk, diary, May 1, 1842.

119. Krahmer, diary, April 28, 1831.

120. Schneider, diary, August 30, 1847.

CONCLUSION: FURNISHING THEIR OWN AGE

1. Jean-Jacques Rousseau, *Émile, or On Education,* trans. and ed. Christopher Kelly and Allan Bloom (Hanover, NH: Dartmouth College Press, 2010), 89.

2. Jennifer Popiel similarly notes that pedagogues following Rousseau ignored his censure of fables for children. *Rousseau's Daughters: Domesticity, Education, and Autonomy in Modern France* (Durham: University of New Hampshire Press, 2008), 123–26.

3. In *Rousseau's Daughters,* Popiel explores how it is that so many eighteenth-century women seeking their own liberation nevertheless admired Rousseau the misogynist.

4. Deborah Levison, Mary Jo Maynes, and Frances Vavrus, "Children and Youth as Subjects, Objects, Agents: An Introduction," in *Children and Youth as Subjects, Objects, Agents: Innovative Approaches to Research across Space and Time,* ed. Deborah Levinson, Mary Jo Maynes, and Frances Vavrus (New York: Palgrave Macmillan, forthcoming).

5. Mona Gleason, "Avoiding the Agency Trap: Caveats for Historians of Children, Youth, and Education," *History of Education* 45, no. 4 (2016): 446–59. Also addressed by Karen Vallgårda, Kristine Alexander, and Stephanie Olsen, "Against Agency" (roundtable, Society for the History of Children and Youth, Camden, NJ, June 22, 2017).

6. See the classic by Samuel Bowles and Herbert Gintis, *Schooling in Capitalist America: Educational Reform and the Contradictions of Economic Life* (New York: Basic Books, 1976).

7. Adelheid Popp, *The Autobiography of a Working Woman,* trans. E. S. Harvey (Chicago: F. G. Browne, 1913), 15–16.

8. See for example Afua Twum-Danso, "A Cultural Bridge, Not an Imposition: Legitimizing Children's Rights in the Eyes of Local Communities," *Journal of the History of Childhood and Youth* 1, no. 3 (2008): 391–409; Dominique Marshall, "Children's Rights and Children's Action in International Relief and Domestic Welfare: The Work of Herbert Hoover between 1914 and 1950," *Journal of the History of Childhood and Youth* 1, no. 3 (2008): 351–75.

9. For counter examples of freer learning projects, see Eli Meyerhoff, *Beyond Education: Radical Studying for Another World* (Minneapolis: University of Minnesota Press, 2019).

10. "Diß Büchlein ist noch weiss, o mög' auf seinen Seiten / Dein Lehrer dir mehr Lob als Tadel hier bereiten. / Dis Büchlein sieht dir gleich, du liebe süße kleine / Du hast noch freien Raum für's Gute u: für's Staune / Dem fülle Gott dir aus! Er schreib ins Herz dir ein / Sei mein du liebes Kind, so bin ich ewig Dein." Notizheft über das Betragen und die Lernfortschritte Bertha Seybolds, 1826–27, Q 3/48 Bü 1, Familiennachlass Schmidt, HSAS.

SELECTED BIBLIOGRAPHY

Abrams, Lynn and Elizabeth Harvey, eds. *Gender Relations in German History: Power, Agency and Experience from the Sixteenth to the Twentieth Century.* Durham, NC: Duke University Press, 1997.

Alexander, Christine and Juliet McMaster, eds. *The Child Writer from Austen to Woolf.* Cambridge: Cambridge University Press, 2010.

Allen, Ann Taylor. "'Let Us Live with Our Children': Kindergarten Movements in Germany and the United States, 1840–1914." *History of Education Quarterly* 28 (1988): 23–48.

Anderson, Michael. *Approaches to the History of the Western Family, 1500–1914.* Cambridge: Cambridge University Press, 1980.

Apgar, Richard B. "Taming Travel and Disciplining Reason: Enlightenment and Pedagogy in the Work of Joachim Heinrich Campe." PhD diss., University of North Carolina, 2008.

Applegate, Celia. *A Nation of Provincials: The German Idea of Heimat.* Berkeley: University of California Press, 1990.

Ariès, Phillipe. *Centuries of Childhood: A Social History of Family Life.* Translated by Robert Baldick. New York: Vintage Books, 1962.

Armitage, David and Sanjay Subrahmanyam, eds. *The Age of Revolutions in Global Context, c. 1760–1840.* New York: Palgrave Macmillan, 2010.

Baggerman, Arianne and Rudolf Dekker. *Child of the Enlightenment: Revolutionary Europe Reflected in a Boyhood Diary.* Leiden: Brill, 2009.

Baggerman, Arianne, Rudolf Dekker, and Michael Mascuch, eds. *Controlling Time and Shaping the Self: Developments in Autobiographical Writing since the Sixteenth Century.* Leiden: Brill, 2011.

Baker, Carolyn and Allan Luke, eds. *Towards a Critical Sociology of Reading Pedagogy.* Amsterdam: John Benjamins Publishing Company, 1991.

Barkin, Kenneth. "Social Control and the Volksschule in Vormärz Prussia." *Central European History* 16, no. 1 (1983): 31–52.

Barth, Susanne. "Das Goldtöchterchen: Zur geschlechtsspezifischen Erziehung von Kleinen Mädchen im Kinderbuch um nach 1800." *Der Deutschunterricht: Beiträge zu Seiner Praxis und Wissenschaftlichen Grundlegung* 42, no. 3 (1990): 61–75.

Barton, David and Nigel Hall, eds. *Letter Writing as a Social Practice.* Amsterdam: John Benjamins Publishing Company, 2000.

Bastian, Ulrike. *Die "Kinder- und Hausmärchen" der Brüder Grimm in der literaturpädagogischenliteratur pädagogischen Diskussion des 19. und 20. Jahrhunderts.* Frankfurt: Haag und Herchen, 1981.

Belgum, Kirsten. "Domesticating the Reader: Women and *Die Gartenlaube.*" *Women in German Yearbook* 9 (1993): 91–111.

Benzaquen, Adriana. "Locke's Children." *Journal of the History of Childhood and Youth* 4, no. 3 (2011): 382–402.

Bérenguier, Nadine. *Conduct Books for Girls in Enlightenment France*. Burlington, VT: Ashgate, 2011.

Blaak, Jeroen. *Literacy in Everyday Life: Reading and Writing in Early Modern Dutch Diaries*. Leiden: Brill, 2009.

Blackwell, Jeannine and Susanne Zantop, eds. *Bitter Healing: German Women Writers 1700–1830: An Anthology*. Lincoln: University of Nebraska Press, 1990.

Blair, Ann. *Too Much to Know: Managing Scholarly Information before the Modern Age*. New Haven, CT: Yale University Press, 2011.

Blamires, David. *Telling Tales: The Impact of Germany on English Children's Books 1780–1918*. Cambridge: OpenBook Publishers, 2009.

Borscheid, Peter. "Romantic Love or Material Interest: Choosing Partners in Nineteenth-Century Germany." *Journal of Family History* 11, no. 3 (1986): 157–68.

Bottigheimer, Ruth B., ed. *Fairy Tales and Society*. Philadelphia: University of Pennsylvania Press, 1986.

———. *Grimms' Bad Girls and Bold Boys: The Moral and Social Vision of the Tales*. New Haven, CT: Yale University Press, 1987.

———. "Ludwig Bechstein's Fairy Tales: Nineteenth Century Bestsellers and Bürgerlichkeit." *Internationales Archiv für Sozialgeschichte der deutschen Literatur* 15, no. 2 (1990): 55–88.

Brandtner, Gerhard. *Die Post in Ostpreussen: ihre Geschichte von den Anfängen bis ins 20. Jahrhundert*. Lüneburg: Verlag Nordostdeutsches Kulturwerk, 2000.

Brosterman, Norman. *Inventing Kindergarten*. New York: Harry N. Abrams, 1997.

Budde, Gunilla. *Auf dem Weg ins Bürgerleben: Kindheit und Erziehung in Deutschen und Englischen Bürgerfamilien, 1840–1914*. Göttingen: Vanderhoeck & Ruprecht, 1994.

———. *Blütezeit des Bürgertums*. Darmstadt: Wissenschaftliche Buchgesellschaft, 2009.

Chakrabarty, Dipesh. *Provincializing Europe: Postcolonial Thought and Historical Difference*. Princeton, NJ: Princeton University Press, 2000.

Chartier, Roger. *The Order of Books: Readers, Authors, and Libraries in Europe between the Fourteenth and Eighteenth Centuries*. Stanford, CA: Stanford University Press, 1994.

Clair, William. *The Reading Nation in the Romantic Period*. Cambridge: Cambridge University Press, 2004.

Cook, Daniel Thomas. *The Moral Project of Childhood: Motherhood, Material Life, and Early Children's Consumer Culture*. New York: New York University Press, 2020.

Darian-Smith, Kate and Carla Pascoe, eds. *Children, Childhood and Cultural Heritage*. London: Routledge, 2013.

Darnton, Robert. *The Kiss of Lamourette: Reflections in Cultural History*. New York: W. W. Norton, 1989.

Davidoff, Leonore. *Thicker than Water: Siblings and their Relations, 1780–1920*. Oxford: Oxford University Press, 2012.

Davidoff, Leonore and Catherine Hall. *Family Fortunes: Men and Women of the English Working Class, 1780–1850*. Chicago: University of Chicago Press, 1987.

Davin, Anna. *Growing Up Poor: Home, School, and Street in London, 1870–1914*. London: River Orams Press, 1996.

Delarue, Paul. *Le conte populaire français: Catalogue raisonnée des versions de France*. Paris: Maisonneuve et Larose, 2002.

Denisoff, Dennis, ed. *The Nineteenth-Century Child and Consumer Culture*. Burlington, VT: Ashgate, 2008.

Desan, Suzanne. *The Family on Trial in Revolutionary France.* Berkeley: University of California Press, 2004.

Díaz, Criss Jones. *Literacies in Childhood: Changing Views, Challenging Practice.* Sydney: MacLennan Petty, 2007.

Dickinson, Edward Ross. *The Politics of German Child Welfare from the Empire to the Federal Republic.* Cambridge, MA: Harvard University Press, 1996.

Dierks, Konstantin. *Letter Writing as a Social Practice.* Amsterdam: John Benjamins Publishing Company, 2000.

Digby, Anne, and Peter Searby. *Children, School, and Society in Nineteenth-Century England.* London: Macmillan, 1981.

Dollerup, Cay. *Tales and Translation: The Grimm Tales from Pan-Germanic Narratives to Shared International Fairy Tales.* Amsterdam: John Benjamins Publishing Company, 1999.

Dundes, Alan. *Little Red Riding Hood: A Case Book.* Madison: University of Wisconsin Press, 1988.

Ellis, John M. *One Fairy Story Too Many: The Brothers Grimm and Their Tales.* Chicago: University of Chicago Press, 1983.

Engelsing, Rolf. *Analphabetentum und Lektüre: Zur Sozialgeschichte des Lesens in Deutschland zwischen feudaler und industrieller Gesellschaft.* Stuttgart: Metzler, 1973.

———. *Der Bürger als Leser: Lesergeschichte in Deutschland 1500–1800.* Stuttgart: J. B. Metzlersche, 1974.

Erlin, Matt. *Necessary Luxuries: Books, Literature, and the Culture of Consumption in Germany, 1770–1815.* Ithaca, NY: Cornell University Press, 2014.

Falzon, Christopher, Timothy O'Leary, and Jana Sawicki, eds. *A Companion to Foucault.* Malden, MA: Wiley-Blackwell, 2013.

Fass, Paula S., ed. *The Routledge History of Childhood in the Western World.* London: Routledge, 2013.

Fergus, Jan. *Provincial Readers in Eighteenth-Century England.* Oxford: Oxford University Press, 2007.

Flanagan, Mary. *Critical Play: Radical Game Design.* Cambridge, MA: MIT Press, 2009.

Flynn, Elizabeth and Patrocinio Schweickart, eds. *Gender and Reading: Essays on Readers, Texts, and Contexts.* Baltimore: Johns Hopkins University Press, 1986.

Frederiksen, Elke P. and Katherine R. Goodman, eds. *Bettina Brentano-von Arnim: Gender and Politics.* Detroit: Wayne State University Press, 1995.

Fronius, Helen. *Women and Literature in the Goethe Era 1770–1820: Determined Dilettantes.* Oxford: Clarendon Press, 2007.

Fronius, Helen and Anna Richards, eds. *German Women's Writing of the Eighteenth and Nineteenth Centuries: Future Directions in Feminist Criticism.* Oxford: Legenda, 2011.

Fuchs, Rachel. *Abandoned Children: Foundlings and Child Welfare in Nineteenth-Century France.* Albany: State University of New York Press, 1984.

Fulford, Tim and Debbie Lee. "Mental Travelers: Joseph Banks, Mungo Park, and the Romantic Imagination." *Nineteenth-Century Contexts* 24, no. 2 (2002): 117–37.

Furet, François and Jacques Ozouf. *Reading and Writing.* Cambridge: Cambridge University Press, 1982.

Ganaway, Bryan. *Toys, Consumption, and Middle-Class Childhood in Imperial Germany, 1871–1918.* Oxford: Peter Lang, 2009.

Gawthrop, Richard and Harvey Graff, eds. *National Literacy Campaigns: Historical and Comparative Perspectives.* New York: Plenum Press, 1987.

Gawthrop, Richard and Gerald Strauss. "Protestantism and Literacy in Early Modern Germany." *Past and Present* 104, no. 1 (1984): 39–53.

Gay, Peter. *The Naked Heart: The Bourgeois Experience, Victoria to Freud.* New York: W. W. Norton & Company, 1995.

Gay-White, Pamela and Adrienne Wadewitz. "Introduction: Performing the Didactic." *The Lion and the Unicorn* 33, no. 2 (2009): 5–7.

Gebhardt, Werner. *Die Schüler der Hohen Karlsschule: Ein biographisches Lexikon.* Stuttgart: Kohlhammer, 2011.

Gerstl, Quirin. *Die Brüder Grimm als Erzieher: Pädagogische Analyse des Märchens.* Munich: Franz Ehrenwirth Verlag, 1964.

Gillis, John. *Youth and History: Tradition and Change in European Age Relations, 1770–Present.* New York: Academic Press, 1981.

Gleixner, Ulrike and Marion Gray, eds. *Gender in Transition: Discourse and Practice in German-Speaking Europe, 1750–1830.* Ann Arbor: University of Michigan, 2006.

Göbels, Hubert. *Das Leipziger Wochenblatt für Kinder (1772–1774): eine Studie über d. älteste deutschsprachige Kinderzeitschrift.* Ratingen: Aloys Henn Verlag, 1973.

———, ed. *Der Kinderfreund: Ein Lesebuch zum Gebrauch in Landschulen.* Dortmund: Harenberg, 1979.

———, ed. *Hundert Alte Kinderbücher aus dem 19. Jahrhundert: Eine illustrierte Bibliographie* Dortmund: Harenberg, 1979.

Goldstein, Jan. *The Post-Revolutionary Self: Politics and Psyche in France, 1750–1850.* Cambridge, MA: Harvard University Press, 2005.

Goodman, Dena. *Becoming a Woman in the Age of Letters.* Ithaca, NY: Cornell University Press, 2009.

Graff, Harvey. *The Literacy Myth.* New York: Academic Press, 1979.

———, ed. *Literacy and Social Development in the West: A Reader.* Cambridge: Cambridge University Press, 1981.

———. *The Legacies of Literacy: Continuities and Contradictions in Western Culture and Society.* Bloomington: Indiana University Press, 1987.

Gray, Marion. *Productive Men, Reproductive Women: The Agrarian Household and the Emergence of Separate Spheres during the German Enlightenment.* New York: Berghahn Books, 2000.

Grenby, Matthew. *The Child Reader, 1700–1840.* Cambridge: Cambridge University Press, 2011.

Haase, Donald, ed. *The Reception of Grimms' Fairy Tales: Responses, Reactions, Revisions.* Detroit: Wayne State Press, 1993.

———, ed. *Fairy Tales and Feminism: New Approaches.* Detroit: Wayne State University Press, 2004.

———. "Kiss and Tell: Orality, Narrative, and the Power of Words in 'Sleeping Beauty.'" *Etudes de Lettres* 289, no. 3–4 (2011): 275–92.

Habermas, Jürgen. *The Structural Transformation of the Public Sphere: An Inquiry into a Category of Bourgeois Society.* Translated by Thomas Burger and Frederick Lawrence. Cambridge, MA: MIT Press, 1991.

Hall, Martin and Patrick Thaddeus Jackson. *Civilizational Identity: The Production and Reproduction of "Civilizations" in International Relations.* New York: Palgrave Macmillan, 2007.

Hamlin, David. "The Structures of Toy Consumption: Bourgeois Domesticity and Demand for Toys in Nineteenth-Century Germany." *Journal of Social History* 36, no. 4 (2003): 857–69.

———. *Work and Play: The Production and Consumption of Toys in Germany, 1870–1914.* Ann Arbor: University of Michigan Press, 2007.

Hauschild-Thiessen, Renate. *Zwischen Hamburg und Chile.* Hamburg: Vorwerk y Cía S. A., 1995.

Headrick, Daniel. *When Information Came of Age: Technologies of Knowledge in the Age of Reason and Revolution, 1700–1850.* Oxford: Oxford University Press, 2000.

Hearne, Betsy. *Beauty and the Beast: Visions and Revisions of an Old Tale.* Chicago: University of Chicago Press, 1989.

Hensel, Paul. *Rousseau.* Leipzig: B. G. Teubner, 1912.

Heywood, Colin. *Childhood in Nineteenth-Century France: Work, Health, and Education Among the "Classes Populaires."* Cambridge: Cambridge University Press, 1988.

———. *Childhood in Modern Europe.* Cambridge: Cambridge University Press, 2018.

Himmesoëte, Marilyn. *Controlling Time and Shaping the Self.* Leiden: Boston, 2011.

Hopkin, David. *Voices of the People in Nineteenth-Century France.* Cambridge: Cambridge University Press, 2012.

Houston, R. A. *Literacy in Early Modern Europe: Culture and Education 1500–1800.* 2nd ed. New York: Routledge, 2013.

Hunt, Lynn. *The Family Romance of the French Revolution.* Berkeley: University of California Press, 1992.

Immel, Andrea. "The Shady Business of Enlightenment: John Trusler's *Progress of Man* and Johann Basedow's *Elementarwerk." Princeton Library Chronicle* 68, no. 3 (2007): 969–86.

Immel, Andrea and Michael Witmore, eds. *Childhood and Children's Books in Early Modern Europe, 1550–1800.* New York: Routledge, 2006.

Jack, Belinda. *The Woman Reader.* New Haven, CT: Yale University Press, 2012.

Jackson, H. J. *Marginalia: Readers Writing in Books.* New Haven, CT: Yale University Press, 2001.

Jackson, Rosemary. *Fantasy: The Literature of Subversion.* London: Methuen, 1981.

James, David. *Rousseau and German Idealism: Freedom, Dependence, and Necessity.* Cambridge: Cambridge University Press, 2013.

Jarzebowski, Claudia and Thomas Max Safley, eds. *Childhood and Emotion Across Cultures 1450–1800.* New York: Routledge, 2014.

Jean, Lydie. "Charles Perrault's Paradox: How Aristocratic Fairy Tales Became Synonymous with Folklore Conservation." *TRAMES: A Journal of the Humanities and Social Sciences* 11, no. 3 (2007): 276–83.

Johnson, Christopher and David Sabean, eds. *Sibling Relations and the Transformations of European Kinship, 1300–1900.* Oxford: Berghahn Books, 2011.

Joosen, Vanessa. *Critical and Creative Perspectives on Fairy Tales: An Intertextual Dialogue between Fairy-Tale Scholarship and Postmodern Retellings.* Detroit: Wayne State University Press, 2011.

Kaestle, Carl F. "The History of Literacy and the History of Readers." *Review of Research in Education* 12 (1985): 11–53.

Kaltz, Barbara. "*La Belle et la Bête:* Zur Rezeption der Werke Mme Leprince de Beaumonts im deutschsprachigen Raum." *Romanistische Zeitschrift für Literaturgeschichte* no. 3–4 (1989): 275–301.

Karier, Clarence J. *The Individual, Society, and Education: A History of American Educational Ideas.* 2nd ed. Urbana: University of Illinois Press, 2014.

Kertzer, David I. and Marzio Barbagli, eds. *History of the European Family.* Vol. 2, *Family Life in the Long Nineteenth Century, 1789–1913.* New Haven, CT: Yale University Press, 2002.

Kirby, Peter. *Child Labour in Britain, 1750–1870.* New York: Palgrave Macmillan, 2003.

Kleinau, Elke and Christine Mayer, eds. *Erziehung und Bildung des weiblichen Geschlechts: Eine kommentierte Quellensammlung zur Bildungs- und Berufsbildungsgeschichte von Mädchen und Frauen.* Weinheim, Germany: Beltz, 1996.

Kocka, Jürgen, ed. *Bürgertum im 19. Jahrhundert.* Göttingen: Vandenhoeck & Ruprecht, 1995.

Kuxhausen, Anna. *From the Womb to the Body Politic: Raising the Nation in Enlightenment Russia.* Madison: University of Wisconsin Press, 2013.

Langbauer, Laurie. *The Juvenile Tradition: Young Writers and Prolepsis, 1750–1835.* Oxford: Oxford University Press, 2016.

Lejeune, Philippe. *On Diary.* Mānoa: University of Hawai'i Press, 2009.

Lewis, Martin W. and Kären E. Wigen. *The Myth of Continents: A Critique of Metageography.* Berkeley: University of California Press, 1997.

Liu, Tessie P. *The Weaver's Knot: The Contradictions of Class Struggle and Family Solidarity in Western Europe, 1750–1914.* Ithaca, NY: Cornell University Press, 1994.

Löffler, Katrin and Ludwig Stockinger, eds. *Christian Felix Weiße und die Leipziger Aufklärung.* Hildesheim: Georg Olms Verlag, 2006.

Marsters, Kate Ferguson. *Travels in the Interior Districts of Africa, by Mungo Park.* Durham, NC: Duke University Press, 2000.

Mascuch, Michael. *Origins of the Individualist Self: Autobiography and Self-Identity in England, 1591–1791.* Stanford, CA: Stanford University Press, 1996.

Maynes, Mary Jo. "Age as a Category of Historical Analysis: History, Agency, and Narratives of Childhood." *Journal of the History of Childhood and Youth* 1, no. 1 (2008): 114–24.

———. *Schooling for the People: Comparative Local Studies of Schooling History in France and Germany, 1750–1850.* New York: Holmes & Meier, 1985.

———. *Taking the Hard Road: Life Course in French and German Workers' Autobiographies in the Era of Industrialization.* Chapel Hill: University of North Carolina Press, 2005.

Maynes, Mary Jo, Jennifer Pierce, and Barbara Laslett. *Telling Stories: The Use of Personal Narratives in the Social Sciences and History.* Ithaca, NY: Cornell University Press, 2008.

Maynes, Mary Jo, Birgitte Søland, and Christina Benninghaus, ed. *Secret Gardens, Satanic Mills: Placing Girls in European History, 1750–1960.* Bloomington: Indiana University Press, 2005.

Maynes, Mary Jo and Ann Waltner. *The Family: A World History.* Oxford: Oxford University Press, 2012.

Maynes-Aminzade, Liz. "Literary Fetishes: The Brontë Miniature Books." *Harvard Library Bulletin* 24, no. 2 (2013): 27–45.

Maza, Sarah. *The Myth of the French Bourgeoisie: An Essay on the Social Imaginary, 1750–1850.* Cambridge, MA: Harvard University Press, 2005.

McGlathery, James M., ed. *The Brothers Grimm and Folktale.* Urbana: University of Illinois Press, 1988.

Merget, Adalbert. *Geschichte der deutschen Jugendlitteratur.* Berlin: Plahn Buchhandlung, 1882.

Merveldt, Nikola. "Multilingual Robinson: Imagining Modern Communities for Middle-Class Children." *Bookbird: A Journal of International Children's Literature* 51, no. 3 (2013): 1–11.

Michaelis-Jena, Ruth. *The Brothers Grimm.* New York: Praeger, 1970.

Miller, Pavla. *Transformations of Patriarchy in the West, 1500–1900.* Bloomington: Indiana University Press, 1998.

Mintz, Steven. "Reflections on Age as a Category of Historical Analysis." *Journal of the History of Childhood and Youth* 1, no. 1 (2008): 91–94.

Murdoch, Lydia. *Imagined Orphans: Poor Families, Child Welfare, and Contested Citizenship in London.* New Brunswick, NJ: Rutgers University Press, 2005.

Murphy, G. Ronald. *The Owl, the Raven, and the Dove: The Religious Meaning of the Grimms' Magic Fairy Tales.* Oxford: Oxford University Press, 2002.

Nazar, Hina. *Enlightened Sentiments: Judgment and Autonomy in the Age of Sensibility*. New York: Fordham University Press, 2012.

Nickel, Petra. *Mädchenzeitschriften: Marketing für Medien*. Münster: Waxmann Verlag, 2000.

Olsen, Stephanie. *Childhood, Youth and Emotions in Modern History: National, Colonial and Global Perspectives*. New York: Palgrave Macmillan, 2015.

Ong, Walter. *Orality and Literacy: The Technologizing of the Word*. London: Methuen, 1982.

Orgel, Stephen. *The Renaissance Text: Theory, Editing, Textuality*. Manchester: Manchester University Press, 2000.

O'Rourke, Stephanie. "Histories of the Self: Anne-Louis Girodet and the Trioson Portrait Series." *Eighteenth-Century Studies* 52, no. 2 (2019): 201–23.

Patterson, Thomas C. *Inventing Western Civilization*. New York: New York University Press, 1997.

Perry, Joe. *Christmas in Germany: A Cultural History*. Chapel Hill: University of North Carolina Press, 2010.

Popiel, Jennifer. *Rousseau's Daughters: Domesticity, Education, and Autonomy in Modern France*. Durham: University of New Hampshire Press, 2008.

Porter, Roy, ed. *Rewriting the Self: Histories from the Renaissance to the Present*. London: Routledge, 1997.

Poster, Carol and Linda C. Mitchell. *Letter-Writing Manuals and Instruction from Antiquity to the Present*. Columbia: University of South Carolina Press, 2007.

Prilisauer, Birgit. "Das Kinderschauspiel der Aufklärung—die Intentionen der Autoren im Kontext der Zeit." Diplomarbeit, Universität Wien, 2009.

Radway, Janice A. "Reading Is Not Eating: Mass-Produced Literature and the Theoretical, Methodological, and Political Consequences of a Metaphor." *Book Research Quarterly* 2 (1986): 7–29.

Randolph, John. *The House in the Garden: The Bakunin Family and the Romance of Russian Idealism*. Ithaca, NY: Cornell University Press, 2007.

Raynard, Sophie, ed. *The Teller's Tale: Lives of the Classic Fairy Tale Writers*. Albany: State University of New York Press, 2012.

Rebel, Hermann. "Why Not 'Old Marie'... Or Someone Very Much Like Her? A Reassessment of the Question about the Grimms' Contributors from a Social Historical Perspective." *Social History* 13, no. 1 (1988): 1–24.

Rogers, Rebecca. *From the Salon to the Schoolroom: Educating Bourgeois Girls in Nineteenth-Century France*. University Park: Pennsylvania State University Press, 2008.

Rölleke, Heinz. *Grimms Märchen und ihre Quellen: Die literarischen Vorlagen der Grimmschen Märchen synoptisch vorgestellt und kommentiert*. Trier: Wissenschaftlicher Verlag Trier, 1998.

Rosenblatt, Louise. *The Reader, the Text, the Poem: The Transactional Theory of the Literary Work*. Carbondale: Southern Illinois University Press, 1978.

Ruberg, Willemijn. "Children's Correspondence as a Pedagogical Tool in the Netherlands, 1770–1850." *Paedagogica Historica* 41, no. 3 (2005): 295–312.

———. *Conventional Correspondence: Epistolary Culture of the Dutch Elite, 1770–1850*. Leiden: Brill, 2011.

Rudetsky, Katharina, ed. *Schwarze Pädagogik: Quellen zur Naturgeschichte der bürgerlichen Erziehung*. Frankfurt: Ullstein, 1977.

Sabean, David. *Power in the Blood: Popular Culture and Village Discourse in Early Modern Germany*. Cambridge: Cambridge University Press, 1984.

Saenger, Paul. *Spaces between Words: The Origins of Silent Reading.* Stanford, CA: Stanford University Press, 1997.

Sánchez-Eppler, Karen. *Dependent States: The Child's Part in Nineteenth-Century American Culture.* Chicago: University of Chicago Press, 2005.

———. "Practicing for Print: The Hale Children's Manuscript Libraries." *Journal of the History of Childhood and Youth* 1, no. 2 (2008): 188–209.

Scherf, Walter. *Die Herausforderung des Dämons: Form und Funktion grausiger Kindermärchen.* Munich: K.G. Saur Verlag, 1987.

Schmid, Pia. "Deutsches Bildungsbürgertum: Bürgerliche Bildung zwischen 1750 und 1830." PhD diss., Goethe-Universität Frankfurt am Main, 1984.

Schrempp, Gregory. "Taking the Dawkins Challenge, or, the Dark Side of the Meme." *Journal of Folklore Research* 46, no. 1 (2009): 91–100.

Schröder, Hans Joachim. *Die Brüder Augustus Friedrich und Gustav Adolph Vorwerk: Zwei Hamburger Kaufleute.* Hamburg: Hamburgische Wissenschaftliche Stiftung, 2007.

Schröder, Iris. *Das Wissen von der ganzen Welt: Globale Geographien und räumliche Ordnungen Afrikas und Europas, 1790–1870.* Paderborn: Schöningh, 2011.

Scott, Joan. *Only Paradoxes to Offer: French Feminists and the Rights of Man.* Cambridge, MA: Harvard University Press, 1996.

Seigel, Jerrold. *The Idea of the Self: Thought and Experience in Western Europe since the Seventeenth Century.* Cambridge: Cambridge University Press, 2005.

Selwyn, Pamela. *Everyday Life in the German Book Trade: Friedrich Nicolai as Bookseller and Publisher in the Age of Enlightenment, 1750–1810.* University Park: Pennsylvania State University Press, 2000.

Sheehan, James. *German History, 1770–1866.* New York: Oxford University Press, 1989.

Shepela, Anja Schoenberg. "'Meine kühnsten Wünsche und Ideen': Women, Space, Place, and Mobility in Late Eighteenth- and Nineteenth-Century Germany." PhD diss., University of Minnesota, 2014.

Sherman, William H. *Used Books: Marking Readers in Renaissance England.* Philadelphia: University of Pennsylvania Press, 2008.

Sobe, Noah W. "Concentration and Civilisation: Producing the Attentive Child in the Age of Enlightenment." *Paedagogica Historica* 46, nos. 1–2 (2010): 149–60.

Stanley, Liz. "Letters, the Epistolary Gift, the Editorial Third-Party, Counter-Epistolaria: Rethinking the Epistolarium." *Life Writing* 8 (2011): 135–52.

Stoddard, Roger. "Looking at Marks in Books." *Gazette of the Grolier Club* 51 (1984): 27–47.

Tang, Chenxi. *The Geographic Imagination of Modernity: Geography, Literature, and Philosophy in German Romanticism.* Stanford, CA: Stanford University Press, 2008.

Tatar, Maria. *The Hard Facts of the Grimms' Fairy Tales.* Princeton, NJ: Princeton University Press, 2003.

———, ed. *The Annotated Brothers Grimm.* London: W. W. Norton, 2004.

Taylor, Charles. *Sources of the Self: The Making of the Modern Identity.* Cambridge, MA: Harvard University Press, 1989.

Tebbe, Jason. "Landscapes of Remembrance: Home and Memory in the Nineteenth-Century Bürgertum." *Journal of Family History* 33, no. 2 (2008): 195–215.

Tilly, Louise and Miriam Cohen. "Does the Family Have a History? A Review of Theory and Practice in Family History." *Social Science History* 6, no. 2 (1982): 131–79.

Turner, Kay and Pauline Greenhill, eds. *Transgressive Tales: Queering the Grimms*. Detroit: Wayne State University Press, 2012.

Uther, Hans-Jörg. *The Types of International Folktales: A Classification and Bibliography, Based on the System of Antti Aarne and Stith Thompson*. Helsinki: Suomalainen Tiedeakatemia, Academia Scientiarum Fennica, 2004.

Vehkalahti, Kaisa. "The Urge to See Inside and Cure: Letter-Writing as an Educational Tool in Finnish Reform School Education, 1915–1928." *Paedagogica Historica* 44, nos 1–2 (2008): 193–205.

Vincent, David. "The Progress of Literacy." *Victorian Studies* 45, no. 3 (2003).

———. *The Rise of Mass Literacy: Reading and Writing in Modern Europe*. Cambridge: Polity Press, 2000.

Wadewitz, Adrienne. "'Spare the Sympathy, Spoil the Child': Sensibility, Selfhood, and the Maturing Reader, 1775–1815." PhD diss., Indiana University, 2011.

Warner, Marina. *From the Beast to the Blonde: On Fairy Tales and Their Tellers*. London: Chatto & Windus, 1994.

Watanabe-O'Kelly, Helen, ed. *The Cambridge History of German Literature*. Cambridge: Cambridge University Press, 2008.

Weber, Eugen. "Fairies and Hard Facts: The Reality of Folktales." *Journal of the History of Ideas* 42, no. 1 (1981): 93–113.

Weber-Kellermann, Ingeborg. *Die deutsche Familie: Versuch einer Sozialgeschichte*. Frankfurt: Suhrkamp, 1974.

———. *Die Kindheit: Kleidung und Wohnen, Arbeit und Spiel, eine Kulturgeschichte*. Frankfurt: Insel-Verlag, 1979.

———. *Kinder- und Hausmärchen gesammelt durch die Brüder Grimm*. Frankfurt: Insel, 1976.

Withers, Charles W. J. and David N. Livingstone. *Geography and Enlightenment*. Chicago: University of Chicago Press, 1999.

Wollons, Roberta, ed. *Kindergartens and Cultures: The Global Diffusion of an Idea*. New Haven, CT: Yale University Press, 2000.

Wurst, Karin. *Fabricating Pleasure: Fashion, Entertainment, and Cultural Consumption in Germany, 1780–1830*. Detroit: Wayne State University Press, 2005.

Zantop, Susanne. *Colonial Fantasies: Conquest, Family, and Nation in Precolonial Germany, 1770–1870*. Durham, NC: Duke University Press, 1997

Zipes, Jack. *The Brothers Grimm: From Enchanted Forests to the Modern World*. New York: Palgrave Macmillan, 2002.

———. *The Complete Fairy Tales of the Brothers Grimm*. 3rd ed. New York: Bantam, 2003.

———, ed. *The Great Fairy Tale Tradition: From Straparola and Basile to the Brothers Grimm: Texts, Criticism*. New York: W. W. Norton, 2001.

———. *The Irresistible Fairy Tale*. Princeton, NJ: Princeton University Press, 2012.

———. *The Oxford Companion to Fairy Tales*. Oxford: Oxford University Press, 2000.

———. *The Trials and Tribulations of Little Red Riding Hood*. New York: Routledge, 1993.

———. "What Makes a Repulsive Frog so Appealing: Memetics and Fairy Tales." *Journal of Folklore Research* 45, no. 2 (2008): 109–43.

INDEX

Page numbers in *italics* refer to illustrations.